Macramé

for Beginners

30 Step-by-Step Projects for Home Decor

Macramé for Beginners

30 Step-by-Step Projects for Home Decor

Knots, Patterns & Motifs
Inspired by Chinese Aesthetics

By Gan Xin

SCPG

On page 1
Fig. 1 ***Segmented Dyed Tapestry***
This is from my friend Qingqing's home. The blue segmented dyed tapestry complements her blue windows beautifully. When making this type of tapestry, which features minimal weaving and generous white space, dyeing techniques can be used to add depth and complexity to the layers.

On pages 2–3
Fig. 2 ***Xia Fei's Garden***
My friend Xia Fei is a floral layout designer. After completing a project, she often places any leftover flowers in vases. With the blooms from her garden arranged in vases wrapped in woven sleeves and a cup of floral tea in hand, you are sure to savor a cozy and delightful afternoon (see PP 180–182 for the project).

Text and Photographs: Gan Xin
Translation: Shelly Bryant
Cover Design: Chen Ruiduo
Interior Design: Hu Bin, Li Jing (Yuan Yinchang Design Studio)

Editors: Cao Yue, Yang Wenjing

ISBN: 978-1-63288-037-6

Address any comments about *Macramé for Beginners* to:

SCPG
401 Broadway, Ste. 1000
New York, NY 10013
USA

or

Shanghai Press and Publishing Development Co., Ltd.
Floor 5, No. 390 Fuzhou Road, Shanghai, China (200001)
Email: sppd@sppdbook.com

Printed in China by RR Donnelley Asia Printing Solutions Limited

1 3 5 7 9 10 8 6 4 2

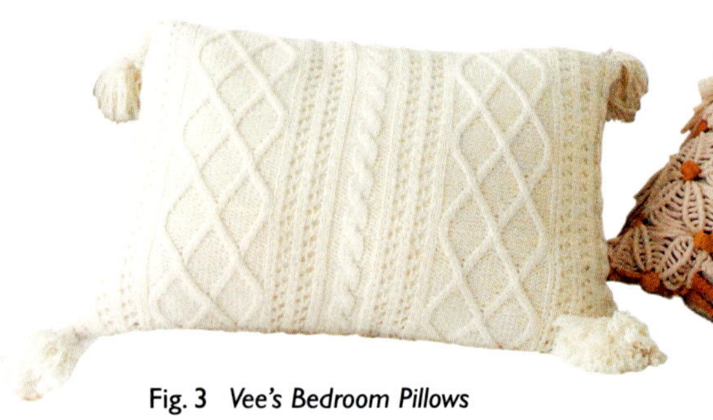

Fig. 3 ***Vee's Bedroom Pillows***
Vee's home features a warm color palette throughout. To enhance the cozy atmosphere in the bedroom, I incorporated bright orange color into the beige-based macramé pillow design, adding both warmth and vibrancy (see PP 164–165 for the project).

CONTENTS

Fig. 4 *Sally's Tassel Tapestry*
Sally enjoys picking up a few bouquets of flowers from the market and arranging them around her home. This light and airy tassel tapestry pairs beautifully with a bouquet, adding a sense of movement and vitality to the space (see PP 211–212 for the project).

CONTENTS

Fig. 5 A basket of threads and a pair of scissors.

CONTENTS

Fig. 6 *Three-Dimensional Flower Designs*
In my friend's room, a wall is adorned with magnolias, featuring interlocking three-dimensional woven flowers in soft pink and white. They appear to be growing out of the wall, creating a dreamy interplay between reality and illusion.

CONTENTS

CONTENTS

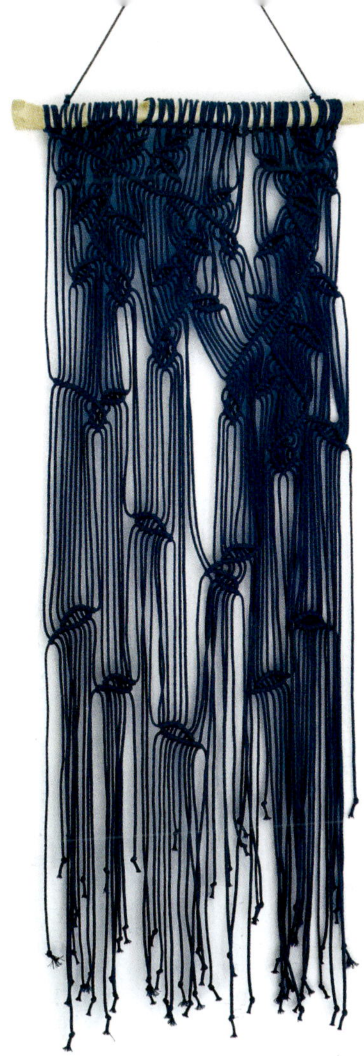

Fig. 7 *Foliage Tapestry*
This foliage tapestry, inspired by the natural branches, is designed to be free and unrestricted, bringing a lively energy to your home. Not only is this design beautiful, but it also fills the space with serenity and peace, creating a cozy little corner of nature where you can relax and unwind (see P 210 for the project).

Preface

My connection with the art of knotting began with the variously shaped Chinese knots that my elders wove by hand at home. As a child, I watched the red strings flutter in their hands, transforming in an instant into exquisite knot ornaments, and my heart was filled with curiosity and longing. As I grew older, through repeated practice and constant exposure, my deep interest in the art of knotting led me to quickly master various weaving techniques. I also gradually came to understand the unique meanings and emotions embodied in the many different types of Chinese knots.

After graduating from university, my weaving work transitioned from a hobby to a career. After several years of refinement, my weaving skills, aesthetics, and styles have all seen significant progress. Today, I constantly challenge myself with intricate and difficult designs. In 2012, when I first saw pictures and descriptions of macramé from abroad, it felt like a revelation. It turns out that simple knots and techniques can create endlessly diverse designs.

Some of the basic knots and techniques in macramé are very similar to those in traditional Chinese knotting. Techniques like the lark's head knot, square knot, spiral knot, and methods of adding and extending cords are strikingly similar to those used in traditional Chinese knots. Slightly different with Chinese knotting, macramé places more emphasis on the overall visual effect, presenting forms that are more free and diverse. It values creating works that combine unique charm and an innovative spirit through various combinations of basic knots.

Through this book, I aim to freely share my nearly twenty years of weaving experience. I have tried to summarize some commonly used knots and techniques and have presented 141 weaving patterns, ranging from basic to advanced. I also want to try to break through the cultural boundaries of knotting art through my creations, skillfully blending Eastern and Western aesthetics and creativity.

On the facing page
Fig. 8 *Cactus Tapestry*
The cactus tapestry, placed between the real and artificial plants, adds a unique focal point and depth to the picturesque setting (see PP 143–145 for the project).

In the creation of this book's tutorials, I hoped the entire process would be authentically realized, so I enlisted my good friends so I could design real life macramé decorations for their homes. In these designs, I began experimenting with blending contemporary macramé styles with traditional Chinese aesthetics, ultimately presenting thirty macramé home decor pieces. Some of these pieces incorporate traditional Chinese colors, such as festive red, elegant gold, and mysterious indigo, into the choice of macramé cords, giving them a unique Asian charm. Many pieces also draw on traditional Chinese patterns, such as cloud shoulders, lotus motifs, butterfly designs, and carp, imbuing the works with a rich cultural heritage.

I would like to thank my husband, Guo Zemin, for assisting with the photography of all the steps, Chen Wenyuan for meticulously drawing diagrams of the knots by hand, Xu Hui and Xiao Cao for helping with the multiple scene photographs, and the pet companions who appeared in the shots. Finally, I want to thank you for opening this book. I hope my sharing allows you to experience the charm of knotting and enriches your handmade home decor.

Fig. 9 *Tranquil Woodland*
Perfect for hanging in forests, meadows, and other outdoor settings, macramé projects showcase a unique style infused with handmade warmth.

MAGIC and MEDICINE of PLANTS
National

CHAPTER ONE

Preparation

This chapter provides a detailed introduction to the basic materials and tools needed for macramé. The right choice of cords and tools not only greatly enhances production efficiency but also makes your work more aesthetically pleasing. We also provide different cord treatment methods for macramé works with different needs and styles, allowing you to unleash your creativity to the fullest.

Materials and Tools

If you're looking to venture into the field of macramé, understanding and becoming familiar with the tools and materials is a prerequisite for successfully embarking on the journey of macramé creation.

1. Cord Materials

Of those available in the market, cords can be categorized according to natural and chemical fibers. Natural fibers include plant, animal, and mineral fibers. This book primarily uses plant fiber cords. Plant fibers are made from organic fibers extracted from plants such as cotton, grasses, and hemp. They have a soft texture and gentle colors. Chemical fibers include artificial and synthetic fibers such as acrylic, polyester, and nylon. These are commonly found in various textile fabrics used in everyday life. Synthetic fiber cords are represented by nylon material, which has high abrasion and corrosion resistance and is commonly used in outdoor settings. There are also many cords and fabrics on the market made from high-tech polymer compounds.

Different cords have distinct characteristics and properties. By understanding these traits, you can select the most suitable cord for various types of woven pieces.

On the facing page
Fig. 10 *Large Segmented Tapestry*
The living room holds a central position in the home and often features large white walls. Hanging a tapestry in this space instantly adds a unique visual effect and a touch of handmade artistry (see PP 158–159 for the project).

Fig. 11 Unbleached cotton cords.

Fig. 12 Colored cotton cords.

Cotton cord is relatively soft and easy to handle. It is commonly used for making woven items. There are two types of cotton cord, unbleached cotton cord and colored cotton cord. Unbleached cotton cord is primarily off-white, and the finished woven items have a clean, minimalist appearance. The selection of colored cotton cords on the market is limited. You can try dyeing your own cords according to the tutorials provided later (see pages 23–26).

Since the number of times each cord is knotted varies, the principle for estimating the length of cord is that it should be longer rather than shorter. If you find that the cord is not long enough during the knotting process, you can refer to the methods for adding cord in Chapter Two (see pages 61–64).

Hemp cord is a natural material cord

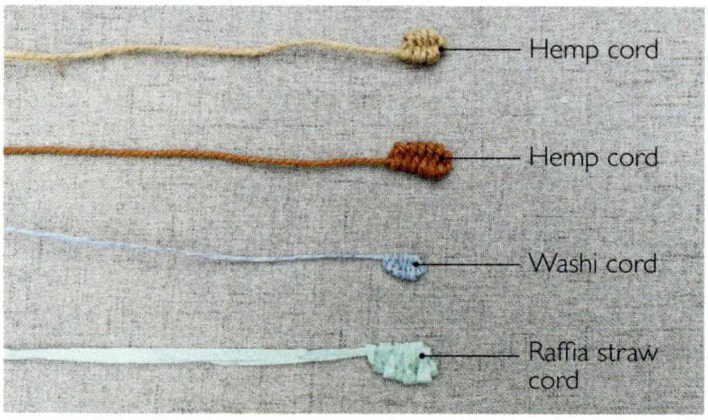

Figs. 13–14 Hemp cords, washi cord, raffia straw cord.

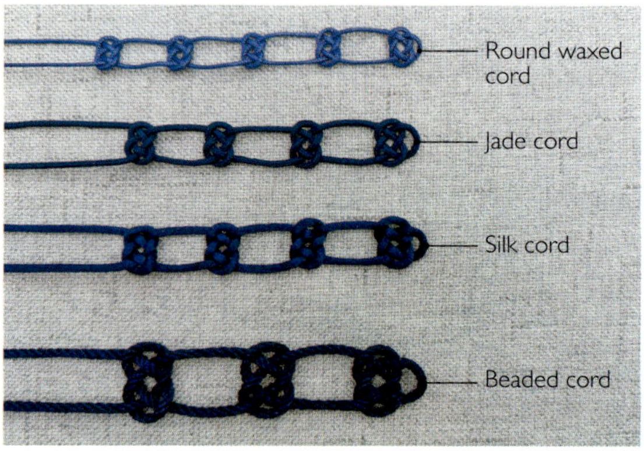

Figs. 15–16 Nylon cords.

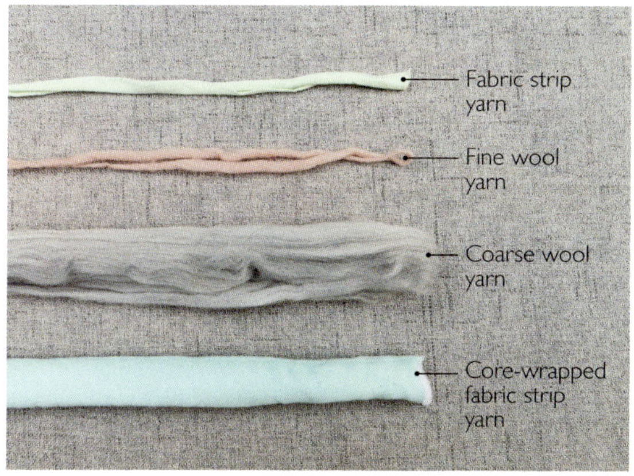

Figs. 17–18 Fabric strip yarns and wool yarns.

with a rough texture, suitable for creating pieces that are intended for natural settings and have a more rustic feel, such as hanging planters, vase decorations, and staircase rail decorations.

Washi cord/raffia straw cord are natural material cords that are very flexible and are suitable for making fresh, natural items such as bags and hats.

Nylon cord, made from synthetic fibers, is available in various thicknesses and is commonly found as round waxed cord, jade cord, silk cord, and beaded cord. The cord has a smooth surface, making it unsuitable for weaving tapestry, but widely used for making jewelry.

Fabric strip yarn is made from natural fibers and is generally thicker in size. It has a soft texture and is suitable for weaving items such as cushions, small blankets, and small bags.

Wool yarn is made from natural fibers and is available in fine and coarse varieties. The texture of the yarn is not very distinct when knotting, and it is primarily used in this book for creating weaving pattern sections.

Decorative yarns such as long haired yarn, nubby yarn, and mixed specialty yarns, are commonly used. Its texture is not very distinct when knotting, and in this book, it is mainly used for making tassels or decorative accents in blank spaces.

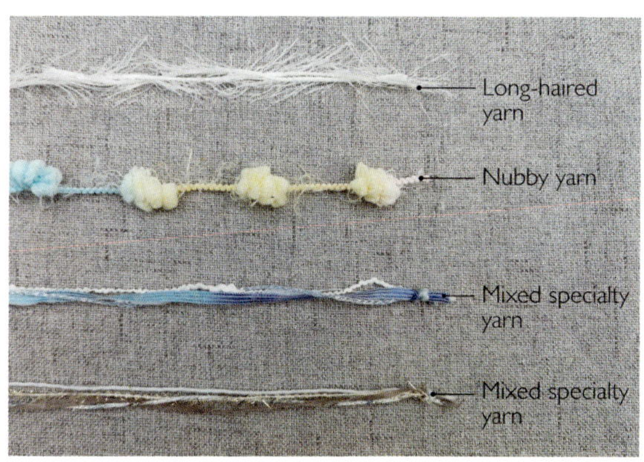

Figs. 19–20 Decorative yarns.

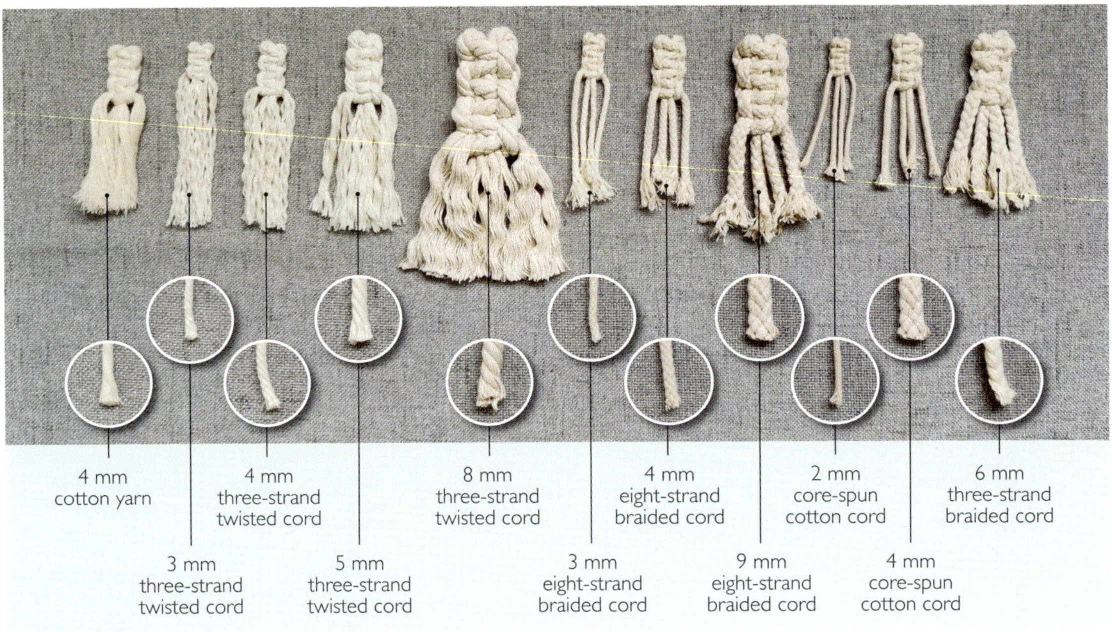

Fig. 21 Different types of cotton cords.

2. Types and Characteristics of Cotton Cords

As one of the most commonly used cords, cotton cord comes in various types and classifications. You can choose different textures and thicknesses of cotton cord to create macramé pieces with a diverse range of appearances.

Cotton yarn has no distinct texture, and the ends are relatively straight when frayed. It is suitable for making tassels, leaves, or feathers.

Three-/four-strand twisted cord has vertical strip textures, and when frayed, it resembles instant noodles. It is suitable for making items with a fluffy or textured finish at the ends, such as tapestries.

Eight-strand braided cord has a braided texture, and its ends are not easily frayed. When the ends are frayed, the cord has a draping quality. It is suitable for making large-scale macramé tapestries and similar projects.

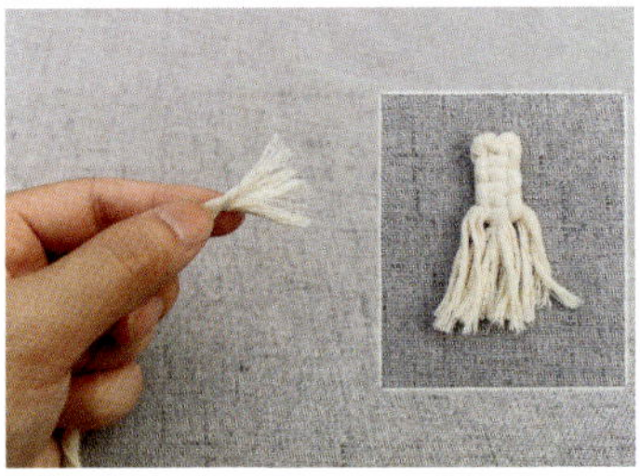

Fig. 22 Cotton yarn.

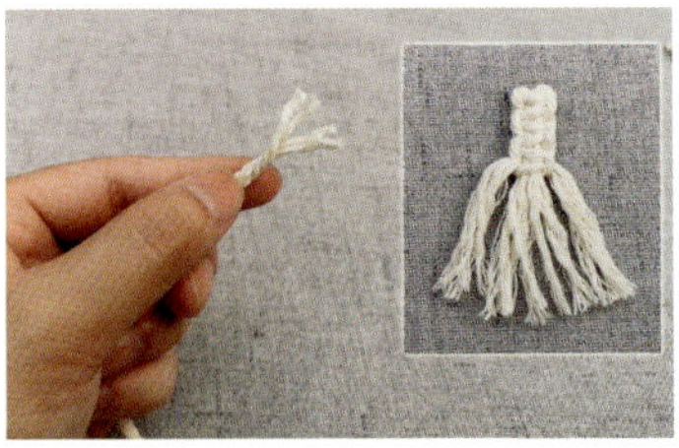

Fig. 23 Three-/four-strand twisted cord.

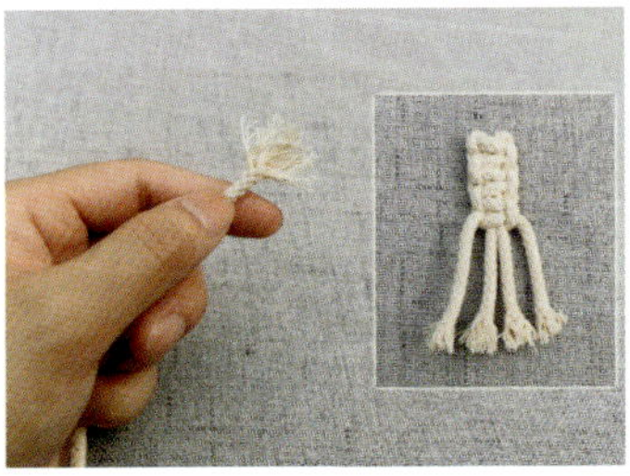

Fig. 24 Eight-strand braided cord.

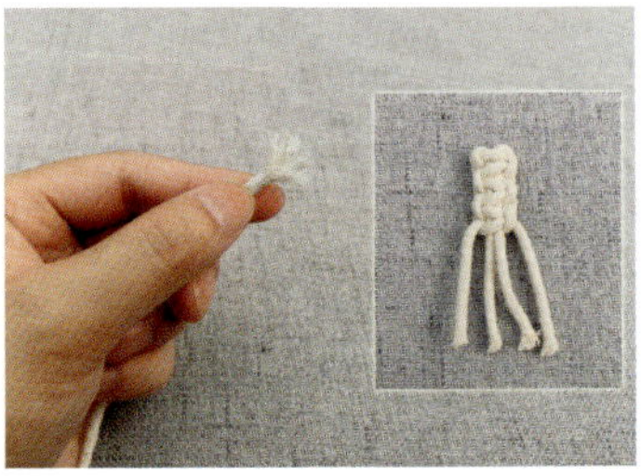

Fig. 25 Core-spun cotton cord.

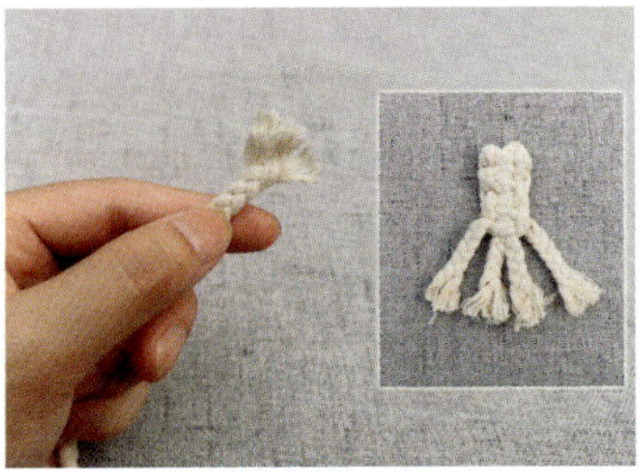

Fig. 26 Three-strand braided cord.

Core-spun cotton cord has a braided texture and is often round in shape. It is relatively stiff, and the ends do not fray easily, making it suitable for creating firm, structured pieces.

Three-strand braided cord has a braided texture and the ends are prone to fraying. It is suitable for making decorative accents in blank spaces and for creating woven patterns.

3. Tools

Although macramé is primarily done by hand to create knots and patterns, making larger, more design-oriented pieces requires some practical tools.

Weaving boards are used for weaving small items like mini tapestries and is typically used in conjunction with clips. It can also be replaced by a drawing board, corkboard, or similar surfaces.

Clips are used to secure cords or wooden rods to the weaving mat. Common types include steel clips and binder clips.

Weaving frames are used for weaving large tapestries, often used in conjunction with S-hooks. A clothes hanger can also be used as an alternative.

S-hooks are used to secure support rods, such as wooden rods, to the weaving frame, making it easier to weave large tapestries.

Fig. 27 Weaving boards.

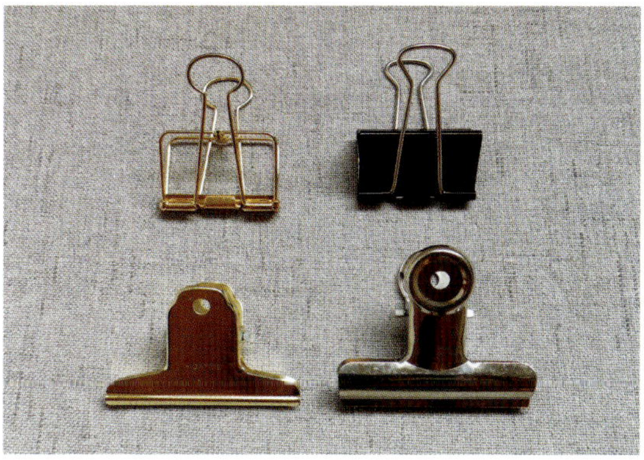

Fig. 28 Clips.

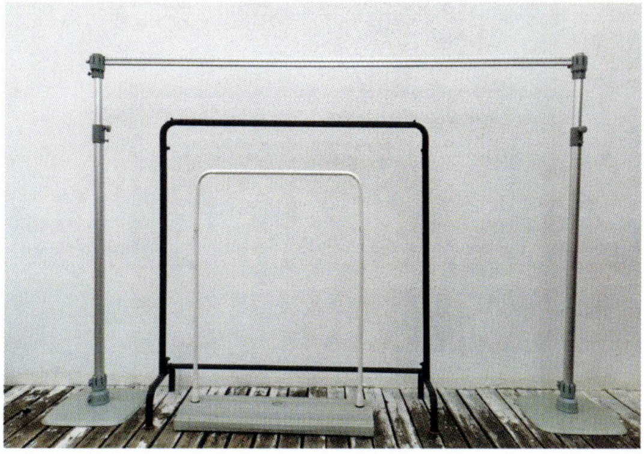

Fig. 29 Weaving frames.

Fig. 30 S-hooks.

Fig. 31 Scissors and other tools.

Scissors are used for trimming cords. The diagram shows a tailor's shears, regular scissors, and thread snips. Scissors can be differentiated by their size for different functions. Larger scissors are used for trimming thicker cords and adjusting tassels, while smaller scissors are used for more detailed tasks, such as trimming thread ends.

Tape measures are used to measure the length of cords and tapestries.

Pins are used to secure cords to the weaving board, making it easier to weave once the positions are fixed.

Crochet hooks are used to hide thread ends.

Large-eye sewing needles are used for sewing in thread ends.

Adhesive tapes are used to stick cords to the weaving board, fixing it in place temporarily. The ends of cotton cord tend to fray easily. Wrapping the end with adhesive tape makes it easier to thread through beads. The diagram shows both transparent tape and masking tape. You can choose either one.

Combs are used to smooth out the ends of the cords.

Glue is used to glue some parts of thread ends after trimming to prevent them from unraveling. The diagram shows both white glue and fabric glue. You can choose either one, but fabric glue is not suitable for non-fiber materials.

Hot glue gun is used for attaching decorative materials.

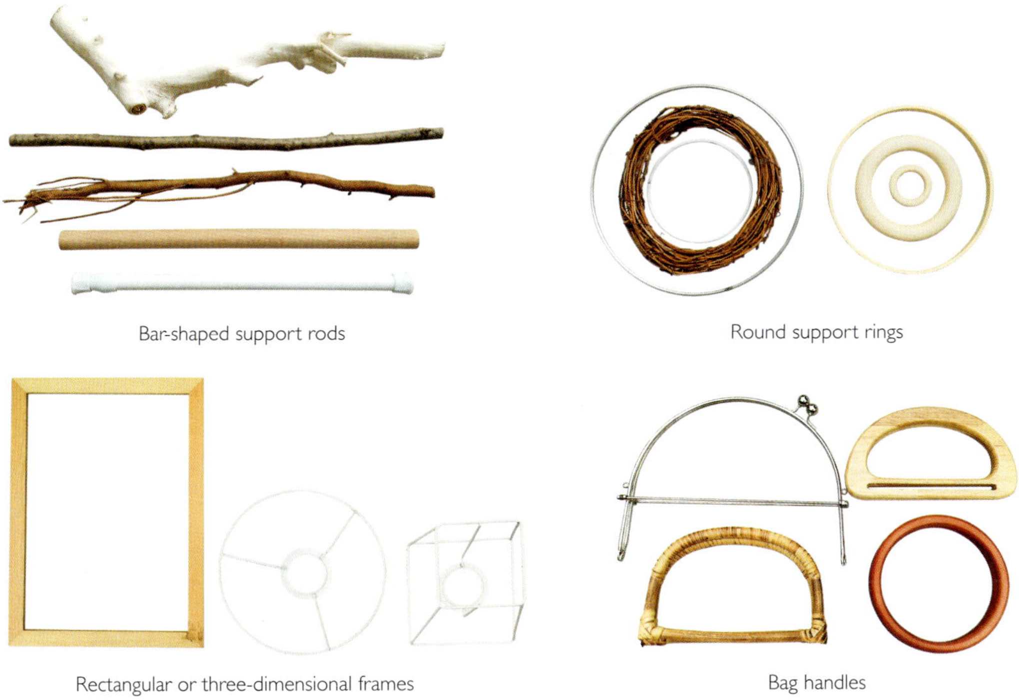

Fig. 32 Decorative accessories.

4. Accessories

Accessories can elevate simple knots or patterns to another level, enhancing the diversity and aesthetic appeal of macramé elements, or they can be used to turn macramé pieces into functional items.

Bar-shaped support rods are wooden rods, natural branches, curtain rods, etc.

Round support rings are wooden rings, rattan rings, metal rings, etc.

Rectangular or three-dimensional frames are picture frames, lamp frames, etc.

Bag handles are wooden handles, bamboo handles, round handles, metal handles, etc.

Decorative materials are wooden beads, acrylic beads, pom-poms, feathers, lace ribbons, artificial flowers, dried flowers, etc.

Fig. 33 Decorative materials.

Handling Cords

Many times, the cords we buy may not fully meet our knotting needs. This chapter explains how to modify the length of cords, how to dye cords, and so on, bringing rich variations to your macramé works.

1. Estimating Length

Properly preparing the cords before weaving will make the knotting process much smoother. Depending on the design, it is necessary to estimate the approximate length of the cords in advance and cut them accordingly for later use. Estimating the length of the cords is the first step in knotting. Based on many years of knotting experience, the following is a method for calculation to serve as a reference.

Calculation formula:

[knotting section length × (6–8 times) + tassel] × 2 = required cord length

Below, we will use an example of knotting a tapestry with a length of approximately 80 cm to demonstrate how to use this formula.

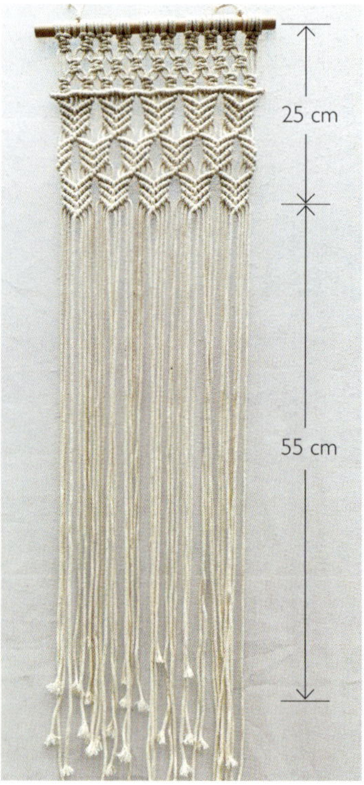

If the knotting section is 25 cm long and the tassel section is 55 cm long, the required cord length is [25 cm × (6–8 times) + 55 cm] × 2 = 410–510 cm (When folded in half, the length would be 205–255 cm).

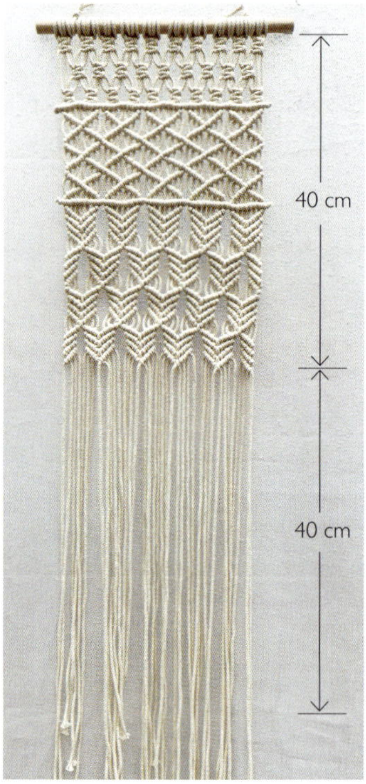

If the knotting section is designed to be 40 cm long and the tassel section is 40 cm long, then the required cord length is [40 cm × (6–8 times) + 40 cm] × 2 = 560–720 cm (which is 280–360 cm when folded in half).

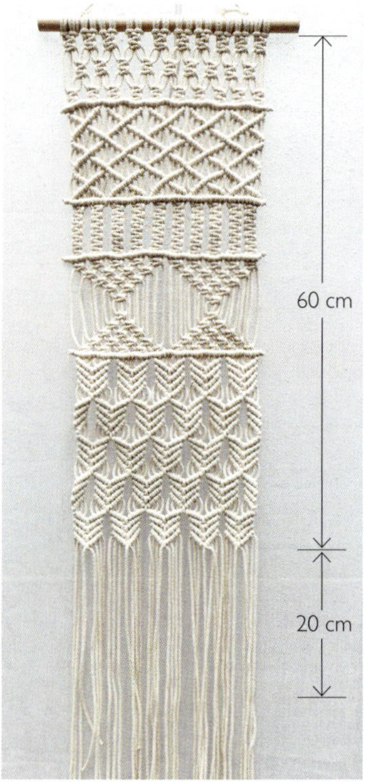

If the knotting section is designed to be 60 cm long and the tassel section is 20 cm long, then the required cord length is [60 cm × (6–8 times) + 20 cm] × 2 = 760–1000 cm (which is 380–500 cm when folded in half).

Since the number of times each cord is knotted varies, the principle for estimating the length of cord is that it should be longer rather than shorter. If you find that the cord is not long enough during the knotting process, you can refer to the methods for adding cord in Chapter Two (see pages 61–64).

2. Cleaning

Wash the trimmed cords first. After being shipped from the factory, the cords may have dust or a strong smell of machine oil. Washing them can help reduce odors and burrs. Using clean cords for knotting can extend the time before the finished product needs to be washed again.

Dilute laundry detergent with room temperature water and soak the cords.

Gently scrub the cords, then soak them for two to four hours. Adjust the number of washes based on how cloudy the water becomes.

Rinse thoroughly, then spread out the cords and hang them in a well-ventilated area to dry. Note that colored cords should not be exposed to direct sunlight for too long.

3. Dyeing

There are different types of dye, plant dye, powder dye, and pigment dye. Based on the dyeing method, it can be divided into dip dyeing, hang dyeing, spray dyeing, and brush dyeing. All dyeing methods will result in colors that look different when dried compared to when they are wet. If the color is not rich enough after drying, you can repeat the dyeing process multiple times.

Plant dyeing is suitable for dyeing cords before knotting, typically using the dip dyeing method.

Prepare the plant dye solution. Here, we will demonstrate using a haematein dye solution.

Boil the cotton cords to remove impurities and bleach them, making the cotton cords easier to color.

Soak the cotton cords in the dye solution. Adjust the number of soakings and the duration based on the quantity of cotton cords and the desired color intensity.

4

Wash the cords multiple times until the water runs clear.

5

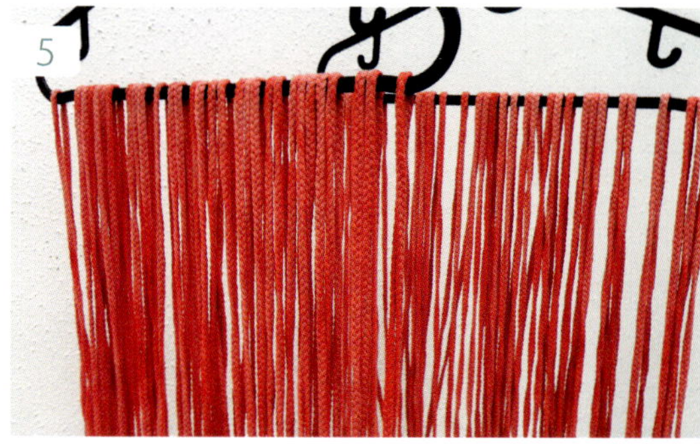

Hang the dyed cotton cords in a well-ventilated area to dry. Avoid exposure to direct sunlight for too long to prevent fading.

Powder dyeing is a method which commonly uses industrial dye powders, which is a quick, convenient procedure. It can be done before knotting or after the product is finished, using either the dip dyeing or hang dyeing method. However, because the color fixing of powder dye is unstable, the finished product needs to be kept in a dry environment to maintain its color.

1

Dissolve the dye powder. Add water according to the instructions, using more water for lighter colors and less water for darker colors.

2

Soak the part of the cords that needs to be dyed in water, then wring it out. This helps the dye to penetrate the cotton cords more effectively.

3

Soak the part of the cords that needs to be dyed in the dye solution. You can gently rub it with your hands to help the dye penetrate the cotton cords (wear gloves for this step). If you want the tassels of the tapestry to have a gradient effect, repeat the dip dyeing process.

4

Hang dyeing. To allow the dye solution to penetrate deeper into the cotton cords, hang dye and soak for 6 to 12 hours.

5

Washing and drying. After dyeing, wash the cords until the water is relatively clear. Hang in a ventilated area away from direct sunlight to dry to avoid fading.

Pigment Dyeing. Using propylene, watercolor, gouache, and other pigments can also achieve a dyeing effect. This method is suitable for coloring finished knotted products and can be done using spray dyeing or brush dyeing techniques. Due to the larger pigment particles, the penetration into the cotton cords is not as deep as that of dye powder. Hang, spray dyeing, or brush dyeing will result in a significant loss of pigment dye solution. Although flat dyeing does not allow the pigment to penetrate the cotton cord evenly and quickly, the remaining pigment dye solution will stay on the waterproof tablecloth. Letting it sit for 6 to 12 hours allows the remaining dye solution to slowly penetrate the cotton cords, and the junctions of the two colors will blend very naturally. Using pigments for dyeing may result in color fading. After washing and drying, avoid contact with water and direct sunlight.

Spray Dyeing Method

Dilute the pigment in a measuring cup.

Pour the diluted dye solution into a spray bottle for later use.

Soak the cotton cords and then wring them dry, ensuring that the areas needing dye are thoroughly moist.

Lay the tapestry flat on a table covered with a waterproof tablecloth.

Spray dye onto the sections that require coloring. For multiple colors, conduct separate sprayings for each color.

Brush Dyeing Method

Dilute the pigment.

Soak the cotton cords and then wring them dry, ensuring that the areas needing dye are thoroughly moist.

Brush dye onto the sections that require coloring repeatedly.

For multiple colors, dye in multiple steps.

After cleaning, hang the cord up to air dry.

Care for Dyed Fabrics

1. Avoid exposure to direct sunlight which can cause fading.
2. Try to keep the fabric away from damp environments.
3. Dust regularly by lightly brushing or using a handheld vacuum cleaner.
4. If stained, gently treat the stains with a stain remover or detergent.
5. Hand wash with gentle rubbing if needed, but avoid using a washing machine or vigorous scrubbing.

Posture and Hand Strength

Due to the varied sizes and styles of macramé crafts, the time required for different projects can vary greatly. For different environments and macramé crafts of different sizes, it is important to adjust your posture and hand strength accordingly to effectively complete the craft.

1. Posture

Small Tapestries. Remain seated in a chair with a backrest. If you are knotting for an extended period, take occasional breaks, leaning against the backrest to relieve pressure on the neck, shoulders, and back. You can place

Fig. 34 Posture for small tapestries.

Fig. 35 Posture for medium tapestries.

the knotting board on your lap, leaning it against the edge of the table to form an angle of approximately 60 degrees.

Medium Tapestries. Sit in front of the knotting frame and adjust its height according to the knotting position. Set the height slightly below your horizontal line of sight. At this position, your arms will not be raised too high, and your neck will not be strained, making the work less tiring. As you continue knotting downward, adjust the height accordingly.

Large Tapestries. Remain standing and adjust the knotting frame to a height taller than your own. At the beginning of the knotting process, you can stand on a chair or ladder. For very large tapestries, the cords are often quite long, so hanging the frame higher can prevent the cords from dragging on the ground. After completing the main section, adjust the knotting frame to the actual height needed for the intended display location to make trimming easier.

Fig. 36 Posture for large tapestries.

2. Hand Strength

Each person has a different tactile perception of the cord, and there will be relative friction between the cotton cords during knotting. The right tension will make the knots and the overall knotted craft more aesthetically pleasing. If knotted too loosely, the knots will be too soft, making them prone to warping under the pull of heavy objects. If knotted too tightly, the knots will be too stiff, which can negatively affect designs that require a draping look. When knotting, adjust the tension of the cords by controlling the force applied with your hands.

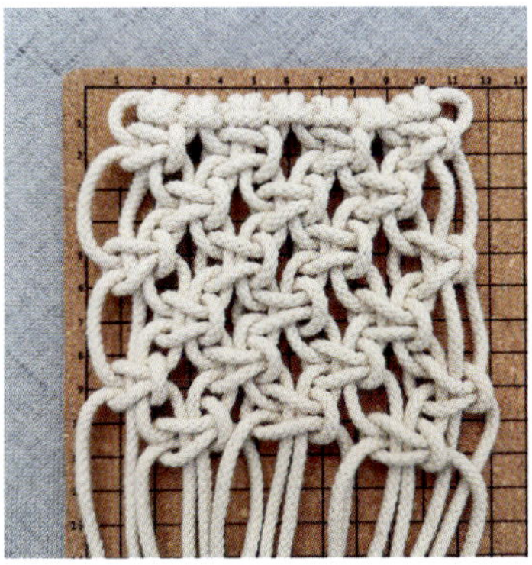

Fig. 37 Too loose.

Fig. 38 Normal.

Fig. 39 Too tight.

CHAPTER TWO

Basic Knots and Techniques

Many beautiful, seemingly complex macramé creations are derived from various combinations of basic knots. Only by mastering the macramé techniques of these basic knots can you freely create your own desired knotting projects.

Basic Knots

Before starting formal instruction, it is helpful to clarify a simple concept: the cord in the middle that provides support is called the holding cord, which generally does not need to be moved. Some knots need to be woven around the holding cord, such as hitch knots, square knot, and diagonal double half hitch knot. The cords that are woven or wrapped around the holding cord are called the working cords.

1. Lark's Head Knot/Reverse Lark's Head Knot

These knots can be used for starting and adding cords midway. The lark's head knot and the reverse lark's head knot are the reverse of each other. For starting, usually the lark's head knot is used, but the reverse lark's head knot can also be used as long as consistency is maintained. The holding cord can be a single or multiple strands of cord, or other materials such as branches or metal rings.

On the facing page
Fig. 40 Basic knots for macramé.

Lark's Head Knot

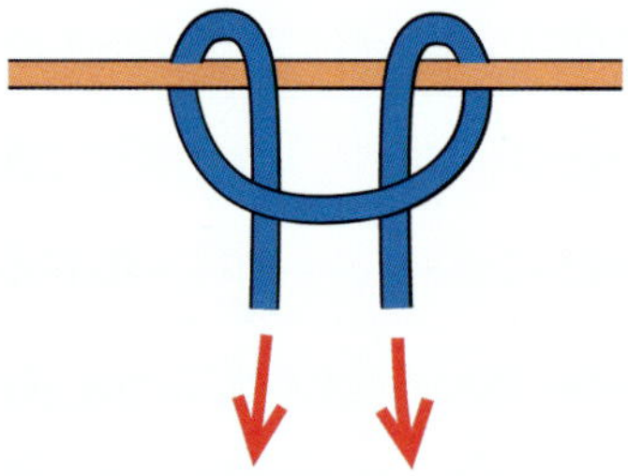

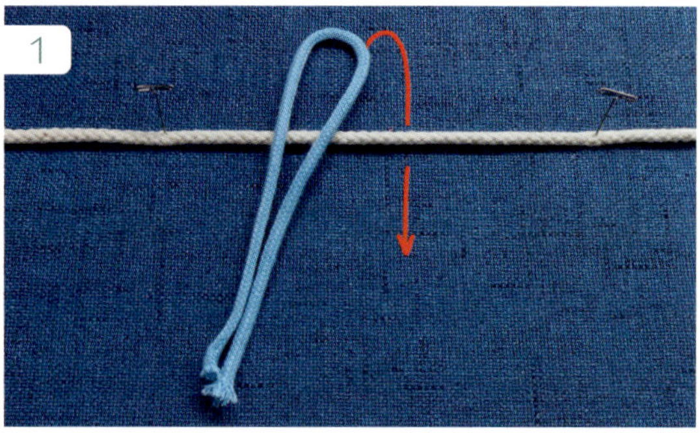

Fold the cord in half and place it over the holding cord.

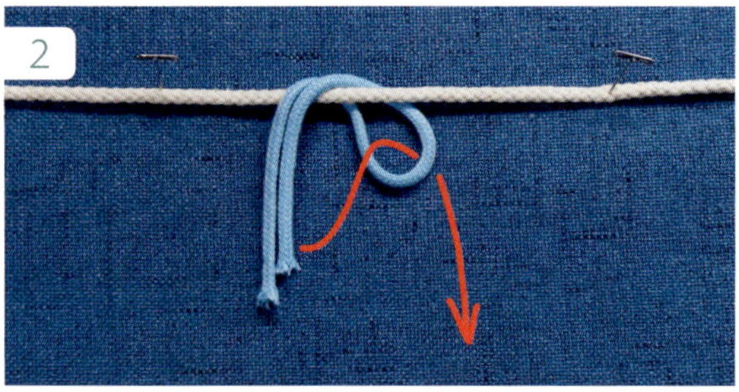

Bend the loop of the cord above the holding cord backwards, and place it below the holding cord. Bring the cord ends through the loop from front to back.

Pull the cord ends downward to secure the knot, with the knot end positioned on the front side.

Reverse Lark's Head Knot

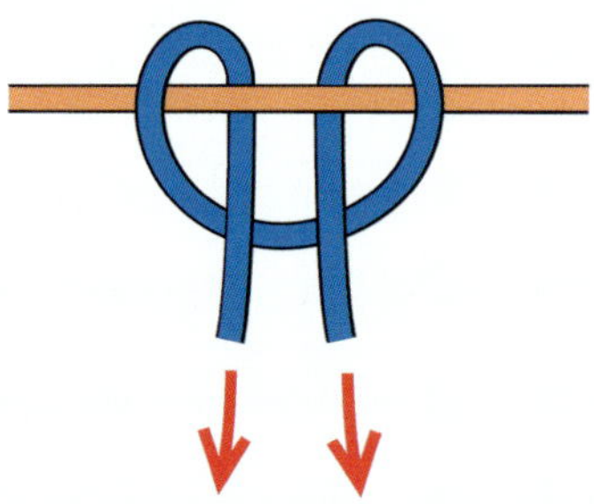

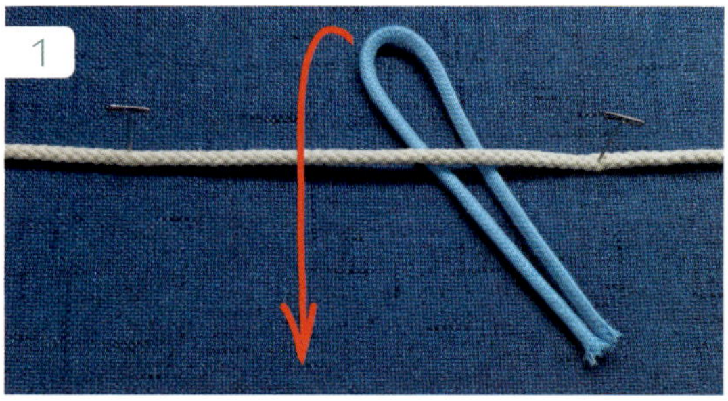

Fold the cord in half and press it underneath the holding cord.

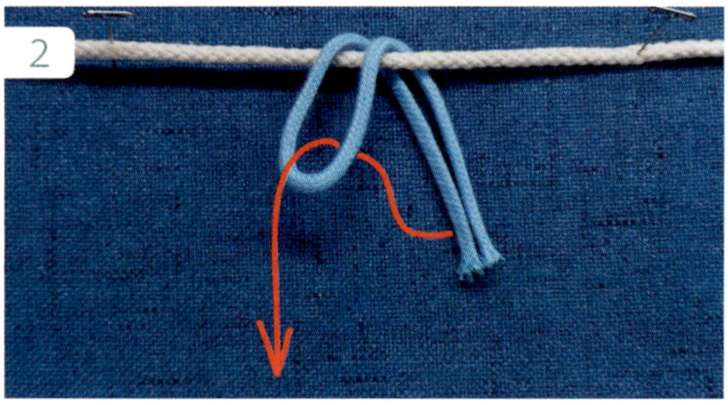

Bend the loop forward and bring the cord end through the loop from back to front.

Pull the cord ends downward to secure the knot, with the knot end positioned on the back side.

2. Overhand Knot

This knot can be used for starting, temporary positioning, finishing, securing, or bead threading. Single-strand or multi-strand cords can be used. Below is a tutorial demonstration using a single-strand cord for an overhand knot.

Overhand Knot with Single Strand

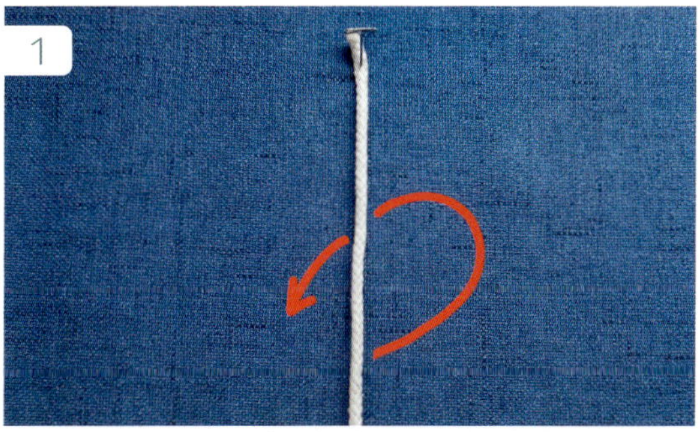

1

Choose the location for the knot. Wrap the lower end of the cord around the upper end, forming a loop.

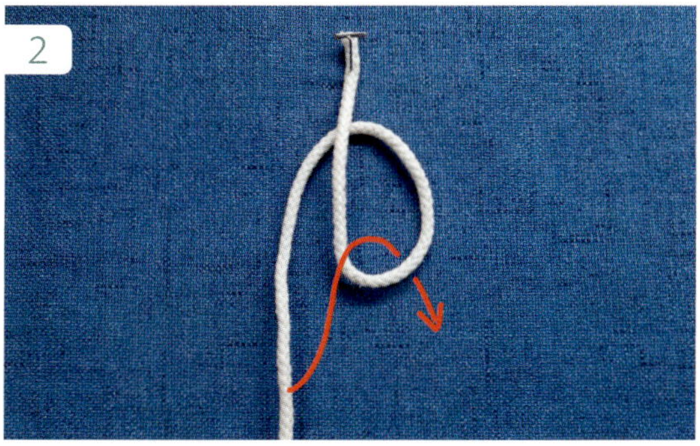

2

Bring the lower end of the cord through the loop from front to back.

3

Pull the cord downward to secure the knot at the chosen location.

3. Hitch Knot

This knot is used for temporary or final securing after knotting. The hitch knot is tied similarly to a overhand knot, but it includes an additional central holding cord. This holding cord can be single or multi-stranded.

Hitch Knot with Single-Strand Holding Cord

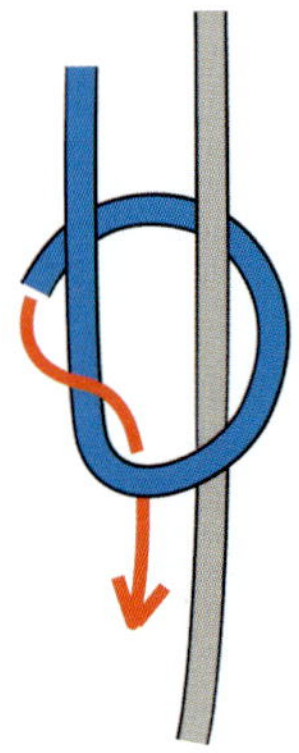

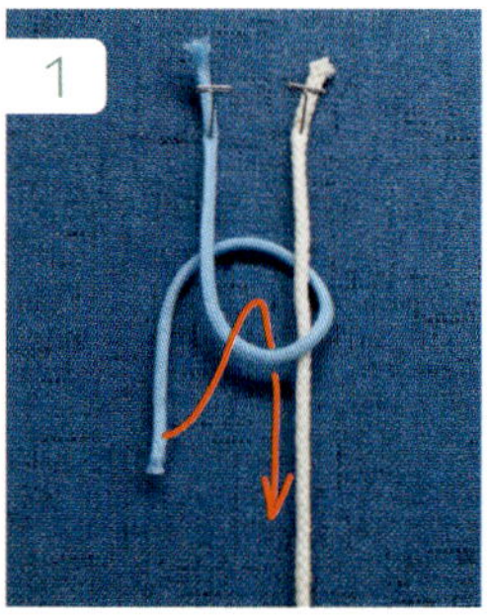

The blue cord is the working cord, and the white cord is the holding cord. Wrap the lower end of the working cord counterclockwise from front to back under both cords to form a loop.

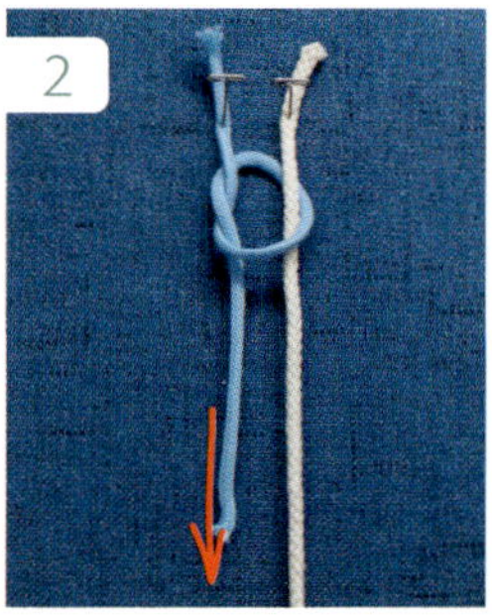

Bring the lower end of the working cord through the loop from front to back.

Pull the cords tight to secure the knot at the chosen position.

Hitch Knot with Multi-Strand Holding Cord

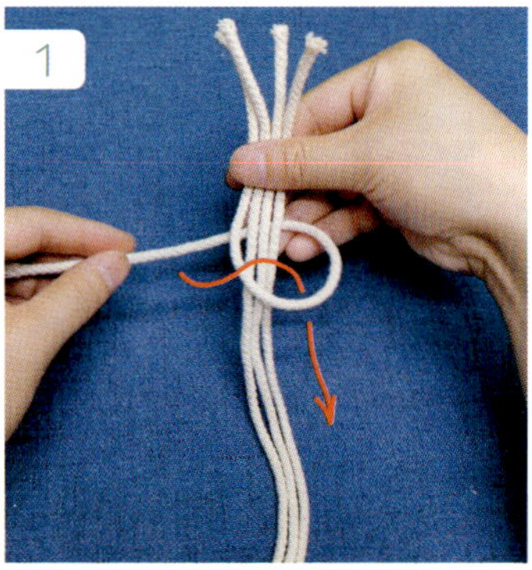

Choose any one cord as the working cord, leaving the rest as holding cords. Wrap the lower end of the working cord counterclockwise from front to back under all cords to form a loop.

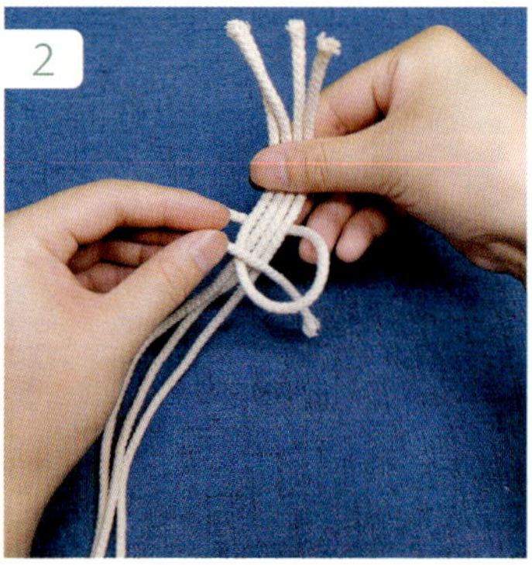

Bring the lower end of the working cord through the loop from front to back.

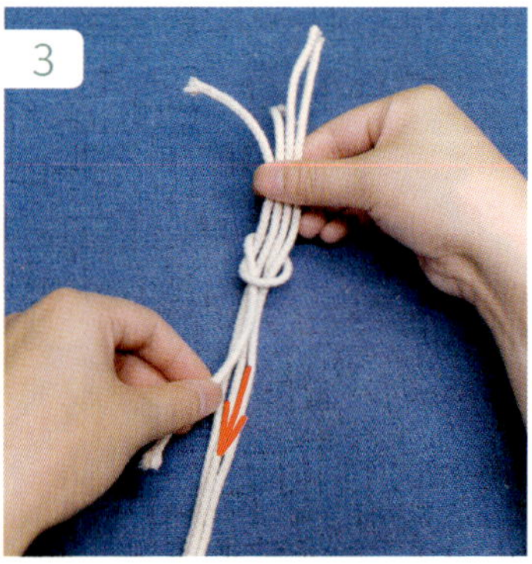

Pull the cord tight to secure the knot at the chosen position.

4. Half Hitch Knot/Half Hitch Sinnet

Used for weaving vertical stripe patterns, repeating half hitch knots in the same direction will create a half hitch sinnet. Based on the position of the working cord and the holding cord, there are four weaving methods as shown in the diagram on the right. From left to right, pictured here are counterclockwise weaving (working cord on top), clockwise weaving (working cord on top), counterclockwise weaving (working cord underneath), and clockwise weaving (working cord underneath).

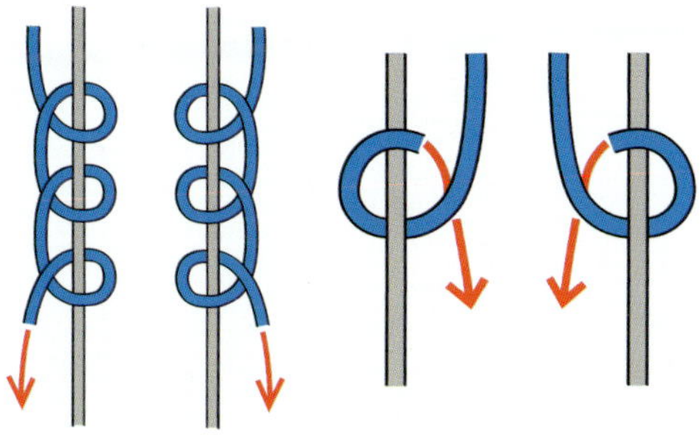

In general weaving situations, if the direction is not particularly emphasized, mastering just one method is sufficient. In the process of weaving half hitch sinnets, the holding cord remains stationary and can consist of a single strand or multiple strands. The working cord is usually a single strand. After wrapping it in the same direction, it will naturally twist. When the working cord rotates to the back, you can adjust it to the front for easier handling. The following tutorial demonstrates the half hitch sinnet knot using counterclockwise weaving with the working cord on top.

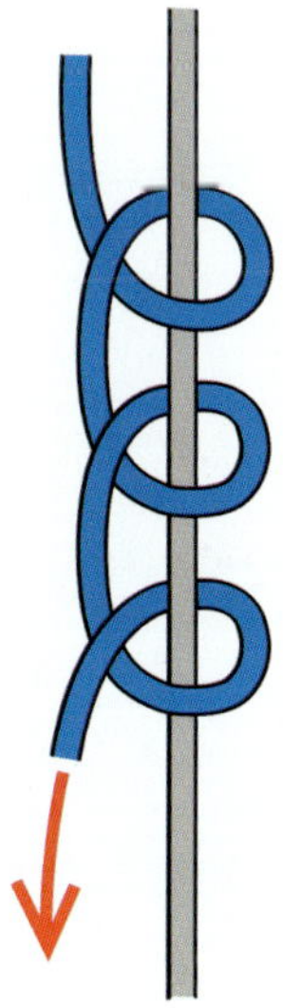

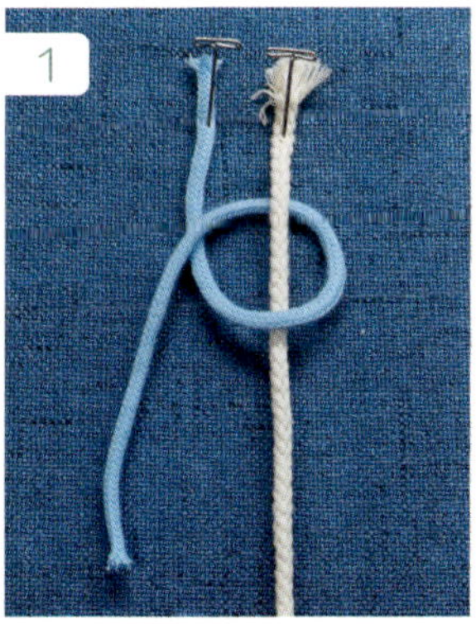

1 The blue cord is the working cord, and the white cord is the holding cord. Wrap the working cord counterclockwise from front to back underneath the holding cord, then pull it through the loop created by the working cord. Tighten to complete a half hitch knot.

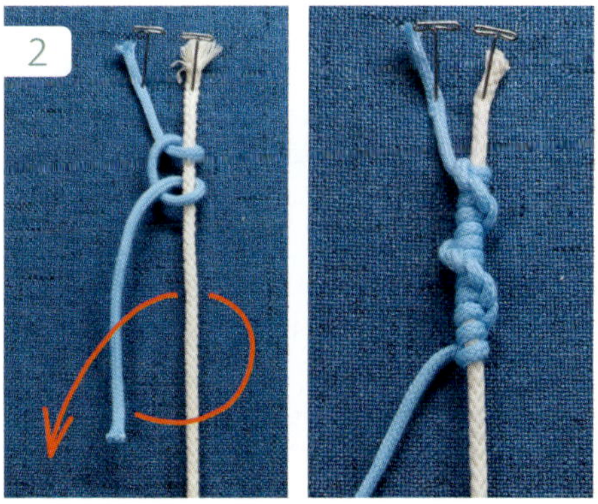

2 Repeat the previous operation, pushing each half hitch knot upward as you go, forming a half hitch sinnet.

5. Alternating Half Hitch Knot

Used for weaving vertical stripe patterns, the alternating half hitch knot is derived from the half hitch knot. Using two cords or multiples of two, alternating the working cords to weave half hitch knots is called the alternating half hitch knot. Unlike the half hitch knot, in the alternating half hitch knot, two cords alternate as the holding cord and working cord. When one cord is the holding cord, the other serves as the working cord. The holding cord should be kept taut.

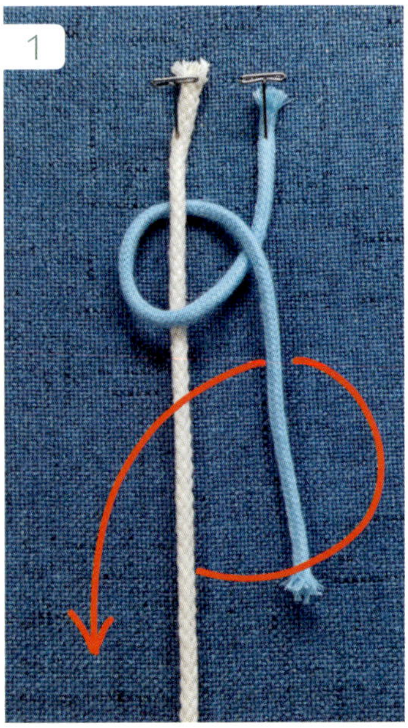

The blue cord is the working cord, and the white cord is the holding cord. Weave a half hitch knot and tighten it.

The white cord is now the working cord, and the blue cord is the holding cord. Weave a half hitch knot and tighten it.

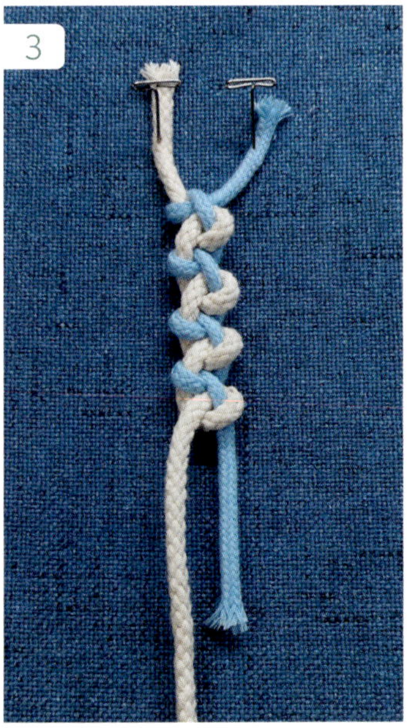

Repeat steps 1–2, with the two cords alternating as the holding cord and working cord, until the desired length is achieved.

6. Reverse Lark's Head Knot Plus a Half Hitch

Also known as the continuous lark's head knot, this knot is used for starting or for decorating blank spaces along the holding cord. It is divided into horizontal and vertical knots, with the weaving method alternating over and under.

Horizontal Reverse Lark's Head Knot Plus a Half Hitch

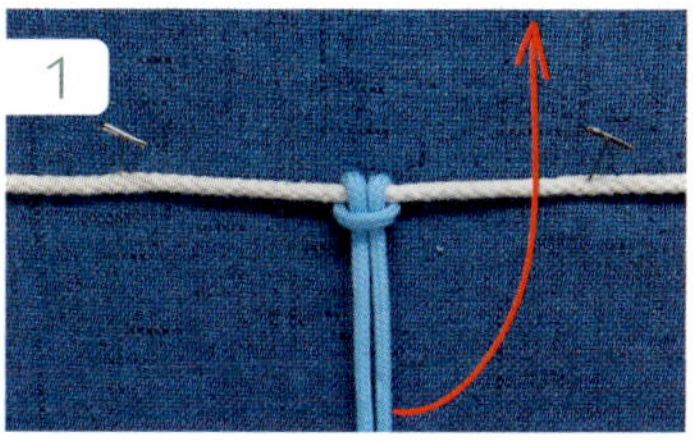

Secure the cord to the holding cord using a lark's head knot.

Bend the right cord upwards and press it over the holding cord to form a loop. Bring the end of the cord through the loop from back to front.

Bend the right cord upwards and place it under the holding cord to form a loop. Bring the end of the cord through the loop from front to back, completing a full lark's head knot.

Repeat steps 2–3 with the left cord. Note that the left cord should first be placed over the holding cord, and then placed underneath it. Following this sequence will ensure that the knot is neat.

Vertical Reverse Lark's Head Knot Plus a Half Hitch

The blue cord is the working cord, and the yellow cord is the holding cord. Weave a half hitch knot counterclockwise (with the working cord on top) and tighten it. Next, weave a half hitch knot counterclockwise (with the working cord underneath) and tighten it. Repeat the above steps until the desired length is achieved.

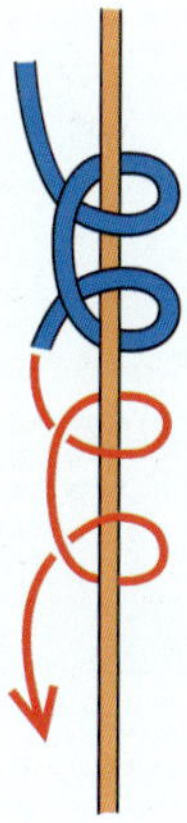

7. Square Knot Without Holding Cord

It is used for decoration and connection. It is woven using two cords or multiples of two. Below are demonstrations of two methods, the threading method and the folding method. The threading method allows for continuous vertical weaving but cannot bear weight. The tension from pulling up and down can cause the knot to deform. The folding method is suitable for creating the starting knot in the middle of two cords and is commonly used when weaving feathers.

Threading Method

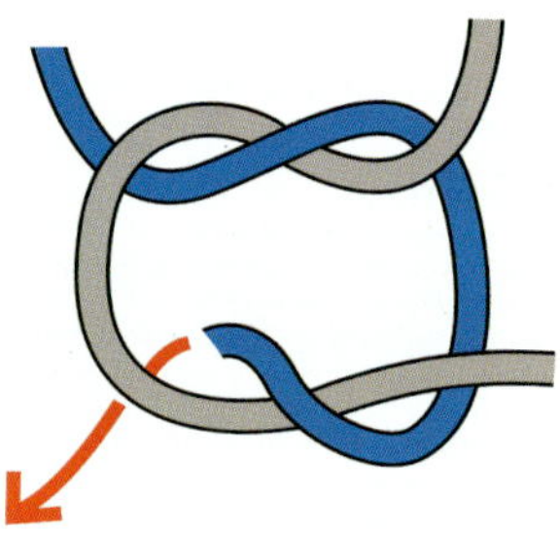

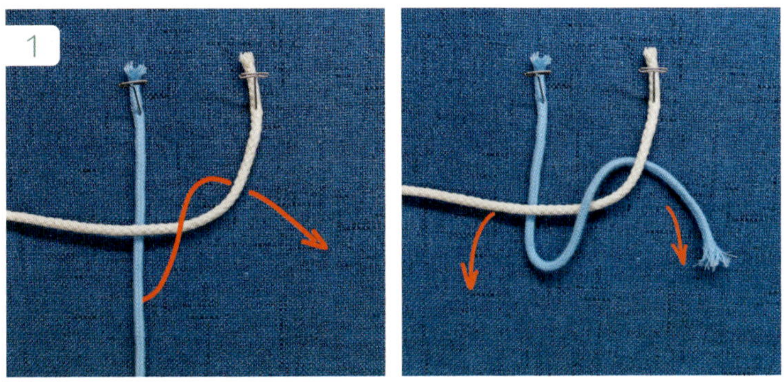

Bend the white cord to the left and place it over the blue cord. Then, take the blue cord to the right and wrap it from the front to the back under the white cord.

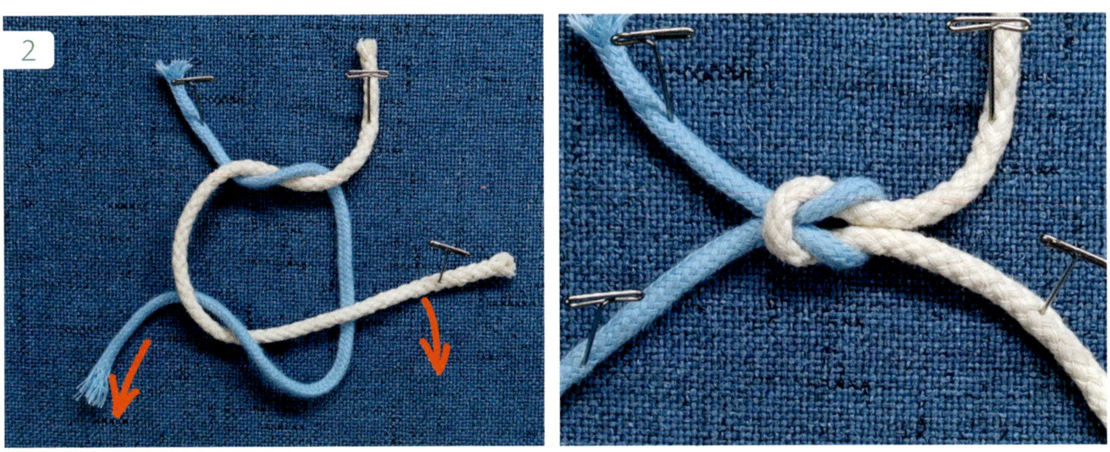

Bend the white cord to the right and place it over the blue cord. Then, take the blue cord to the left and wrap it from the front to the back under the white cord. Tighten the cords to complete the square knot without holding cord, with the knot end positioned on the left side.

Folding Method

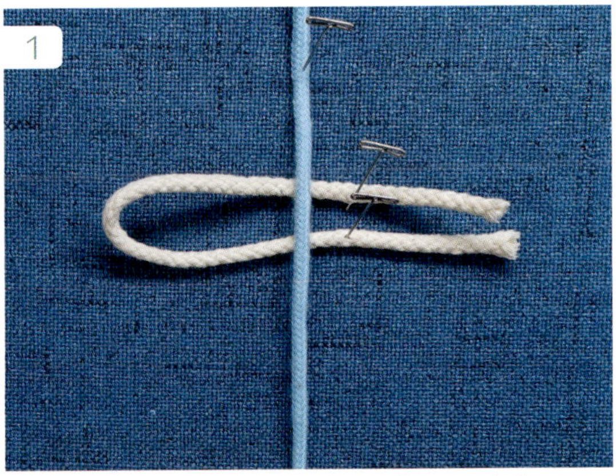

Fold the white cord in half to form a loop and place it below the midpoint of the blue cord.

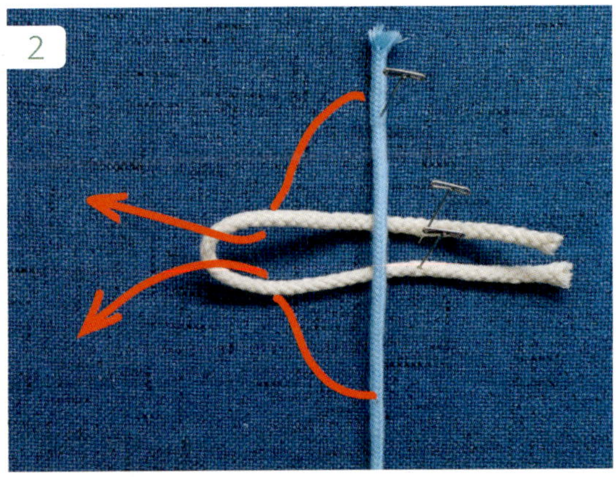

Bring both ends of the blue cord through the white loop, moving upward from below.

Tighten both ends of the cords to complete the square knot without holding cord. The knot end will be positioned on the right side.

8. Square Knot

Derived from the square knot without holding cord, the difference between it and this knot is that the square knot has an holding cord, whereas the square knot without holding cord does not. The square knot is often used in tapestry weaving. Starting from the initial knot end, the number of knot ends will equal the number of square knots. A square knot requires at least three strands of cord. The central cord serves as the holding cord and can be one or multiple strands, while the cords on either side are the working cords. In this book, the square knot generally uses four strands of cord. Using four strands makes it easier to calculate the amount of cord needed and facilitates pattern design.

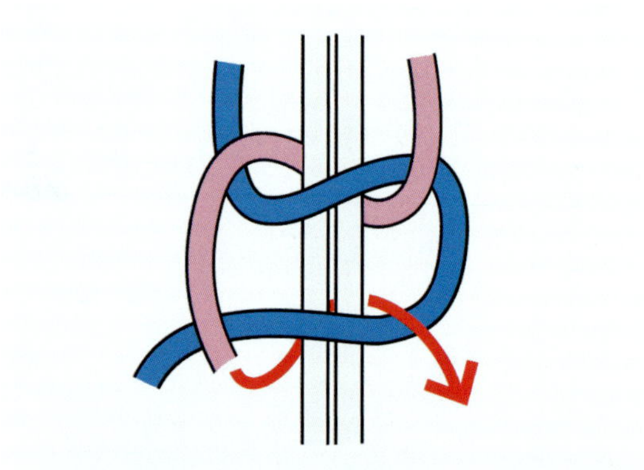

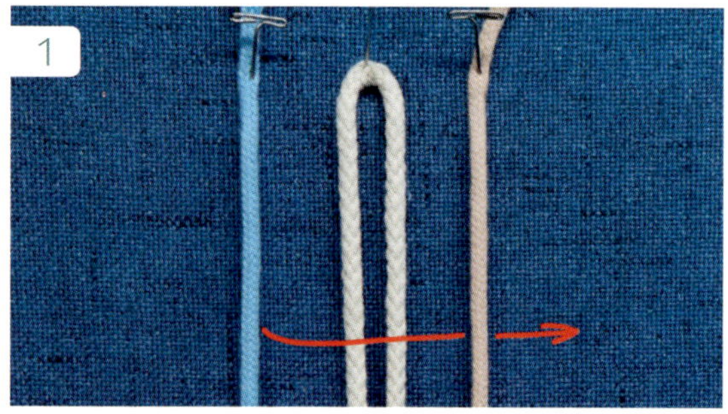

The two white cords in the center are the holding cords, while the blue and pink cords on either side are the working cords.

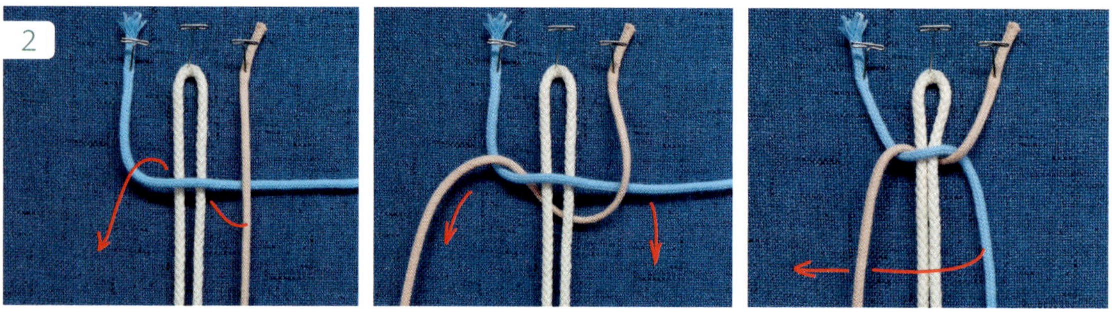

Bend the blue cord to the right, placing it over the holding cords, and position it under the pink cord. Bend the pink cord to the left, wrap it downward around the holding cords, and thread it through the blue cord. Tighten the cords, completing half of the square knot.

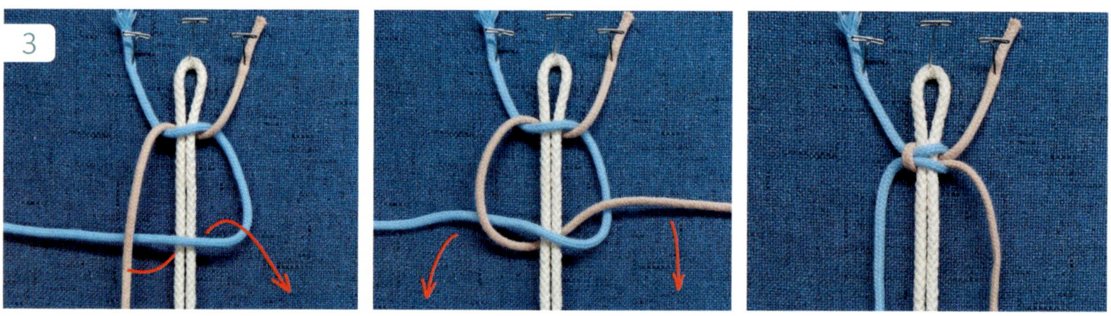

Bend the blue cord to the left, placing it over the holding cords, and position it under the pink cord. Bend the pink cord to the right, wrap it downward around the holding cords, and thread it through above the blue cord. Tighten the cords to complete a square knot, with the knot end positioned on the left side.

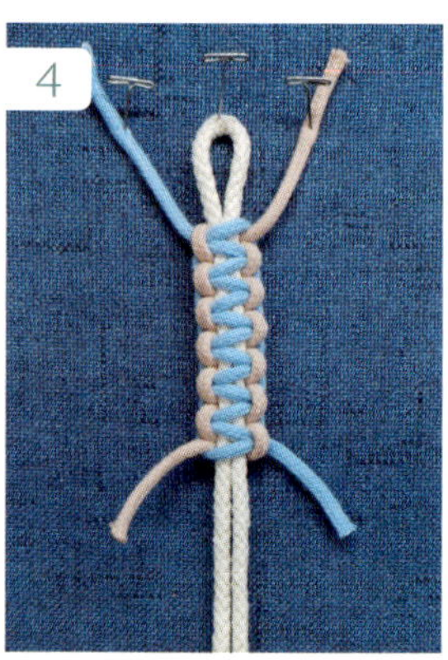

Repeat the above steps to achieve a vertical strip of square knots.

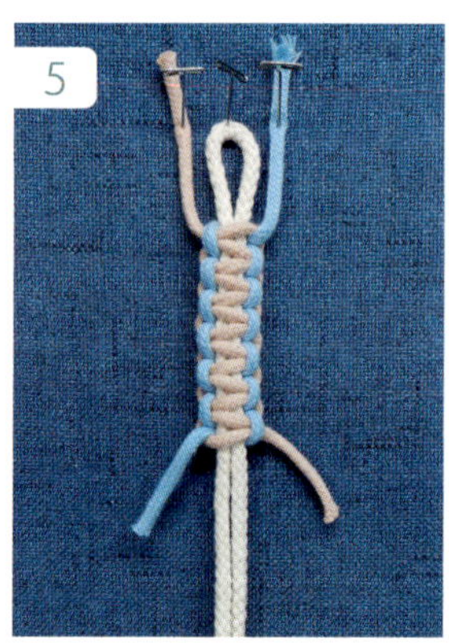

When using two different colors of working cords, the front and back sides will be the exact opposite, as shown in the illustration. If using cords of the same color, the front and back sides will be the same.

9. Square Knot Button

The square knot button is used to create a three-dimensional effect in a tapestry. Usually, three to five square knots are sufficient. The more square knots, the higher the elevation.

1 Leave a small gap before starting the square knot button, then weave four square knots.

2 Thread the working cords on both sides from front to back through the gap.

3 Tighten the working cords, then weave another square knot to secure.

10. Spiral Knot

Also known as a single direction square knot, the spiral knot differs from the square knot in that it involves repeating half square knots in the same direction to create a spiral pattern. The spiral knot requires at least three strands of cord. The middle strand serves as the holding cord, which can be one or more strands, while the working cords on the sides repeat half square knots in the same direction. In this book, the spiral knot is generally made with four strands of cord, as four strands make it easier to calculate cord usage and simplify pattern design.

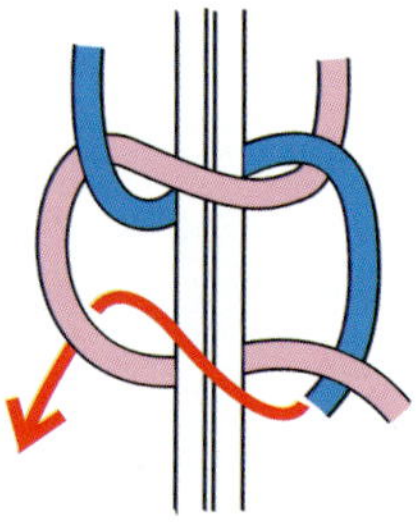

The white cord serves as the holding cord, while the blue and pink cords are the working cords. The blue cord bends to the right, passes downward through the holding cord, and rests on top of the pink cord. The pink cord bends to the left, goes up over the holding cord, and passes under the blue cord. Tighten the cords to complete a half square knot.

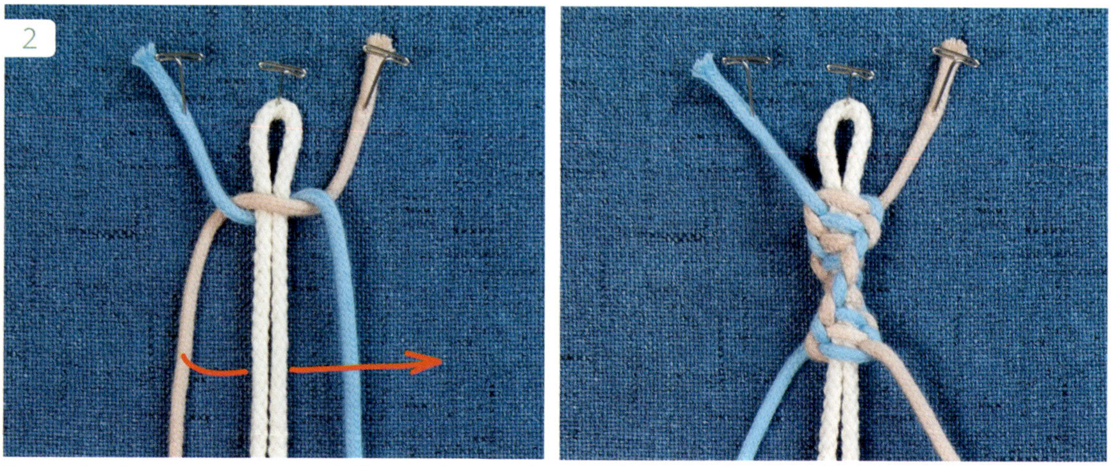

Repeat the above process, weaving half square knots in the same direction. The knot will automatically twist, forming a spiral knot.

11. Double Half Hitch Knot

The double half hitch knot is commonly used in designs like tapestries and has many variations. The double half hitch knot consists of a holding cord and a working cord. The holding cord remains stationary while the working cord wraps around it in a regular pattern twice to complete a double half hitch knot.

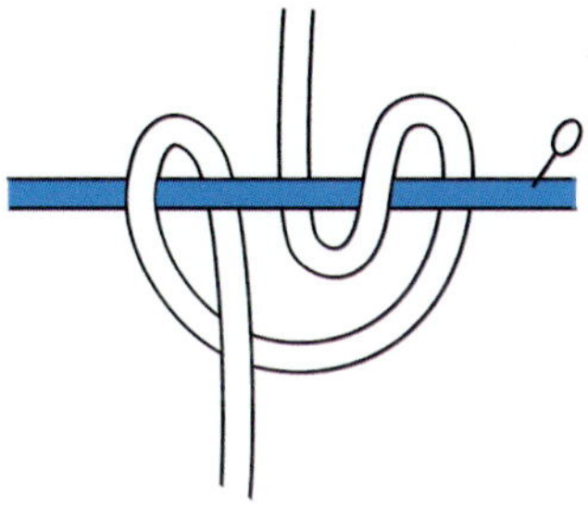

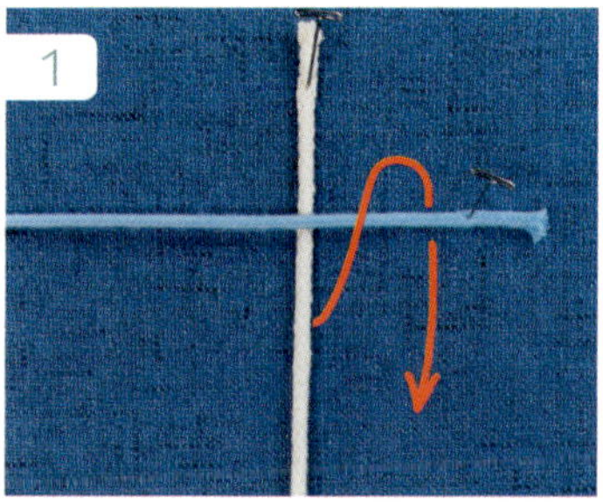

The blue cord is the holding cord, and the white cord is the working cord. At the start, the holding cord must be positioned above the working cord.

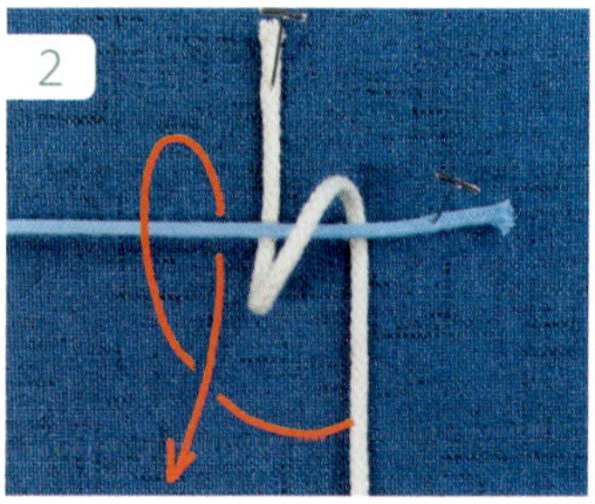

Bend the working cord upward to the right and wrap it around the holding cord from behind. Make sure the holding cord remains straight.

Bend the working cord upward to the left to form a loop, then wrap it around the holding cord from behind and bring it through the loop.

Straighten the holding cord, tighten the working cord, and complete a double half hitch knot.

Horizontal Double Half Hitch Knot

This is a type of knot in which several working cords are continuously wrapped around the same horizontal holding cord.

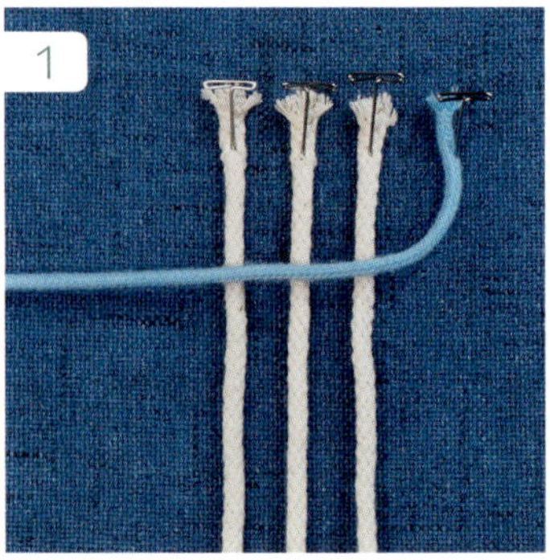

Position the right blue cord as the holding cord, and stretch it horizontally above the left working cords.

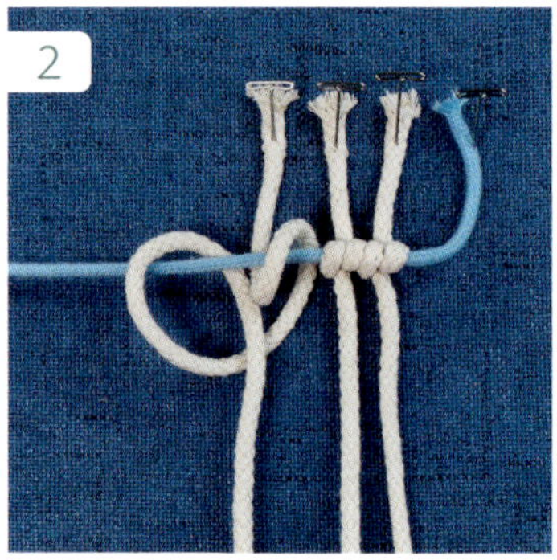

Starting from the cord closest to the holding cord, create a series of double half hitch knots, ensuring that each knot is adjacent to the previous one.

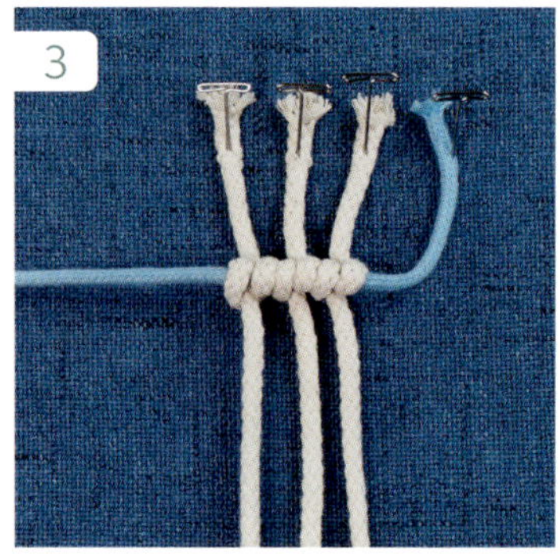

Multiple double half hitch knots can be weaved on a single holding cord, creating a horizontal double half hitch knot.

Vertical Double Half Hitch Knot

Unlike the horizontal double half hitch knot, the vertical double half hitch knot involves wrapping the same working cord continuously around different holding cords.

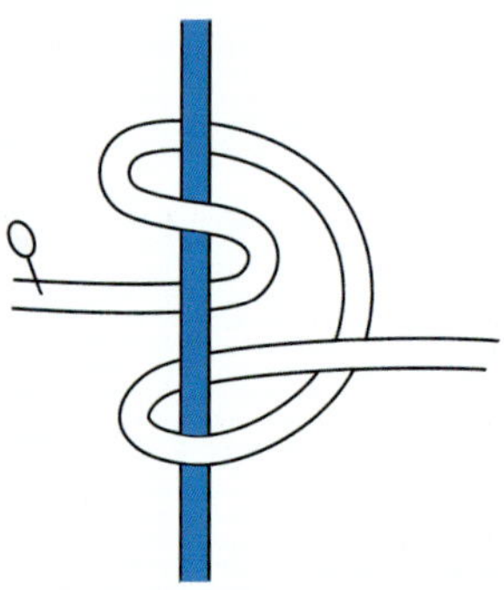

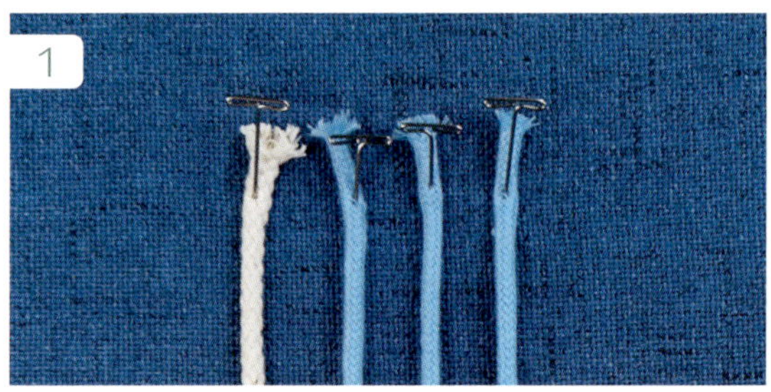

The white cord on the left is the working cord, and the blue cords are the holding cords. While you are weaving, the holding cords must be positioned above the working cord.

Start weaving the double half hitch knot on the holding cord closest to the working cord, making sure to keep the holding cord straight.

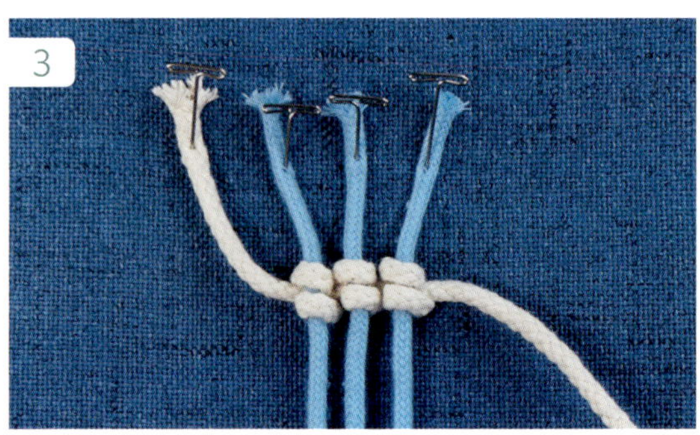

On each of the following holding cords, use the same working cord to weave double half hitch knots, forming a vertical double half hitch knot.

Diagonal Double Half Hitch Knot

Diagonal double half hitch knots are commonly used in woven works like tapestries, primarily for line design, allowing for the creation of richly varied patterns. The weaving method is the same as for horizontal double half hitch knots, except the holding cord is slanted.

Tips

Regardless of whether you are weaving horizontal, vertical, or diagonal double half hitch knots, there are a few key points to keep in mind regarding the double half hitch knot technique.

1. When using double half hitch knots in designs such as tapestries, any strand can serve as the holding cord, allowing for a wide variety of knot combinations and variations.
2. When weaving, first confirm the holding cord and its direction. Pull the holding cord straight with the hand on the side where the holding cord extends. If beginners find it difficult to determine the direction of the holding cord while weaving, they can use a pin to secure the tail end. After more practice, the pin can be removed.
3. When weaving a double half hitch knot, the holding cord should be positioned above the working cord.
4. The holding cord must be kept straight and should not become tangled with the working cord.

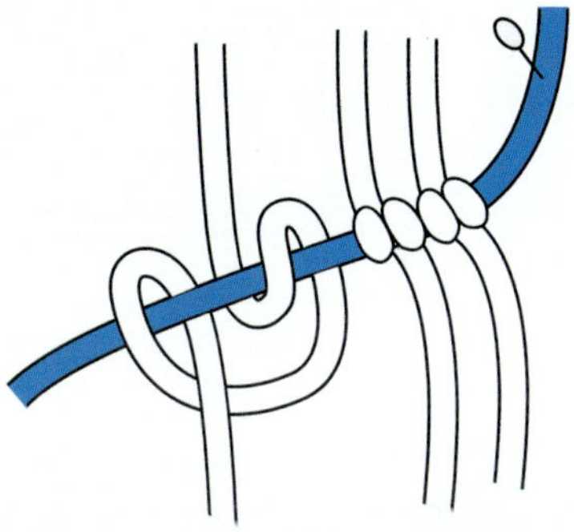

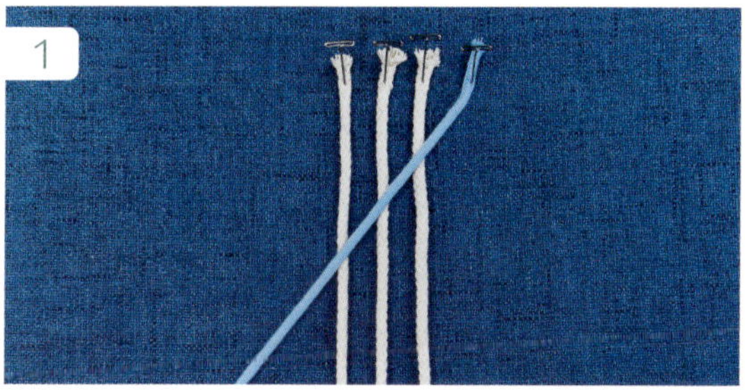

1

The blue cord on the right serves as the holding cord, while all white cords are the working cords. Tilt the holding cord to the left and pull it above the working cords.

2

Starting with the working cord closest to the holding cord, weave double half hitch knots one by one toward the lower left. Each double half hitch knot should be placed tightly against the previous one.

3

Multiple double half hitch knots can be woven on a single holding cord, forming a diagonal double half hitch knot.

12. Reverse Double Half Hitch Knot

This knot is typically used at the midpoint of symmetrical patterns. When we create diagonal double half hitch knots or other double half hitch knots on the front side, the reverse side actually resembles a reverse double half hitch knot.

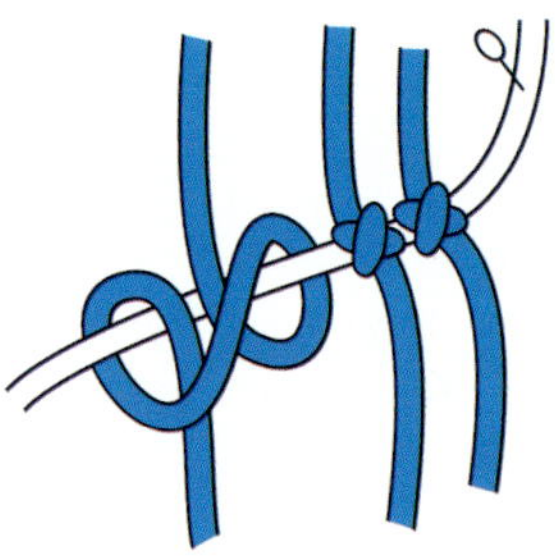

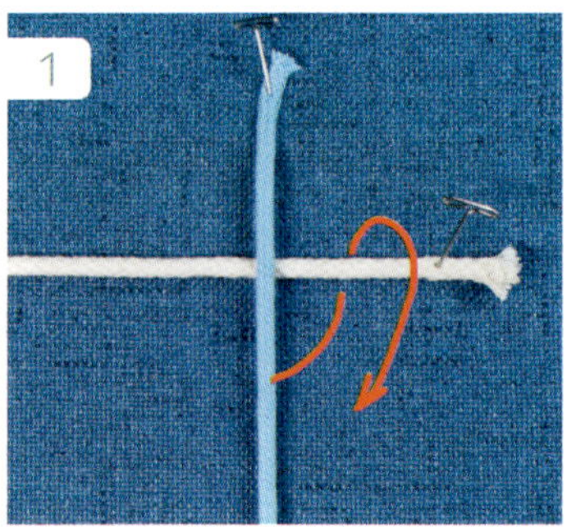

The white cord is the holding cord, and the blue cord is the working cord. During weaving, the holding cord is positioned below the working cord.

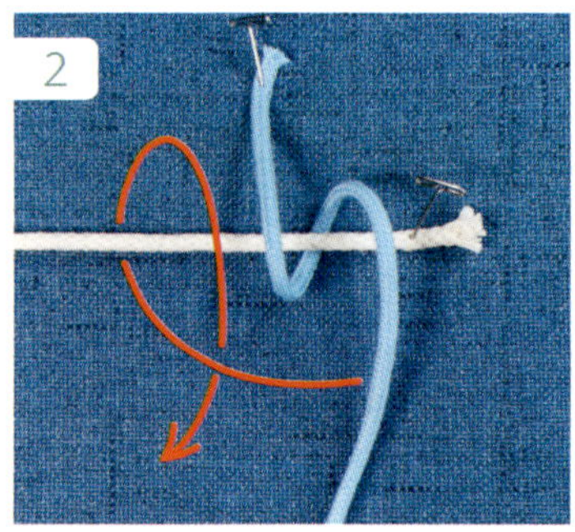

The working cord loops from the back right over the holding cord and bends downward.

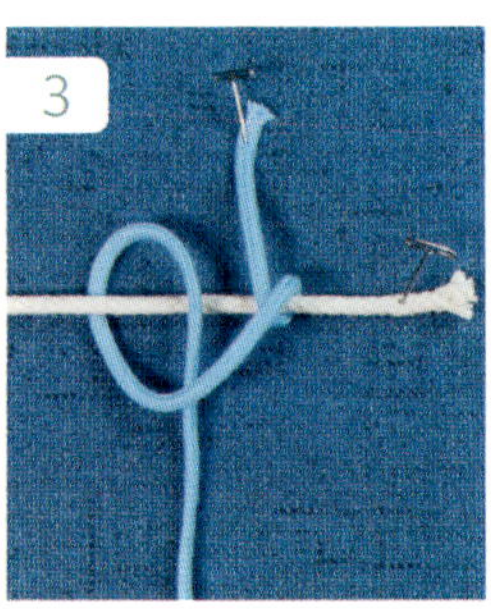

Bend the working cord upward to the left, forming a loop, then pass it from back to front over the holding cord and through the loop.

Tighten the cord, and the knot will form an X shape.

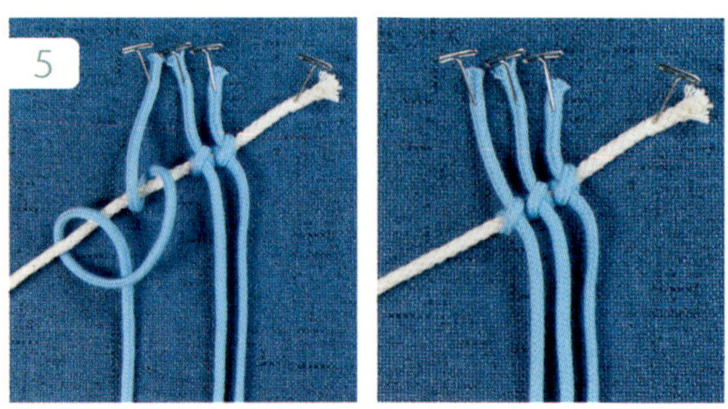

On the same holding cord, use different working cords to weave reverse double half hitch knots to the left.

13. Three-Strand Simple Braid

Used for weaving vertical stripe patterns, this technique involves using three strands or a multiple of three strands of cord.

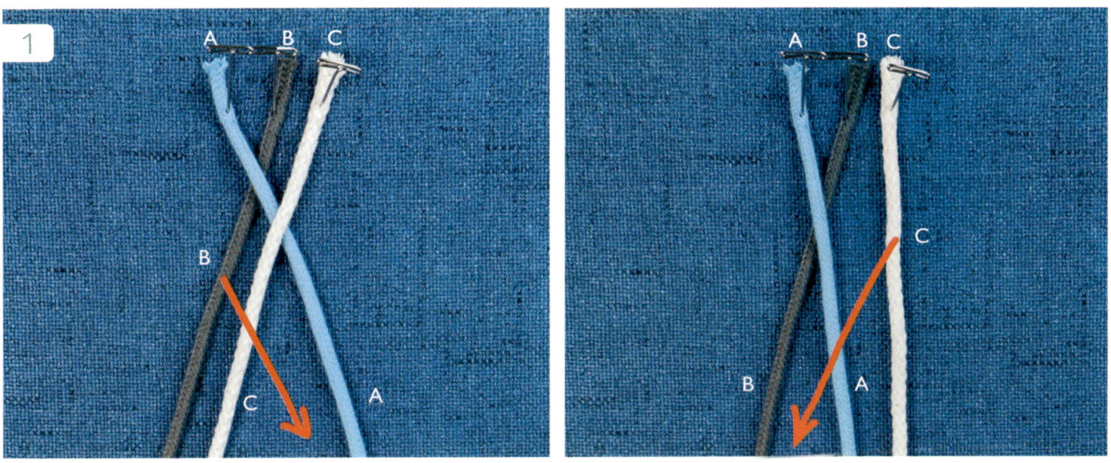

Place cord A over cord B, and then place cord C over cord A.

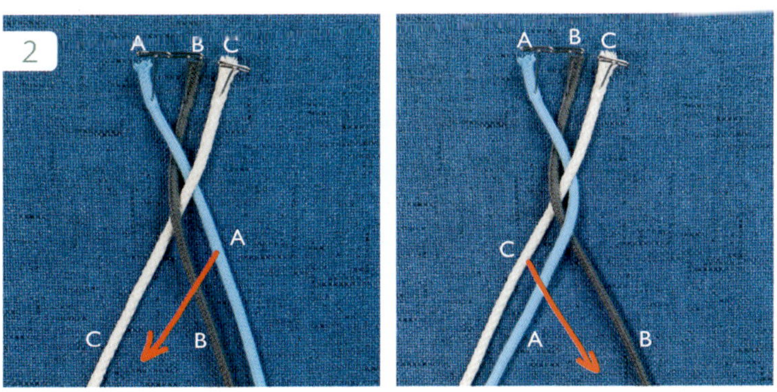

Place cord B over cord C, and then place cord A over cord B.

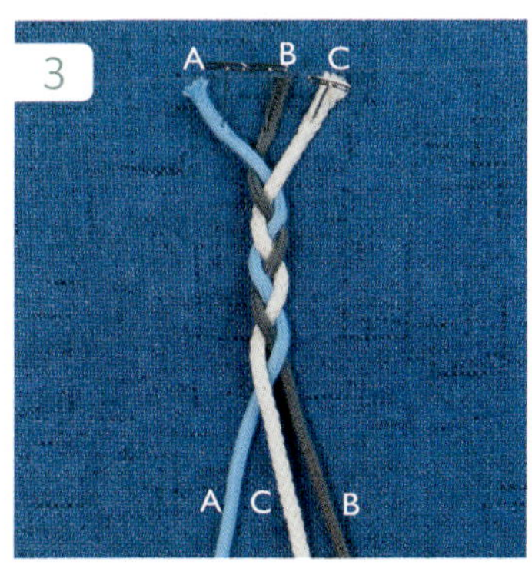

Repeat the above steps by placing the left cord over the middle cord and the right cord over the middle cord, continuing until you reach the desired length.

14. Four-Strand Simple Braid

Used for weaving vertical stripe patterns, using four strands or multiples of four strands of cord. The weaving mnemonic can be summarized as follows. The leftmost cord presses the 2nd cord, picks up the 3rd cord, and presses the 4th cord.

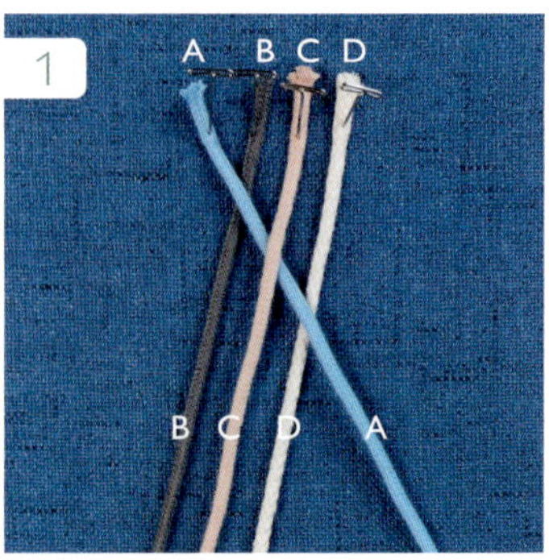

Cord A presses cord B, picks up cord C, and presses cord D.

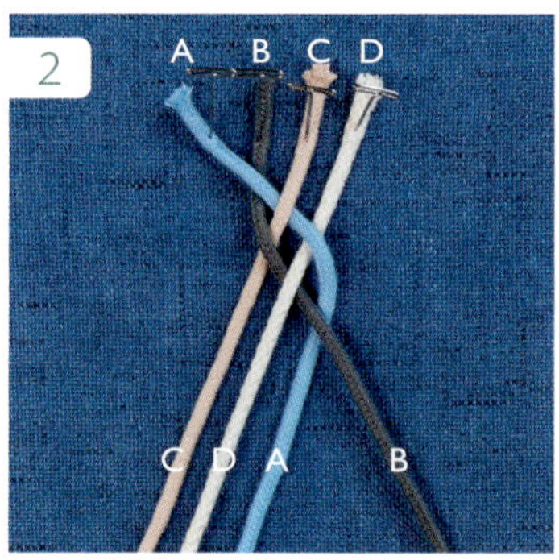

Cord B presses cord C, picks up cord D, and presses cord A.

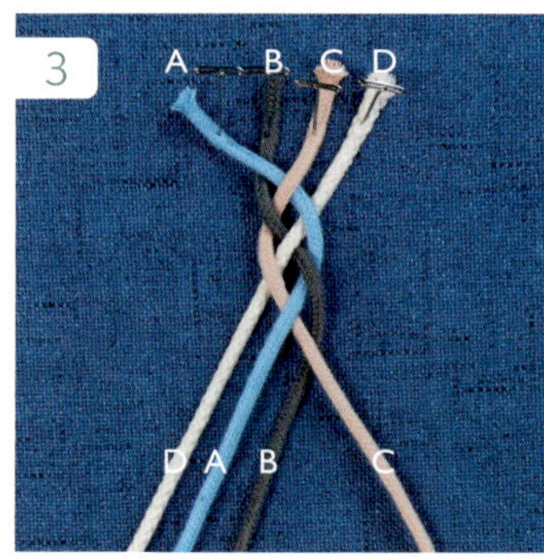

Cord C presses cord D, picks up cord A, and presses cord B.

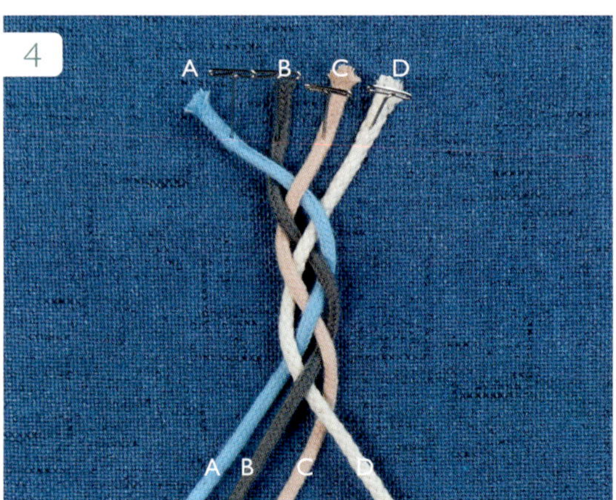

Cord D presses cord A, picks up cord B, and presses cord C.

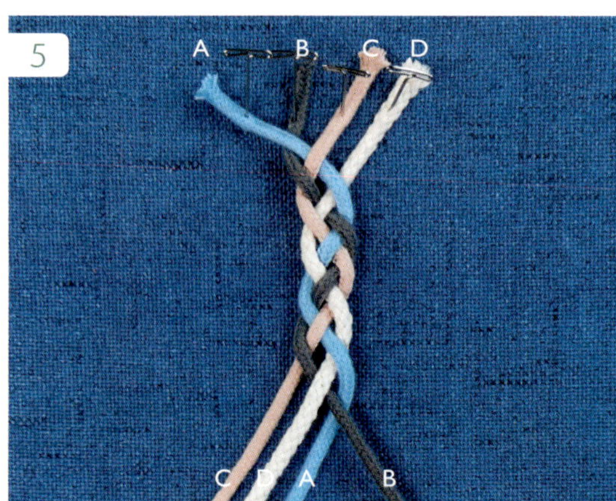

Repeat the above steps, tightening the knots as you go until you reach the desired length.

15. Chinese Crown Knot

Used for continuously weaving vertical stripe patterns, the Chinese crown knot has both clockwise and counterclockwise variations. Below is a demonstration of the clockwise method. The continuous combination of Chinese crown knots can form round Chinese crown knots and square Chinese crown knots.

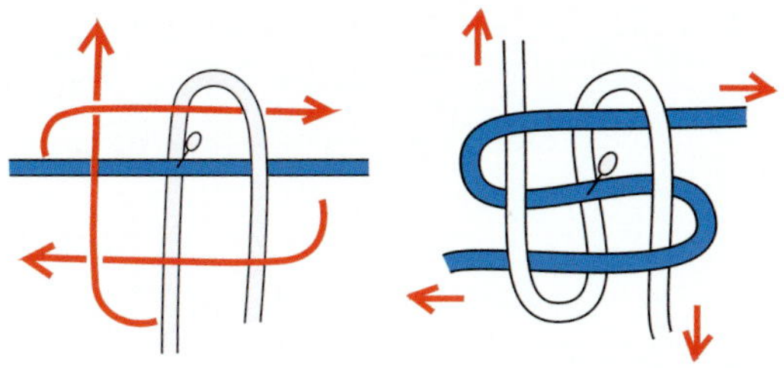

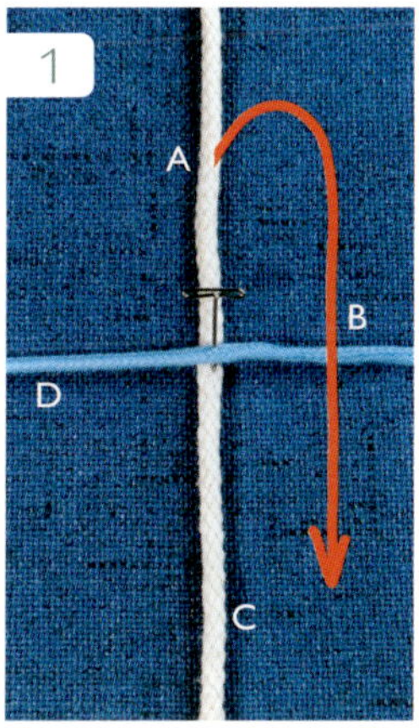

As shown in the diagram, place two or four strands of cord perpendicular to each other.

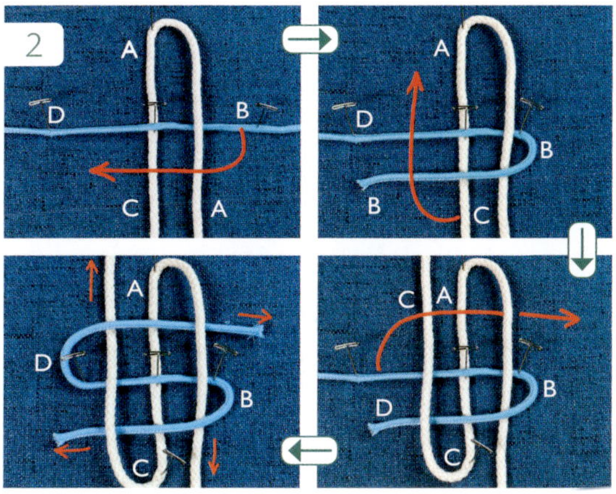

In a clockwise direction, fold the strands as follows: Cord A presses cord B. Cord B presses cord A and cord C. Cord C presses cord B and cord D. Cord D presses cord C and cord A, then passes through the loop formed by cord A.

Pull the cords tightly in all four directions to form a grid pattern. Repeat steps 1–2 to complete a section of the crown knot.

Round Crown Knot (Cylindrical Knot)

Repeating weaving crown knots in the same direction (either clockwise or counterclockwise) creates a round crownknot.

Square Crown Knot (Square Column Knot)

This knot alternates between clockwise and counterclockwise directions when weaving crown knots, creating a square crown knot.

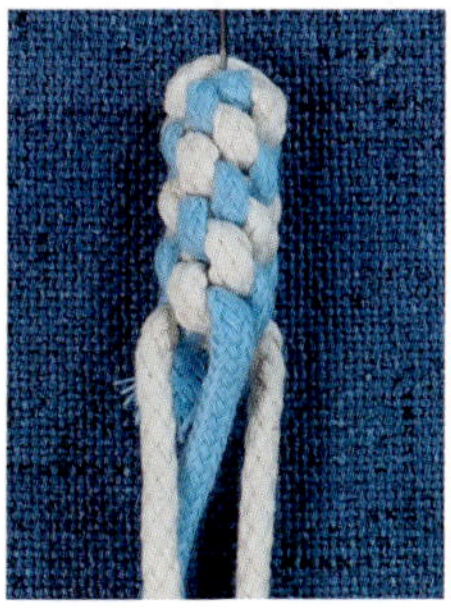

Round crown knot (cylindrical knot).

Square crown knot (square column knot).

16. Barrel Knot

This knot is used for single-cord endings, adding cords, or decoration, and is typically completed with a single strand of cord.

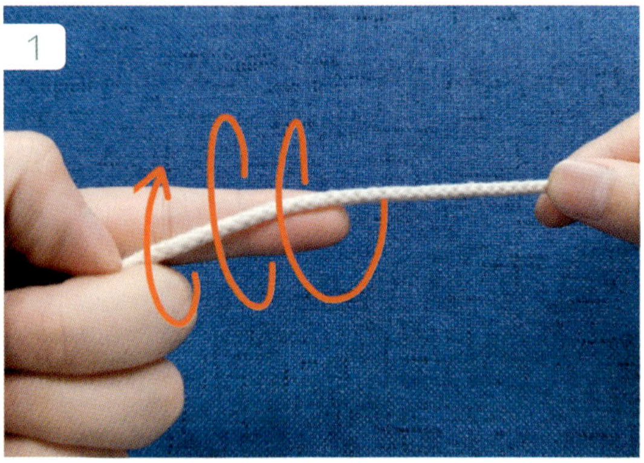

Hold one end of the cord with your left hand while holding the other end with your right hand.

Wrap the end of the cord in your right hand around your left index finger and the other end of the cord about three times. For a longer knot, you can wrap it more times.

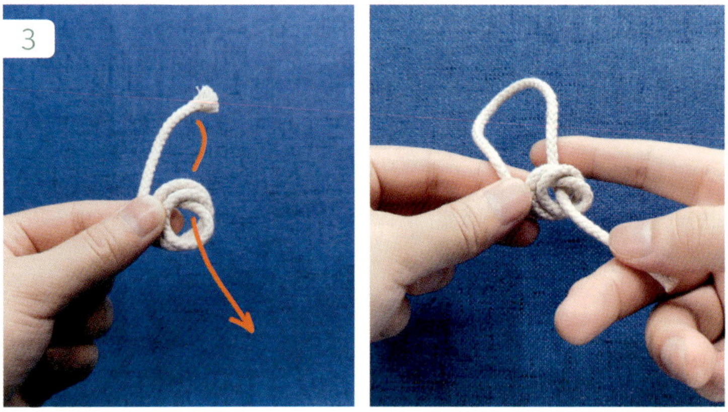

Remove the cord loop from your index finger, making sure to hold the loop so it doesn't come undone. Thread the end of the cord in your right hand through the loop.

Slowly pull both ends of the cord to tighten the knot and adjust the cord so that it is even.

17. Leaf Knot

This knot is often used for end decoration and is typically made with a single strand of cord.

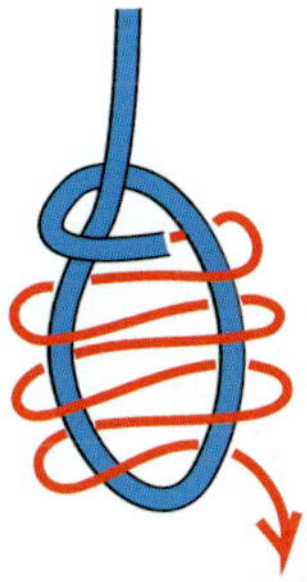

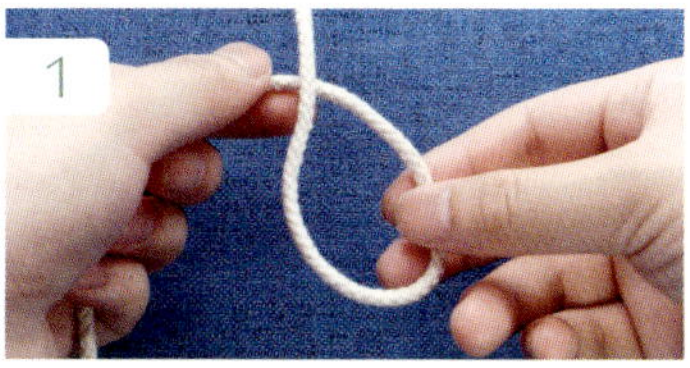

Secure the top end of the cord. Leave the bottom end slightly longer, then bend it counterclockwise and upward and place it underneath the cord.

Thread the bottom end through the loop and pull it to the right.

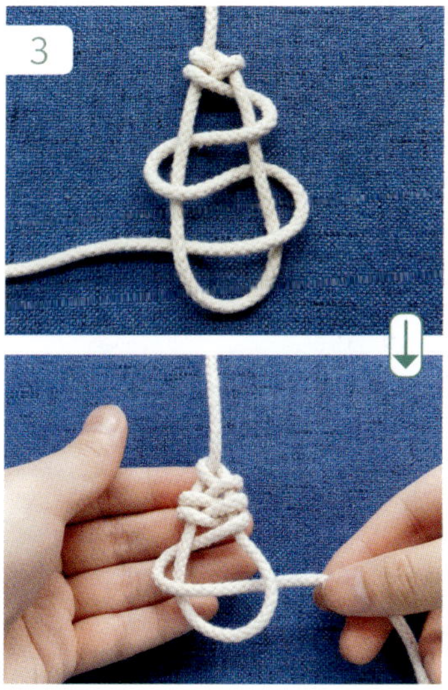

Alternately pass the bottom end through the loop from left to right and pull tight, until the desired length is achieved (typically six to eight times).

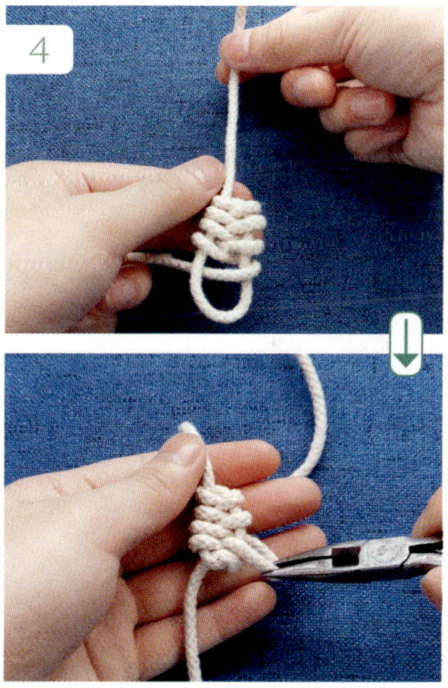

Pull the cord upward to tighten it, and use pliers to tidy up the knot.

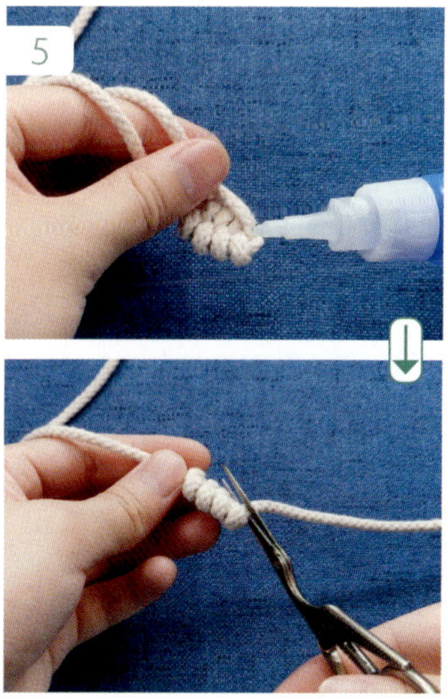

Apply glue to secure the junction of the cord and the loop to prevent it from coming apart, then trim off the excess end of the cord.

18. Sailor Knot

The sailor knot is mainly used as a decorative knot and is not suitable for load bearing purposes. Applying weight may cause the knot to deform.

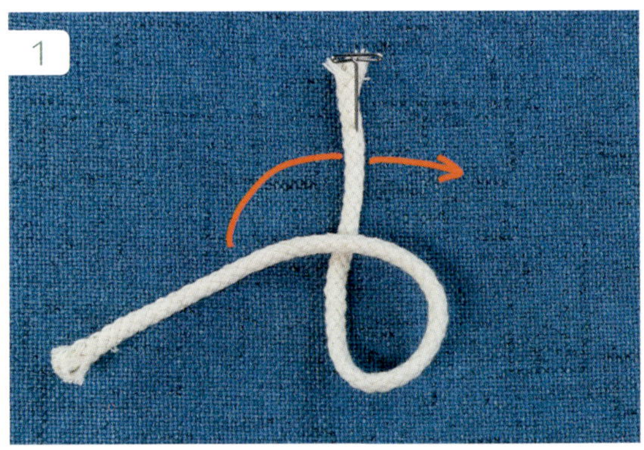

Secure the upper end of the cord. Bend the lower end upward in a counterclockwise direction, crossing it over the cord to form a loop.

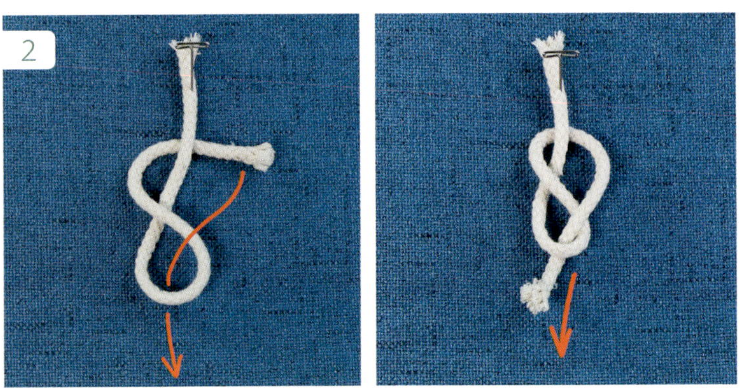

Bend the lower end of the cord to the right, placing it under the upper cord. Then, pass it from front to back through the lower loop.

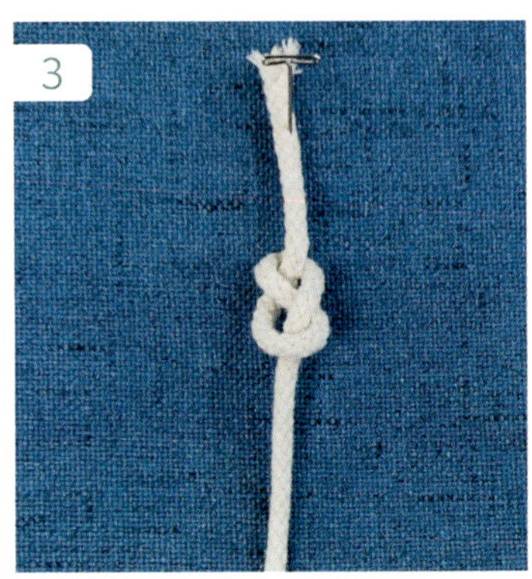

Tighten both ends of the cord and adjust the knot's tension and structure to form a "figure 8" shape.

19. Josephine Knot

Primarily used as a decorative knot, the Josephine knot cannot bear weight, as pulling the knot up and down will cause it to deform.

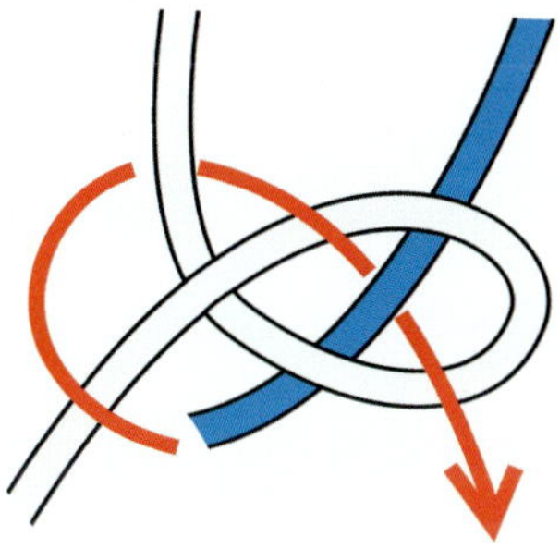

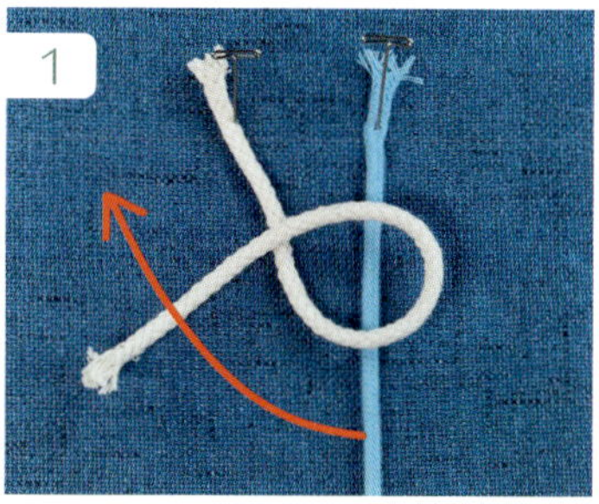

Secure the upper ends of the white and blue cords. Bend the white cord to form a loop and press the loop over the blue cord.

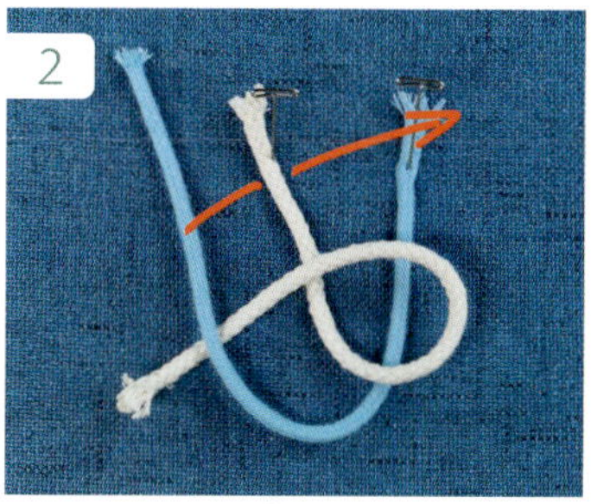

Bend the lower end of the blue cord upward to the left, pressing it over the lower end of the white cord.

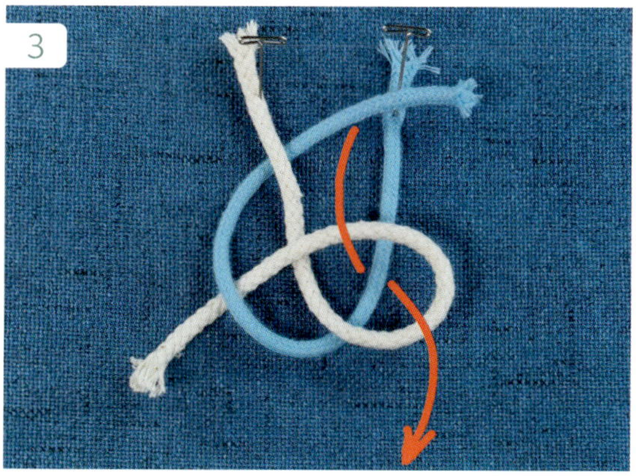

Pass the lower end of the blue cord to the right, through the upper end of the white cord.

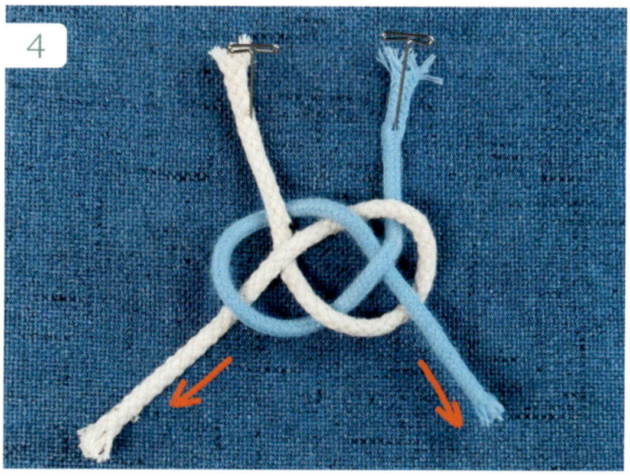

The lower end of the blue cord goes over the white cord, under the blue cord, and then over the white cord again. Then, tighten the cords and adjust the tension and structure of the knots.

20. Monkey's Fist Knot

It is often used as a decorative knot. The following demonstrates with a three-loop monkey's fist knot as an example.

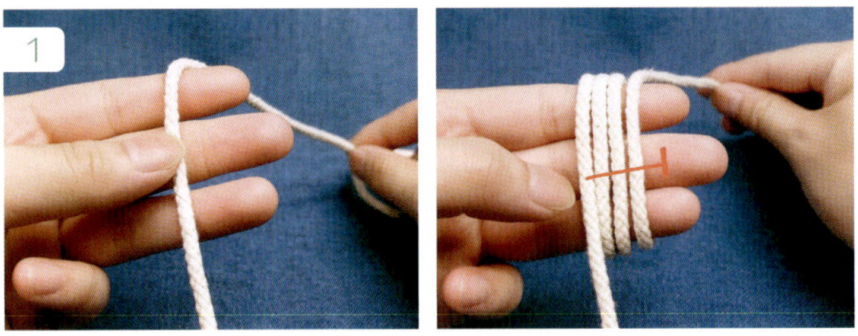

Place the cord on your fingers, using them as a wrapping tool, and wrap the cord around your fingers three times.

Insert a pin horizontally through the cord loops to fix it in place temporarily, and thread the end of the cord through the loops.

Use the cord loops as a winding tool and wrap horizontally around them for three turns.

Insert the pin vertically into the cord loop to temporarily secure it.

Thread the end of the cord through the second loop. Use the second loop of the cord as the wrapping tool and wrap it three times.

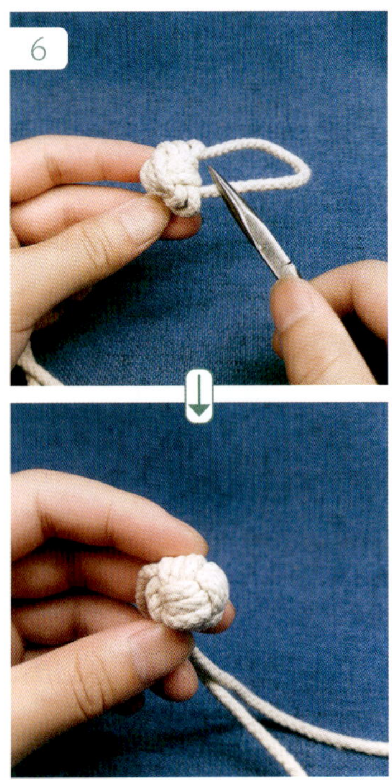

Tighten the loops in the wrapping order, using tweezers if necessary, to complete the three-loop monkey's fist knot.

21. Wrapping Knot

This knot is used for securing cords, starting hanging designs, and finishing the ends of cords.

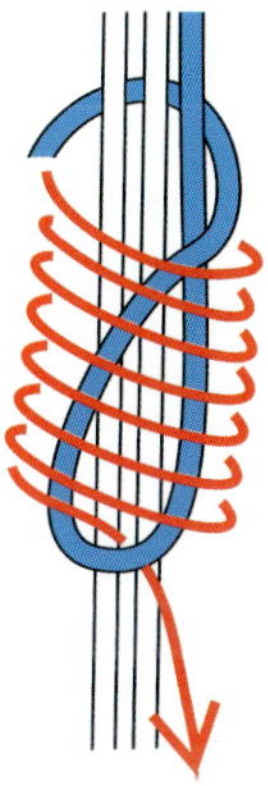

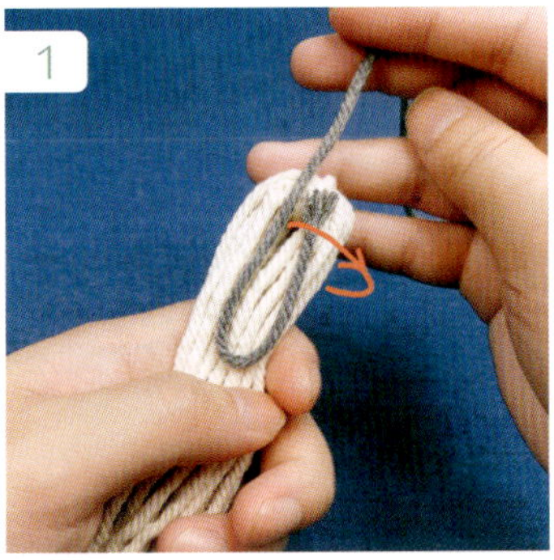

Bend the gray cord to form a loop, placing the short end on top of the white cord that needs to be secured.

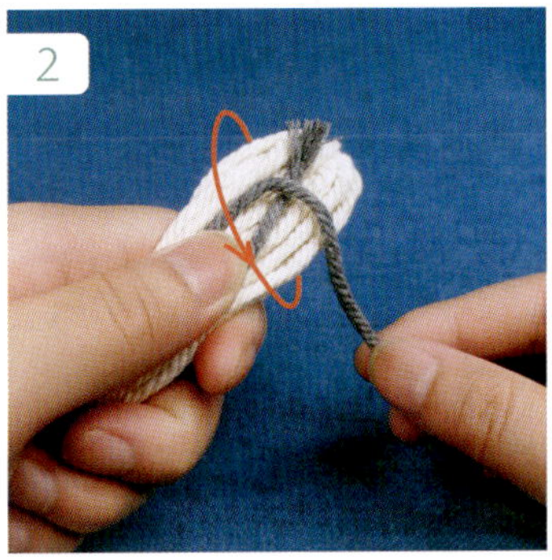

Bend the long end over the short end, ensuring that a small portion of the short end is left sticking out

Wrap the long end counterclockwise until the desired length is achieved (seven to ten turns recommended). Pass the end of the cord through the lower loop.

Pull the end of the cord from step 2 upward, and the cord end and loop will be tucked inside the wrapping knot.

Cut off the excess ends of the cord and apply glue if needed to secure them in place.

Starting Techniques

We choose different starting methods based on the different macramé designs. Below are four types of starting methods for macramé.

1. Horizontal Starting Techniques

This is commonly used in tapestry making and can be initiated on any strip like support, such as branches, wooden rods, curtain rods, etc. Here are demonstrations of three commonly used horizontal starting techniques.

Lark's Head Knot/Reverse Lark's Head Knot Starting Technique

When starting with a lark's head knot or reverse lark's head knot (see PP 29–30), make sure the front and back knot heads remain consistent.

Secure the cords sequentially on the support rod using lark's head knots or reverse lark's head knots, arranging them neatly.

The back side will show reverse lark's head knots.

When weaving large tapestries, the cords can be very long, making it time consuming and labor intensive to pull each cord through to weave a lark's head knot. Here's a simple technique to save time and effort.

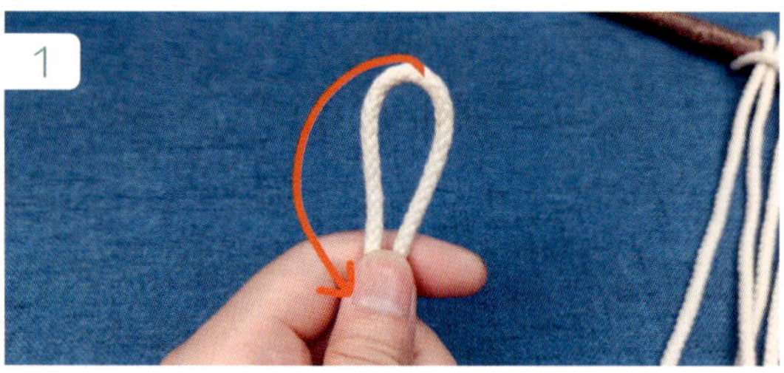

Fold the cord in half.

Bend the apex downward to create two loops, holding the apex in place with your fingers.

Bend the two loops backward together, merging them into a single loop.

Insert the support rod through the loop and pull it tight, aligning the strands neatly.

Square Knot/Spiral Knot Starting Technique

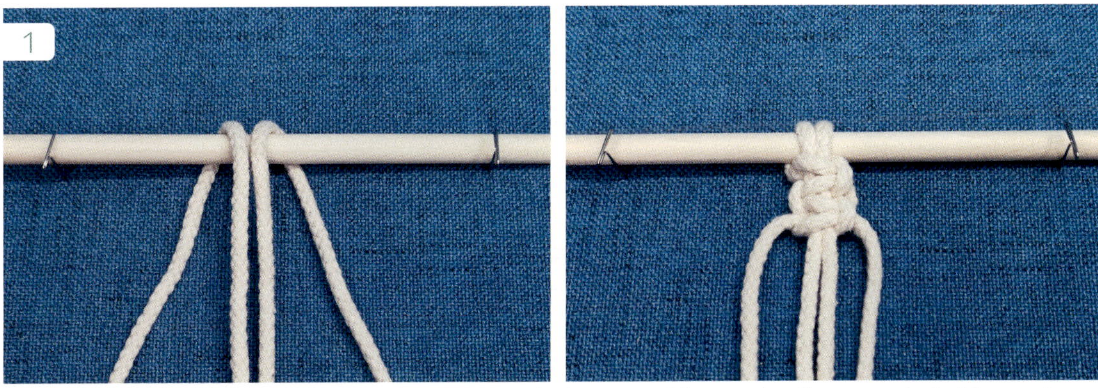

Fold two cords in half and hang them on the support rod. The two middle strands will serve as the holding cords, while the outer two strands will be the working cords. Weave square knots (see PP 37–38) or spiral knots (see P 40).

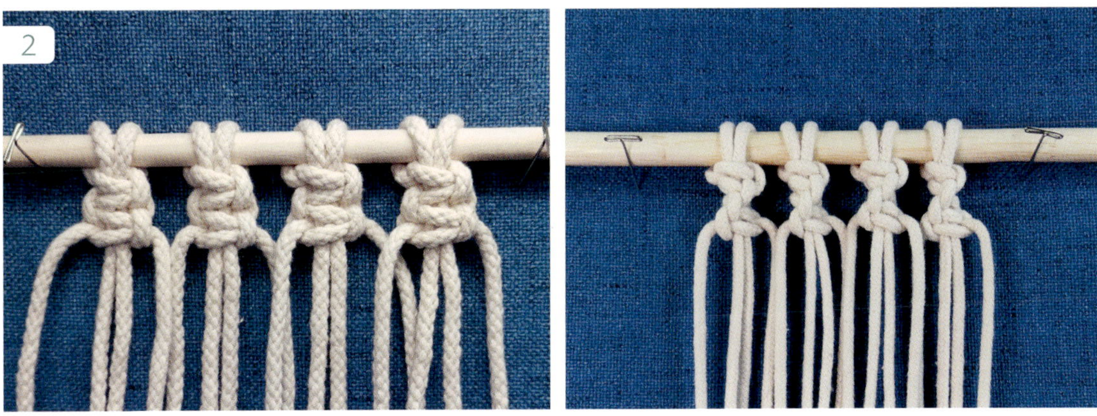

Weave to the desired length.

Double Half Hitch Knot Starting Technique

Fold the cord and hang it on the support rod. Bend the leftmost cord horizontally to serve as the holding cord while the remaining cords act as the working cords. Use the first two cords to weave a double half hitch knot (see P 41).

Pull the cord tight, ensuring the knot is snug against the support rod.

Continue to weave double half hitch knots using the remaining working cords. Once finished, wrap the holding cord around the support rod once and pull the cord tight.

2. Suspension Starting Techniques

This is commonly used for projects that require hanging, such as hanging baskets or chandeliers. This method can be completed either by using wooden rings or by creating the hanging loops with knots. Here is a demonstration of five commonly used suspension starting methods.

Overhand Knot Starting Technique

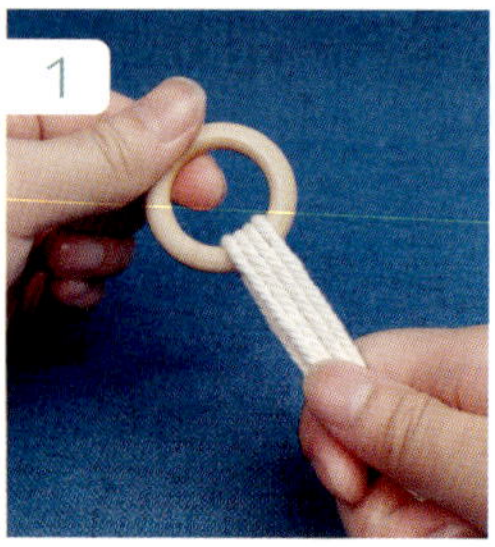

Thread multiple strands of cord through the wooden ring.

Use multiple strands to weave an overhand knot (see P 31).

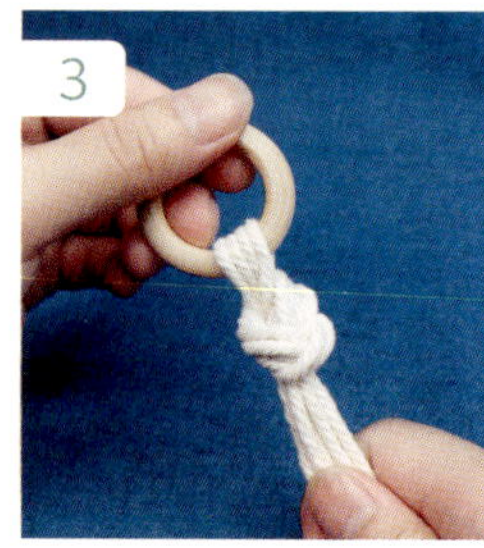

Tighten the cords so that the knot is snug against the wooden ring.

Wrapping Knot Starting Technique

Thread multiple strands through the wooden ring.

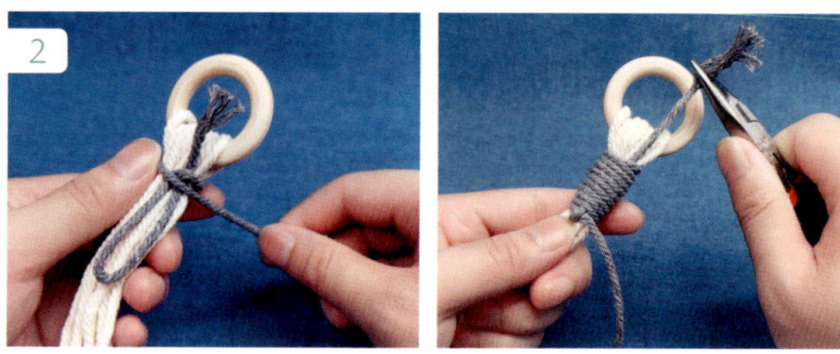

Take another cord and weave a wrapping knot (see P 53).

Spiral Knot/Square Knot Starting Technique

Pass multiple strands of cord through the wooden ring, selecting the left and right strands at the edge as the working cords, while the rest serve as the holding cords.

Braid a spiral knot (see P 40) or square knot (see PP 37–38) to the desired length.

Chinese Crown Knot Starting Technique

Thread multiple cords (in multiples of four) through the wooden ring and divide them into four groups.

Weave a Chinese crown knot (see P 47).

Weave round crown knots or square crown knots to the desired length.

Vertical Stripe Weaving Pattern Starting Technique

In the middle section of the multi-strand cord, weave either alternating half hitch knots (see P 34), square knots (see PP 37–38), three-strand simple braids (see P 45), or four-strand simple braids (see P 46).

After weaving to the desired length, fold the cord and use a wrapping knot (see P 53) to bind the multi-strand cord together, forming a cord loop. Since the number of strands used in each knot varies, the total number of strands in the loop will be twice the initial number. You can adjust the total number of strands according to the pattern you plan to weave next.

3. Center Starting Techniques

Form a center with cord loops and radiate outward. Here are three common methods for creating a center start.

Encircling Technique

When using the encircling method for starting, the center will have only a small hole after tightening, resulting in the best no-trace effect.

Cross the ends of the cord to form a loop, creating a partial overlap.

Secure the cords to the loop using a lark's head knot or a reverse lark's head knot (see PP 29–30).

Tighten both ends of the loop and adjust the tightness of the lark's head knots.

Group the strands into sets of four, including the initial two holding cords. Each group of cords starts by using the two middle cords as the holding cords for weaving the square knots (see PP 37–38).

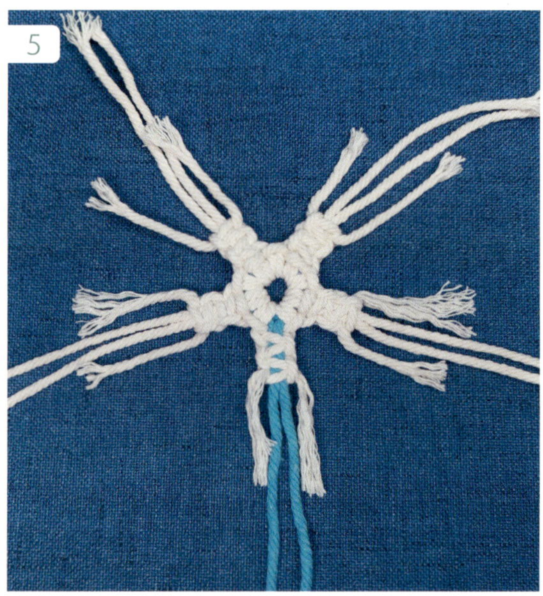

This example demonstrates the weaving of five sets of square knots.

Coil Technique

In general, four to six lark's head knots are enough to close a loop. The more lark's head knots used, the larger the hole in the center.

Fold the holding cord in half and position it. Secure the cord to the holding cord using a lark's head knot. Leave a small hole near the folded section of the holding cord.

Thread the end of the holding cord through the small hole.

Pull the cord tight and adjust the knot.

Loop Knotting Technique

The loop knotting technique requires less cord and is more suitable as a holding cord after the weaving is completed. After adding cords and weaving a section, it's important to adjust the loop again. If the loop is too loose and lacks sufficient support, the center may collapse.

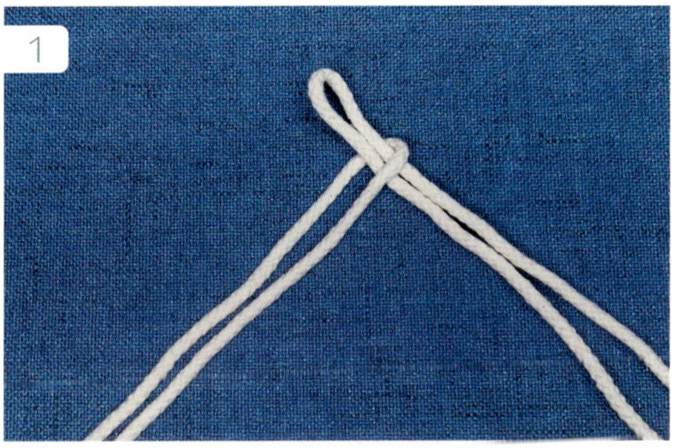

Fold the cord in half. Take another cord, fold it in half, and loop it around the first cord.

Fold each subsequent cord in half and loop it around the previous cord, linking them together in a chain.

Pass the tail end of the last cord through the loop left by the first cord.

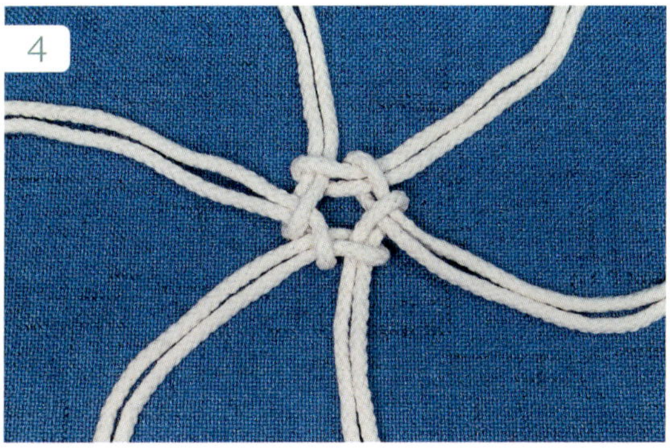

Tighten the cords and adjust the loops, ensuring they are as tight as possible.

4. Closed-Loop Starting Techniques

Closed shapes like circles, squares, and triangles can all be started using this method. Below, I'll demonstrate two common methods for starting a closed loop using a circular ring as an example.

Lark's Head Knot Starting Technique

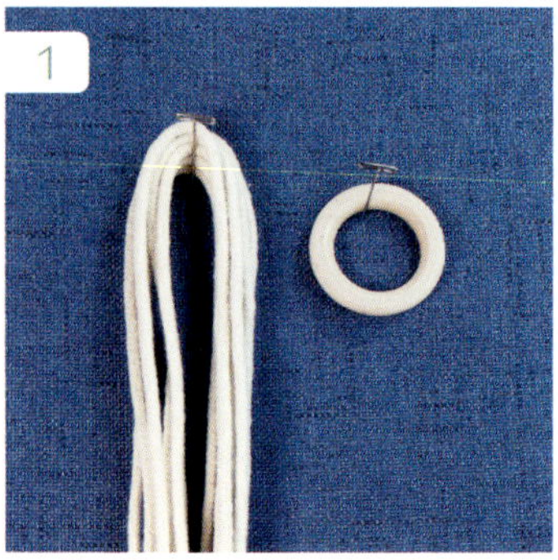

Prepare the cord and the circular ring.

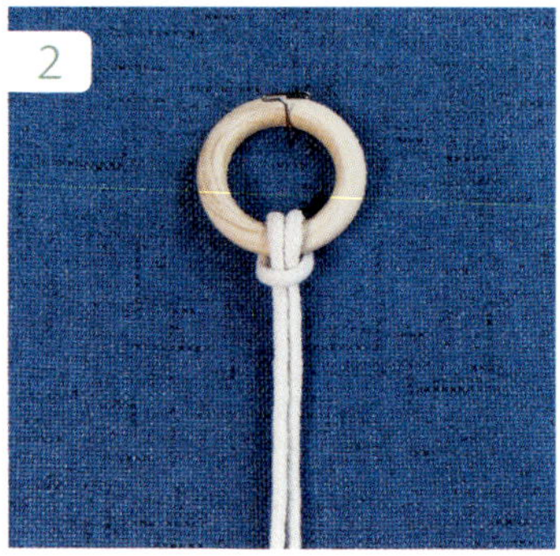

Fold the cord in half and use a lark's head knot (see P 37) to secure it to the circular ring.

Secure all the cords to the circular ring sequentially using lark's head knots and arrange them neatly.

Double Half Hitch Knot Starting Technique

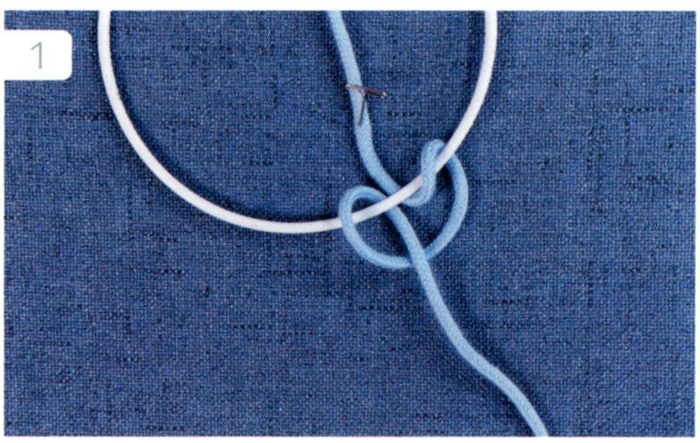

Place the cord under the circular ring. Using the ring as the holding cord for the double half hitch knot, weave the knot (see P 41).

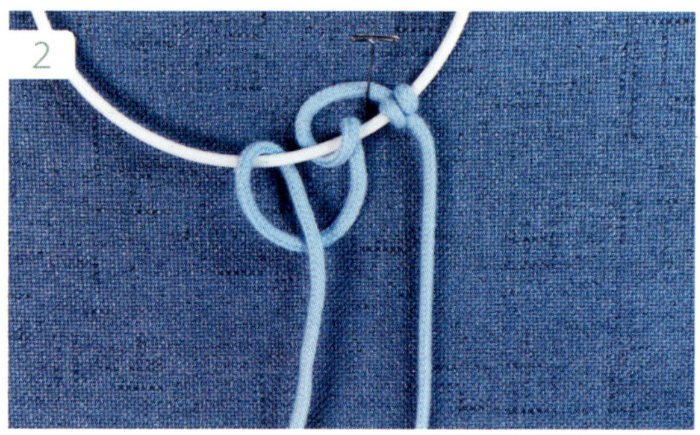

Place one end of the working cord under the circular ring and continue weaving double half hitch knots.

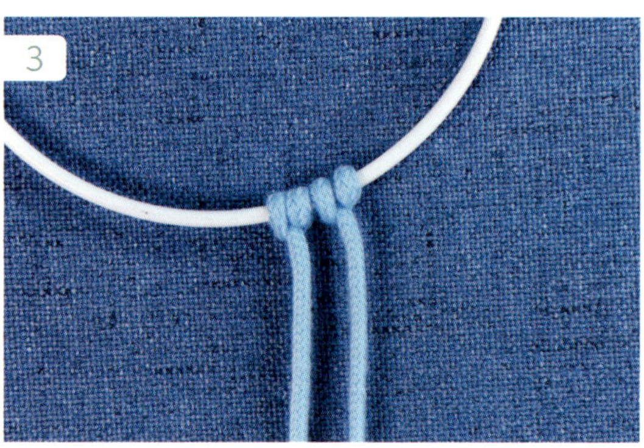

Tighten the cord and secure the knot.

Continue adding cord using double half hitch knots until the entire ring is filled.

Cord Adding and Extending Techniques

In the process of crafting, it is common to encounter situations where the cord quantity or length is insufficient. Here are a few methods to address these issues.

1. Adding Cord

Here are seven commonly used methods for adding cord.

Adding Cord with Lark's Head Knot

The method for adding cord with a lark's head knot is similar to the lark's head knot starting technique. However, instead of securing the knot to a support rod, it is attached to another cord.

Number of cords to be added: Increase from two strands to multiple strands.

Weave two lark's head knots (see P 37) successively with a gap left between them.

Secure the remaining cords onto the empty cord with lark's head knots until the desired number is achieved.

Adding Cord with Square Knots

Add cords to the existing holding cord and weave square knots (see PP 37–38).

Number of cords to be added: Increase from two cords to four cords.

Fold the white cord in half and place it under the gray holding cord, with the loop positioned on the left side.

Take the upper white cord and pass it down through the white cord, then pass it from front to back through the loop on the left side.

Tighten both ends of the cord.

Bend the white cord on the right side to the left, placing it under the holding cord, with the loop on the right side.

The upper white cord repeats step 2 and step 3 by passing through the lower white cord, then from front to back through the loop on the right side, completing a square knot.

Adding Cord with Spiral Knots

Add cord to weave a spiral knot (see P 40) on the existing holding cord.

Number of cords to be added: Increasing from two strands to four strands.

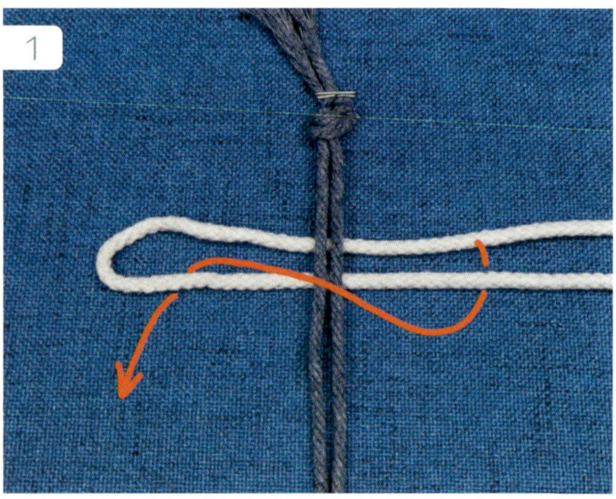

Fold the white cord in half and place it under the gray holding cord, with the loop positioned on the left side.

Take the upper white cord and pass it down through the lower white cord, then thread it from front to back through the loop on the left side.

Tighten both ends of the cord.

Bend the left white cord to the right, placing it under the holding cord, with the loop on the left side.

Repeat the above steps to weave spiral knots until the desired length is reached.

Adding Cord Horizontally on Both Sides

Number of cords to be added: For each additional set of square knots, add four cords.

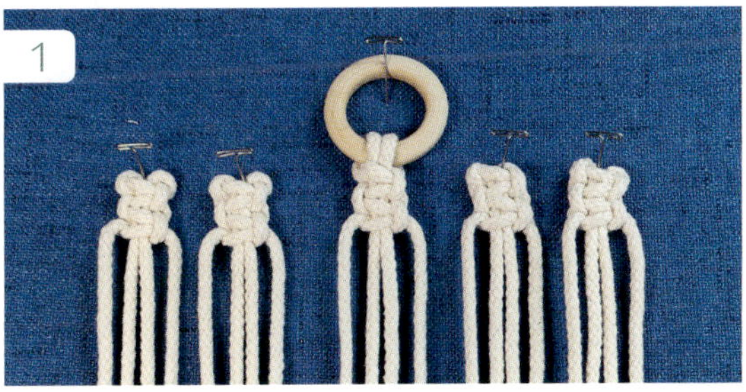

Prepare individual square knots based on the number of cords to be added.

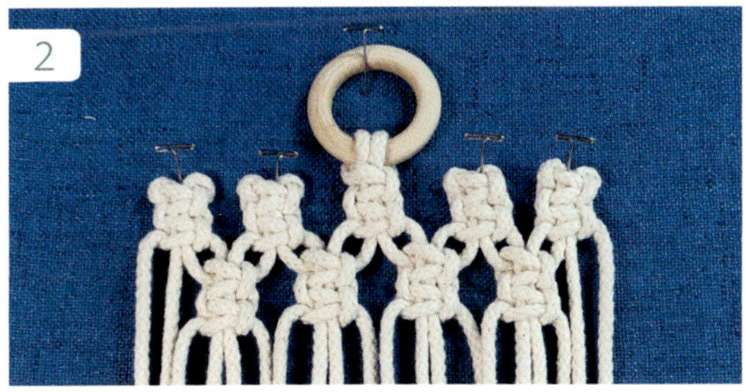

On both sides of the initial square knot, add individual square knots one by one. Take the left and right cords from the initial square knot and weave them into new square knots, connecting each section together.

Adding Cord Diagonally on Both Sides

Number of added cords: For each additional set of square knots, add two strands.

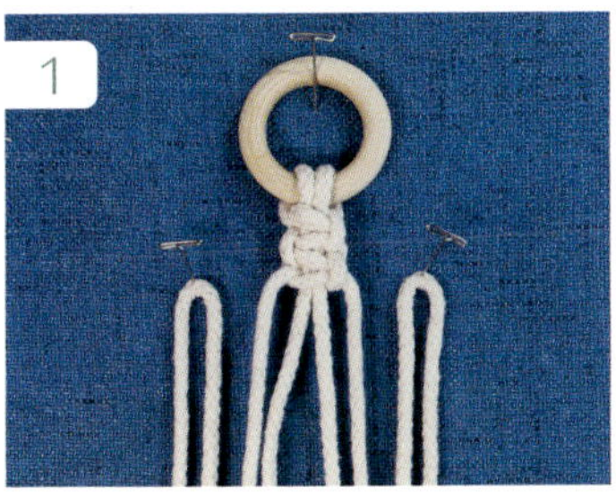

Place a folded cord on each side of the initial square knot.

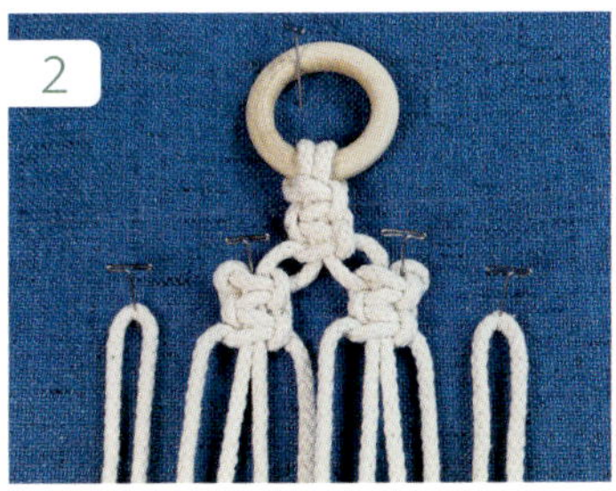

Use a square knot to connect the new cords with the initial square knot, and place a folded cord on each side.

Continue in this manner, adding cords until the desired number or length is achieved.

Adding Cord with Diagonal Double Half Hitch Knots

Number of cords added: Add one cord for each additional double half hitch knot.

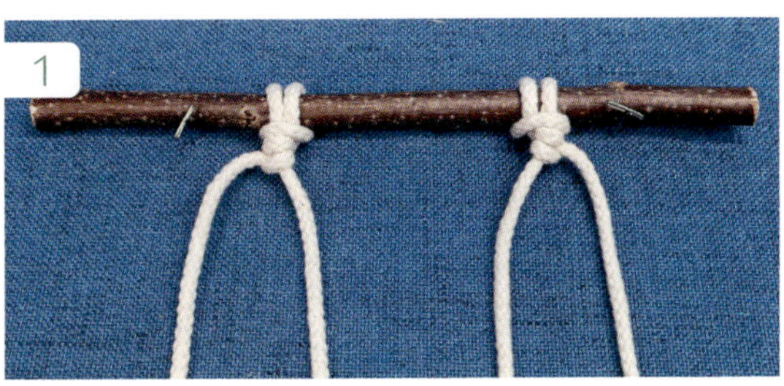

Fold two cords and use a lark's head knot (see P 30) to attach them to a branch. Use the middle two cords as the holding cords, and use the two cords on the left and right side to weave a double half hitch knot (see P 41) for each.

Add a new cord to the left-side holding cord. Use the ends of this cord to weave a double half hitch knot on each side.

Similarly, add a new cord to the right-side holding cord and braid two double half hitch knots.

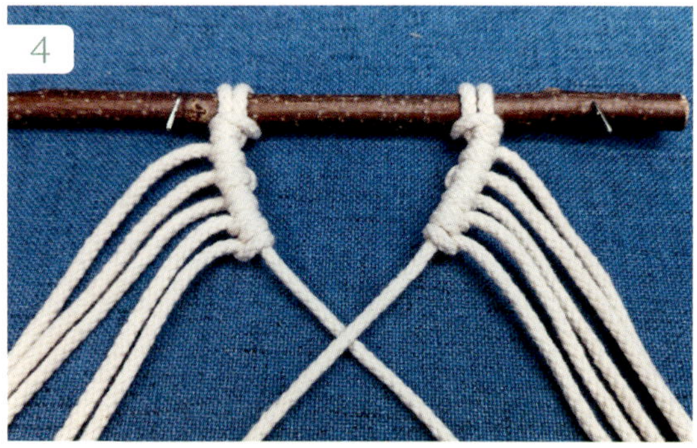

Continue adding until the desired quantity or length is achieved.

Adding Cord with Circular Shape

Number of cords added: Add two strands with each reverse lark's head knot added.

Begin with the coil technique (see P 59). On the holding cord, weave four reverse lark's head knots (see P 30).

Use the right-side holding cord as the working cord to weave a double half hitch knot on the left-side holding cord.

In a counterclockwise direction, sequentially weave double half hitch knots on the holding cord. Add a new strand of cord (the blue cords in the diagram) behind every two strands of working cord with a reverse lark's head knot, completing one round of adding cords. The interval for adding cords in each round does not need to be uniform. As long as the current double half hitch knot is not directly below the double half hitch knot of the previous round, you can add cords in the gaps. This ensures that the double half hitch knots of the same strand are aligned on the same extension cord in any round. Adding cords at the appropriate positions will make the woven circular pattern more compact and even.

2. Extending Cord

In the weaving process, it is common to encounter situations where the length of the cord is insufficient. We can utilize the structure of the knots to extend the cord while hiding the ends. Below are seven common methods for extending the cord.

One of the Working Cords in a Square Knot Is Too Short

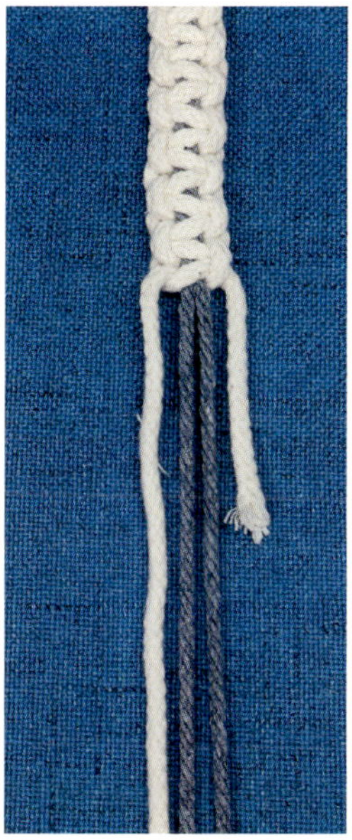

Swap the positions of the holding cord and the short working cord, creating new holding and working cords.

Continue weaving square knots with the new holding cord and working cord.

Both Working Cords in a Square Knot Are Too Short

Use the method of adding cords with square knot (see PP 37–38) to add new working cords.

Use the original short working cords as the new holding cords and incorporate them into the knot.

After weaving a few square knots, pull the original short working cords to the back and trim them off.

One of the Holding Cords in a Square Knot Is Too Short

Overlap the new holding cord with the original short holding cord.

Continue weaving the square knots, incorporating both the new and old holding cords.

After weaving several square knots, turn to the back, apply glue to reinforce, and trim off the ends of both the old and new holding cords.

Both Holding Cords in a Square Knot Are Too Short

Bend the two short holding cords upwards. Fold the new holding cord in half and place it over the original holding cord.

Continue to weave square knots, incorporating both the new and old holding cords.

After weaving several square knots, flip the piece to the back, apply glue to reinforce, and trim off the ends of the old holding cords. The method for extending cords in square knots can also be used for spiral knots.

One of the Working Cords in a Double Half Hitch Knot Is Too Short

At the position where the short working cord is woven, use a double half hitch knot to add a new working cord, with one end being shorter.

Replace the old working cord with the new one and continue weaving double half hitch knots.

After weaving two rows of double half hitch knots, turn the work over to the back.

Hide the ends of the new and old working cords inside the knots. Apply glue and trim the ends of both the new and old working cords.

The Holding Cord in a Double Half Hitch Knot Is Too Short

Add a new holding cord, overlapping it with the original short holding cord.

Continue weaving double half hitch knots on the new and old holding cords.

After weaving a few double half hitch knots, flip the work to the back, apply glue to secure it, and trim the ends of the new holding cords.

Uneven Spacing or Tassel Length

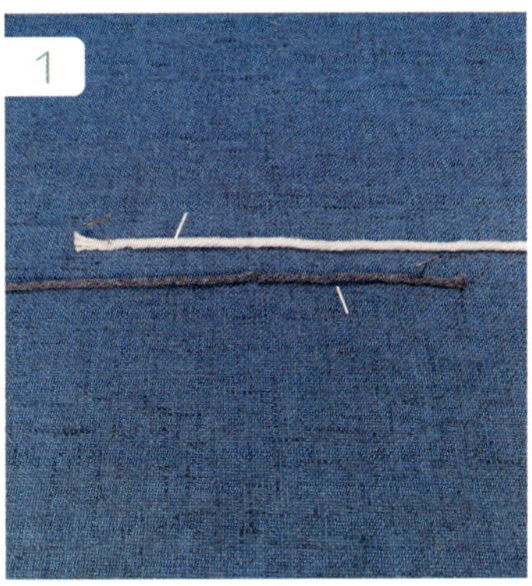

The white cord is the original cord, and the gray cord is the extending cord.

Use the gray cord to weave a barrel knot (see P 48), hiding the white cord inside the barrel knot.

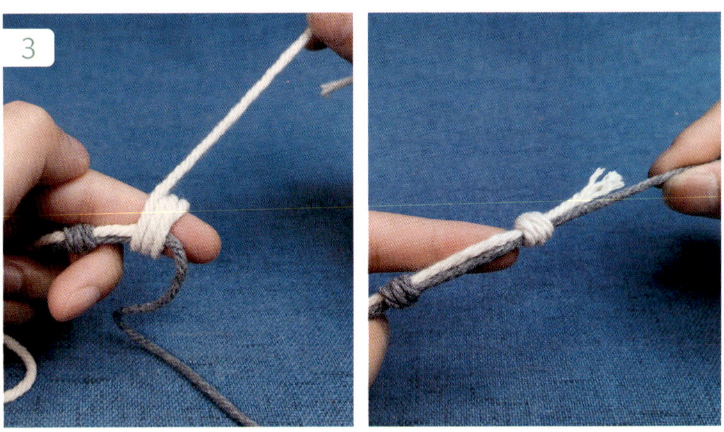

Turn it over and use the white cord to weave a barrel knot, enclosing the gray cord inside the barrel knot.

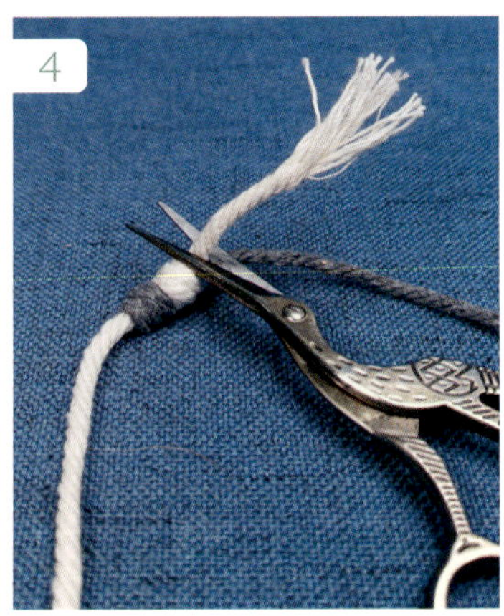

Pull on both ends to join the two barrel knots together, apply glue, and trim the ends of the new and old cords.

Finishing Techniques

In the tapestry-making process, choose the following appropriate finishing methods based on the design requirements. For specific examples, refer to the finishing methods displayed in Chapter Four of the projects.

No trimming: Leave the ends of the cords casual (see P 159).

Trimming: Flat cutting method (see PP 145, 153, 155, 201, 204), pointed cutting method (see PP 151, 206, 209), overhand knot flat cutting method (see P 157), staggered trimming method (see P 161).

Gathering: Use the wrapping knot gathering method, where multiple strands are gathered together as an holding cord and wrapped with a knot to secure them. See the tassel pattern (see PP 138–139). Similarly, the barrel knot gathering method involves weaving barrel knots to gather multiple strands together (see P 177). These two gathering methods mostly appear in the form of tassels, with the trimming length determined by the designer.

Hanging Cord Techniques

After completing a tapestry, the final step is to prepare a cord to hang the tapestry. One of the most common methods is to use a barrel knot to secure the hanging cord.

On the support rod's ends or within the hitch knot, choose two points that can maintain balance. Weave a barrel knot, wrapping with the shorter end of the cord.

Apply glue and trim the excess ends. The hanging cord is now complete.

Fig. 41 Different types of unbleached cotton cords.

CHAPTER THREE
Patterns

Once you have mastered the basic knots and macramé techniques for different situations, you can unleash your creativity by repeating, arranging, and combining different basic knots, to create various patterns and designs. Macramé patterns can be created by stacking and arranging basic knots to form regular, orderly designs or by combining multiple knots to piece together various patterns. This chapter demonstrates a total of 141 macramé patterns with step-by-step instructions, providing a reference for your designs.

Patterns with Square Knots

The square knot is the most common knot in macramé. Learning to combine different types of square knots will provide a solid technical foundation for your own designs.

1. Patterns by Alternating Square Knots

No. 1 Alternating Square Knots (8 Strands)

Divide eight strands of cord into four strands on the left and four strands on the right. Tie a square knot on each side.

Using the middle four strands as a group, tie a square knot, arranging it in an alternating pattern with the two square knots above.

Repeat steps 1–2 until you reach the desired length.

No. 2 Two-Color Alternating Square Knots (6 Strands)

Refer to No. 1, replacing one of the strands with a colored cord.

No. 3 Alternating Single Square Knot Plane Extension (16 Strands)

Group every four strands into a set. Tie a square knot with each set, making a total of four square knots.

Leave a gap below the previous row of square knots, then tie a second row of square knots in an alternating pattern, making a total of three square knots.

At intervals, repeat steps 1–2 until you reach the desired length.

No. 4 Alternating Double Square Knots Plane Extension (16 Strands)

Refer to No. 3, tie two square knots continuously and then weave the next row in an interlaced pattern.

No. 5 Square Knots Houndstooth Pattern (24 Strands)

The finished product in the image below uses 24 strands. The following is a demonstration using 16 strands as an example.

Arrange the colored and white strings alternately as shown in the diagram, with four strands in each group.

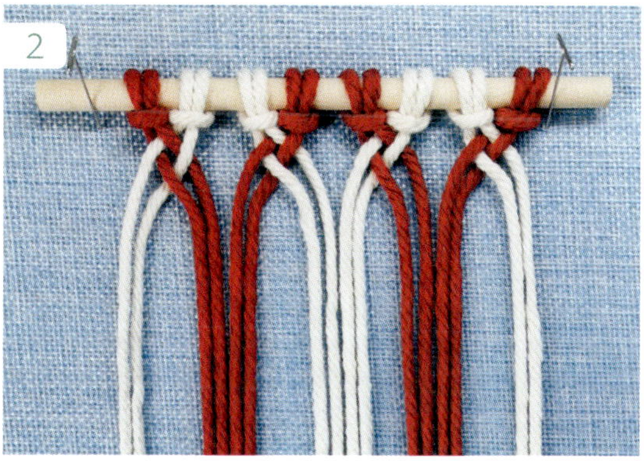

Interlace the four strands of each group.

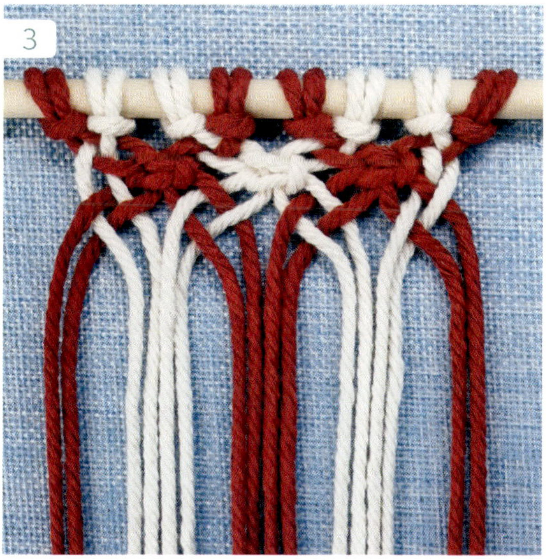

Use the four strands of the same color to weave a square knot.

Repeat steps 2–3, interlacing each group of four strands and weaving a square knot, until the desired length is achieved.

2. Patterns by Exchanging Holding Cords and Working Cords

No. 6 Single Square Knot with Exchanging Holding Cords and Working Cords (4 Strands)

Weave a square knot using four strands of cord.

Move the middle strands to the sides to form the new working cords, and move the side strands to the middle to form the new holding cords, with a gap in between. Weave a square knot.

Repeat the above steps until the desired length is achieved.

No. 7 Double Square Knot with Exchanging Working Cords and Holding Cords (4 Strands)

Refer to No. 6. Weave two consecutive square knots before and after each exchanging working cord and holding cord.

No. 8 Three Square Knots with Exchanging Working Cords and Holding Cords (4 Strands)

Refer to No.6. Weave three consecutive square knots before and after each exchanging working cord and holding cord.

No. 9 Single Square Knot with Exchanging Working Cords and Holding Cords Plane Extension (16 strands)

Refer to No. 3 and No. 6. After completing each row of alternating square knots, switch the holding cord and the working cord when weaving the next row of alternating square knots.

3. Braid Patterns with Square Knots

No. 10 Four-Strand Simple Braid Pattern with Square Knots, Style A (16 strands)

For each group of four cords, weave square knots. In the middle two groups, weave 12 square knots, and in the left and right groups, weave six square knots each.

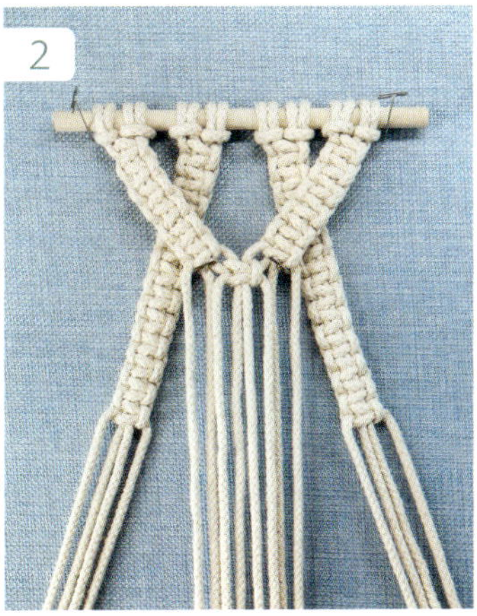

Move the square knots from the sides to the center. Use the four central cords to weave one square knot, connecting the two groups together.

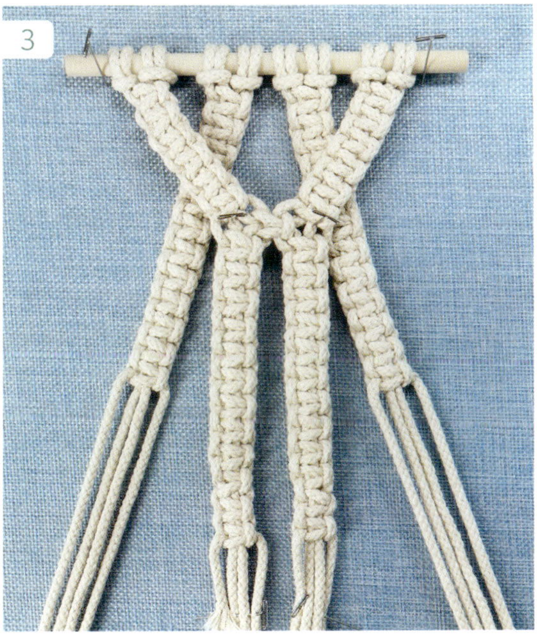

Divide the eight central cords into two groups, and weave 12 square knots in each group.

Repeat steps 2–3 until the desired length is achieved.

No. 11 Two-Tone Four-Strand Simple Braid Pattern with Square Knots, Style A (16 strands)

Refer to No.10. Place the colored cords in the center position and weave square knots.

No. 12 Four-Strand Simple Braid Pattern with Square Knots, Style B (16 strands)

For each group of four cords, weave eight square knots.

Using the four central cords between the first and third groups, and between the second and fourth groups, weave one square knot for each connection, joining the two sets together.

Weave 12 square knots in each group, and cross the two central groups.

Use the four central cords between adjacent groups to weave square knots. Repeat step 3 until the desired length is achieved.

No. 13 Two-Tone Four-Strand Simple Braid Pattern with Square Knots (16 strands)

Refer to No. 12. Put the colored cords in the positions of the first and third groups.

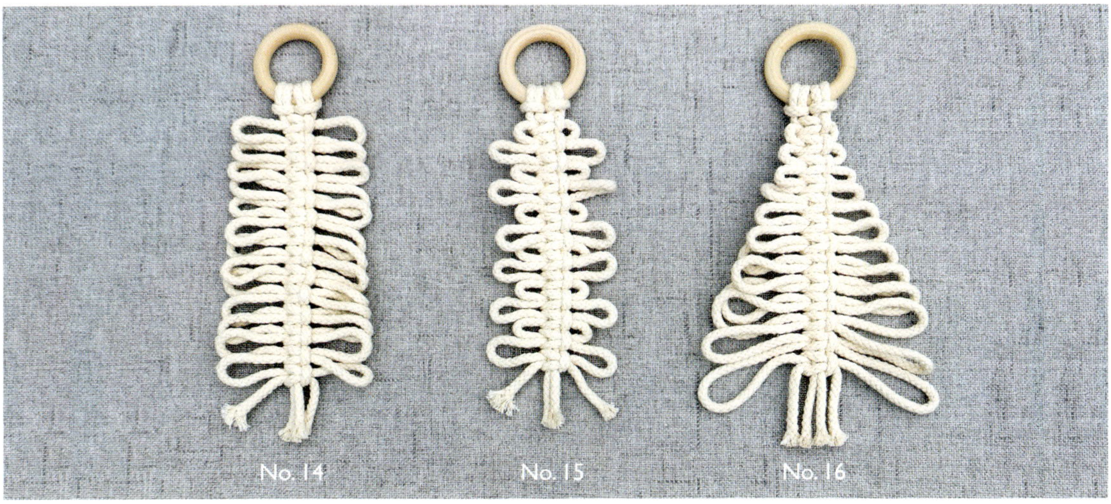

4. Patterns with Square Knot Picots

No. 14 Pattern with Square Knot Picots, Style A (4 strands)

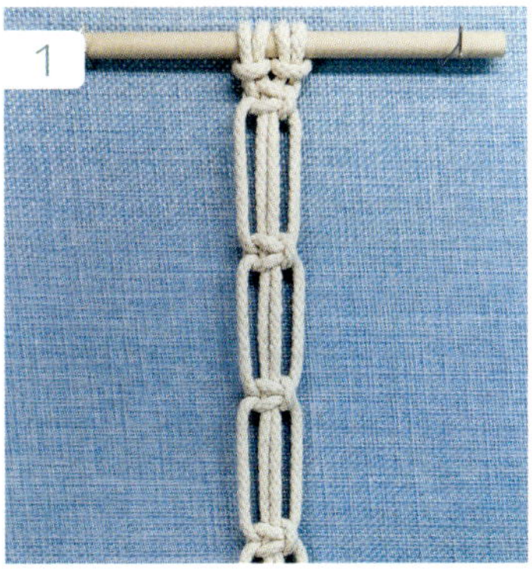

Begin with four cords and start with a square knot. Weave additional square knots at equal distances.

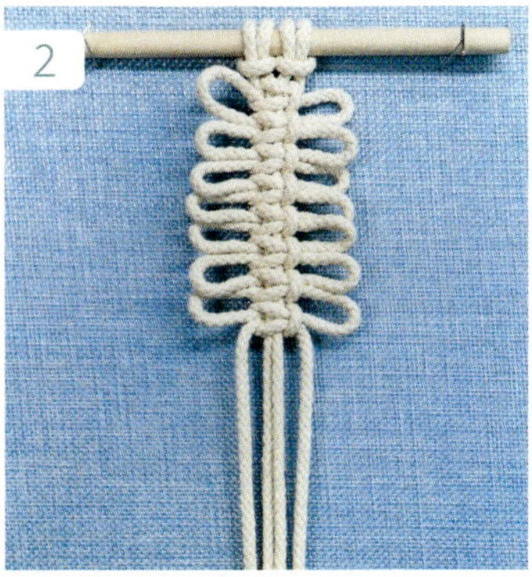

Straighten the holding cords and push the square knots upwards to form a fringe.

No. 15 Pattern with Square Knot Picots, Style B (4 strands)

Start with a square knot, then weave additional square knots with alternating short and long intervals.

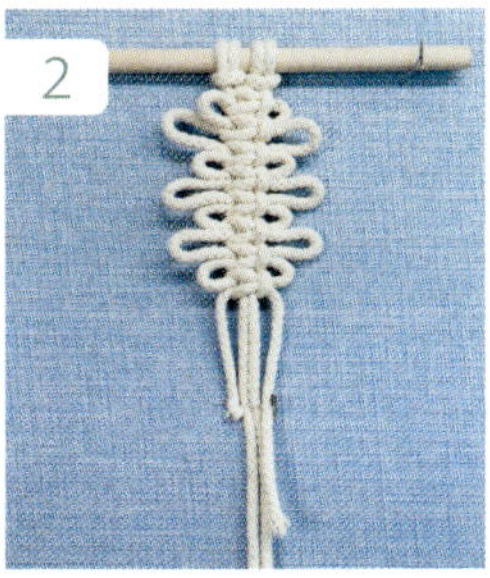

Straighten the holding cords and push the square knots upwards to form a fringe.

No. 16 Pattern with Square Knot Picots, Style C (4 strands)

Begin with a square knot and weave additional square knots with intervals increasing from short to long.

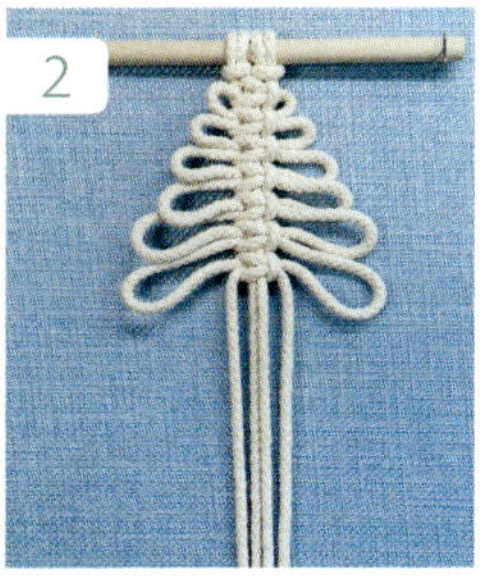

Straighten the holding cords and push the square knots upwards to form a fringe.

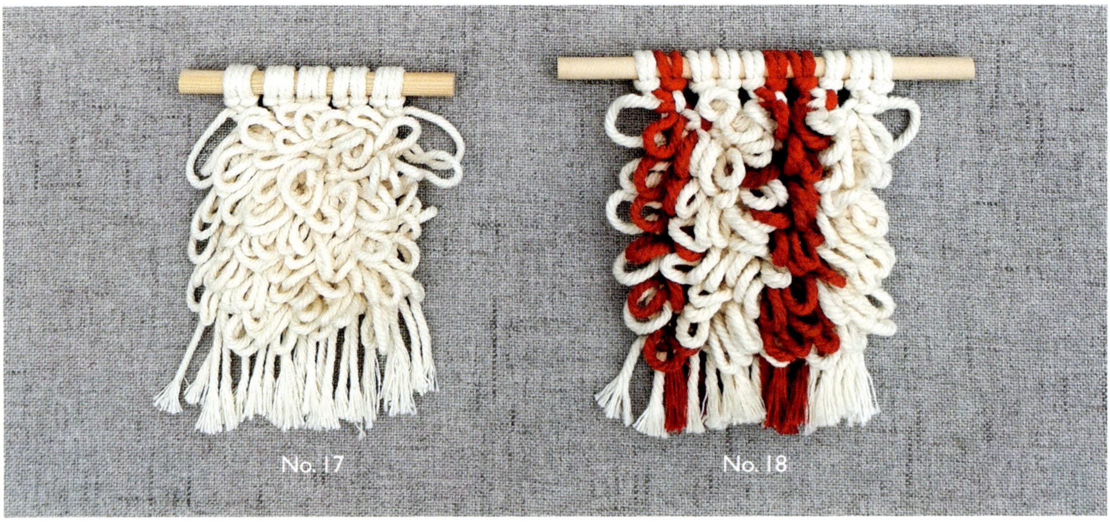

No. 17 Pattern with Square Knot Picots Plane Extension (20 strands)

For each group of four cords, weave square knots. After a short interval, weave a row of alternating square knots.

Push the alternating square knots upwards to form a fringe.

Weave alternating square knots at equal intervals.

Push the knots up to form a fringe and repeat the above steps until the desired length is achieved.

No. 18 Two-Tone Pattern with Square Knot Picots Plane Extension (20 strands)

Refer to No. 17. Place the colored cords in any position and weave square knots.

5. Fishbone Patterns with Square Knots

No. 19 Fishbone Pattern with Square Knots (8 strands)

Using a total of eight cords, designate the two central cords as the holding cords, while the remaining cords serve as the working cords. Use the first set of working cords on either side of the holding cord to weave a square knot.

Then, use the adjacent second and third groups of working cords to sequentially weave square knots.

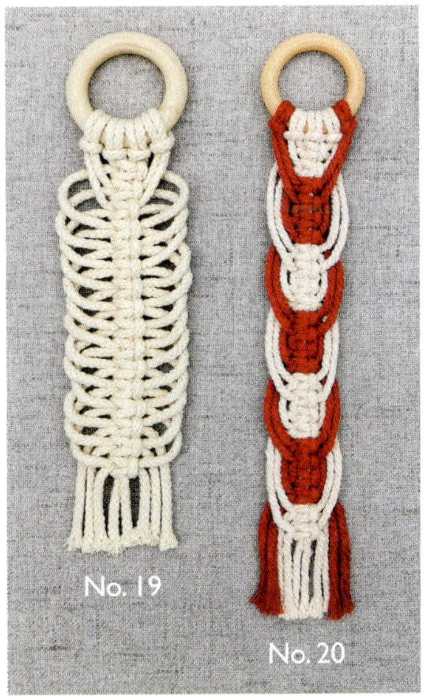

After a short interval, continue weaving square knots with the first group of working cords. Push the knots upwards to form a fringe.

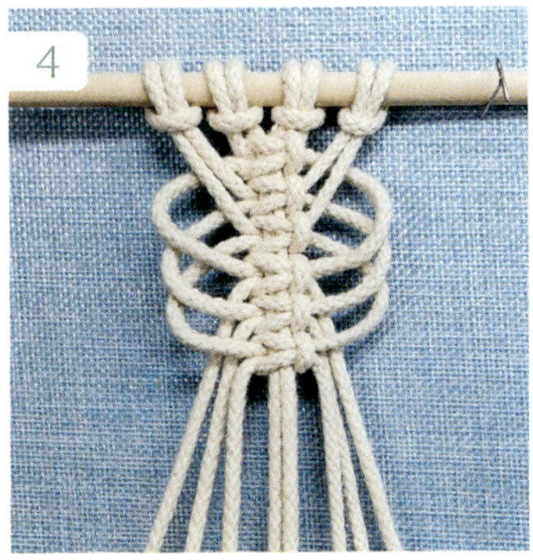

With the second and third groups of working cords, repeat steps 3 and 4 at the same intervals. Continue weaving until you reach the desired length.

No. 20 Two-Tone Fishbone Pattern with Square Knots (10 strands)

Place the white cord in the center and the colored cords on both sides.

Use the two cords in the center as the holding cords, with the remaining cords as working cords. From the inside out, weave square knots on the holding cords one by one.

Taking the two working cords from the lowest square knot, continue weaving downward, creating four consecutive red square knots.

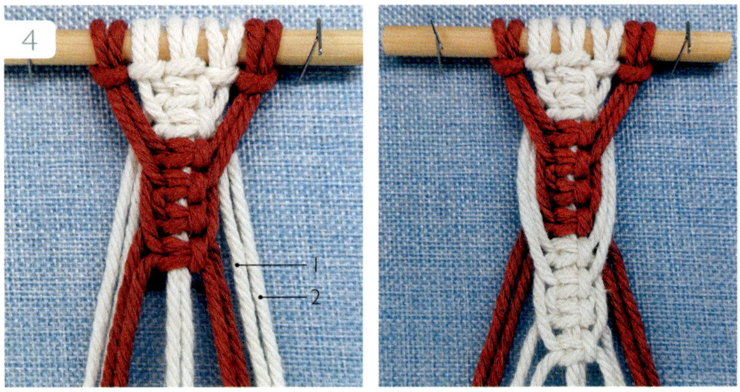

Take the white cords on the two sides in sequence, White Cord 1 and White Cord 2 (as shown in the figure), using them as the working cords to create two white square knots. Repeat step 3 to complete two more white square knots. Using the red and white cords as color dividers, create a cycle of four square knots per group. Continue weaving in this pattern until the desired length is achieved.

No. 21 Fishbone Pattern with Square Knots and Wooden Beads (8 strands)

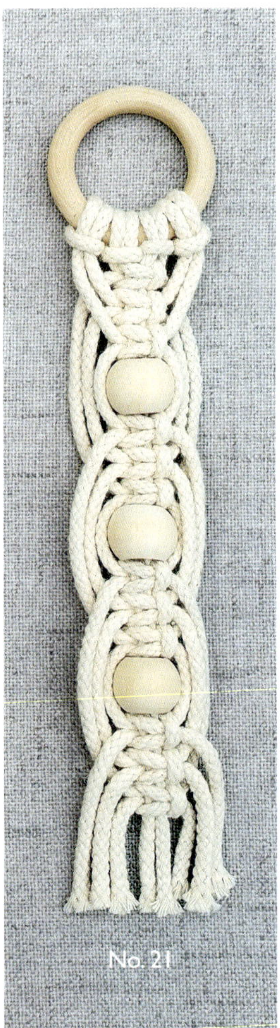

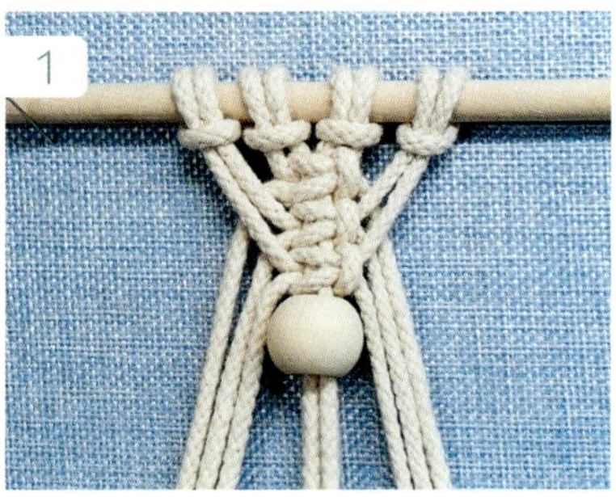

Use the two central cords as the holding cords, with the remaining cords as working cords. Weave square knots on the holding cords from the inside out sequentially and thread wooden beads onto the holding cords.

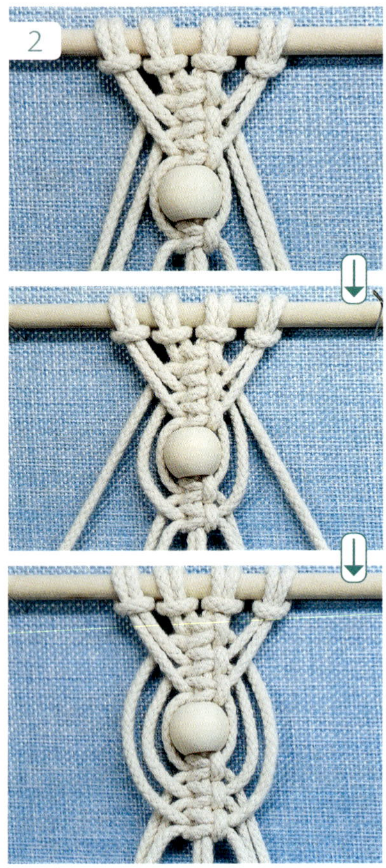

Take the working cords from the square knots positioned from bottom to top in a sequence above the wooden bead and use them to weave square knots below the bead.

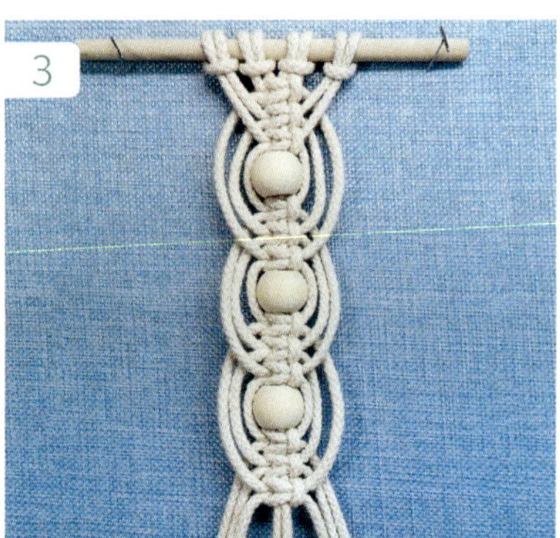

Thread a wooden bead after every four square knots. Repeat the above steps until you reach the desired length.

6. Net Patterns with Square Knots

No. 22 Net Pattern with Square Knots, Style A (34 strands)

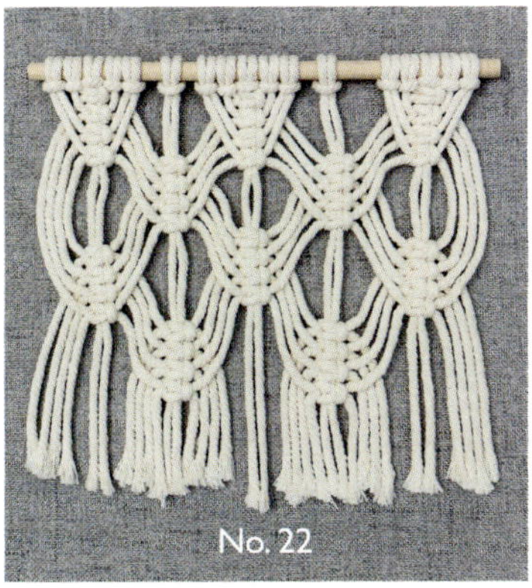
No. 22

For each group of ten cords, refer to No. 19. Use the two central cords as the holding cords and the remaining cords as the working cords. Weave square knots on the holding cords from the inside out. Additionally, add two more cords to the center of each group to serve as the holding cords for step 2.

Take one working cord from the first square knot of each adjacent group and weave a square knot on the newly added holding cord.

Sequentially take the left and right working cords from the second, third, and fourth square knots of each adjacent group and weave square knots on the new holding cords. Repeat the weaving process until the desired length is achieved. Note that it's not recommended to weave the net pattern too long, as the net structure is not designed to bear weight. Under load, it may deform and cause the sides to curve inward.

No. 23 Net Pattern with Square Knots, Style B (30 strands)

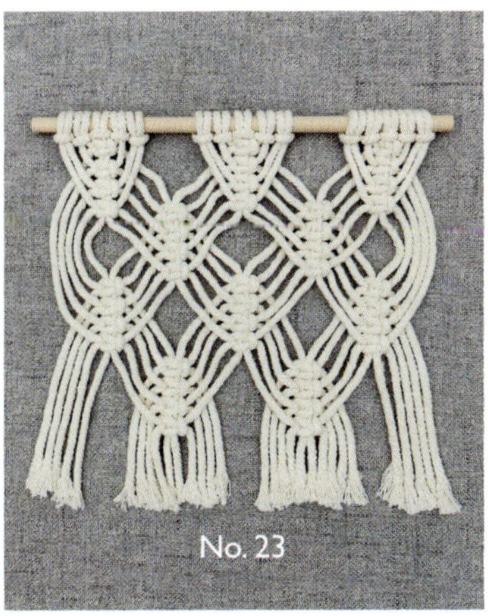
No. 23

Using ten cords as one group, refer to No. 19. The middle two cords will act as the holding cords, while the remaining cords will be the workingcords. From the inside out, weave square knots along the holding cords.

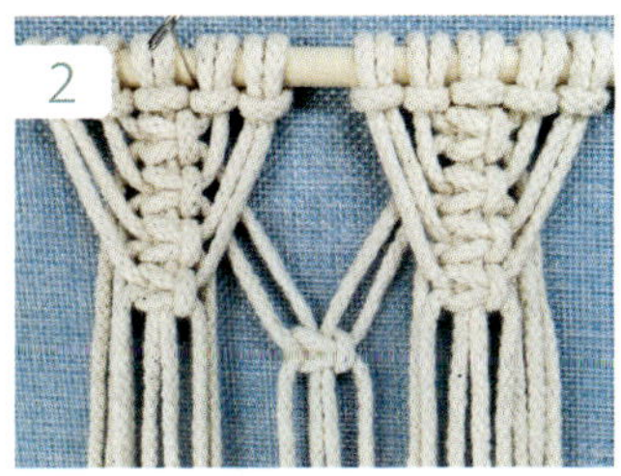

From the first square knot of two adjacent groups, take one working cord from each to form a new holding cord. Then, take one working cord from the second square knot of each group as new working cords, and weave the first square knot of the second row.

From top to bottom, take the working cords from the third square knot of the first row, the working cords from the fourth square knot, and the holding cord from the fourth square knot to continue weaving the square knot group for the second row. Repeat until the desired length is achieved.

No. 24 Net Pattern with Square Knots, Style C (30 strands)

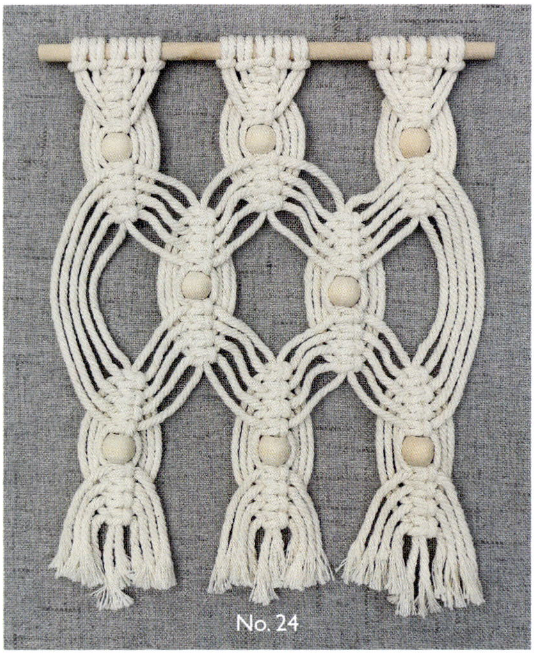

For each group of ten cords, refer to No. 21. Use the two central cords as the holding cords to weave square knots on the holding cords from the inside out. Thread wooden beads onto the holding cords as you go. Then, take the working cords from the square knots above each wooden bead, starting from the bottom and working your way up, and continue weaving square knots.

From the first square knot below the wooden bead in each of the adjacent groups, take one cord from each as the new holding cords. Then, from the second square knot, take one cord from each as the working cords and weave a square knot.

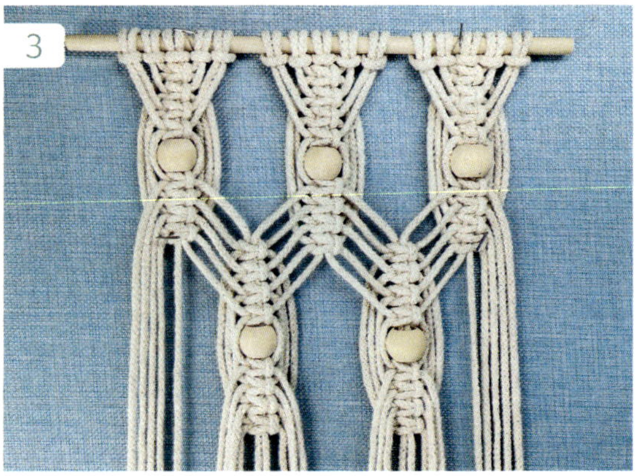

Sequentially take the working cords below the wooden bead from top to bottom, weave square knots on the new holding cords and thread in a wooden bead. Repeat the above steps, weaving until the desired length is achieved.

No. 25 Net Pattern with Square Knots, Style D (30 strands)

Refer to No. 24. Follow the same weaving steps as described, but do not thread wooden beads.

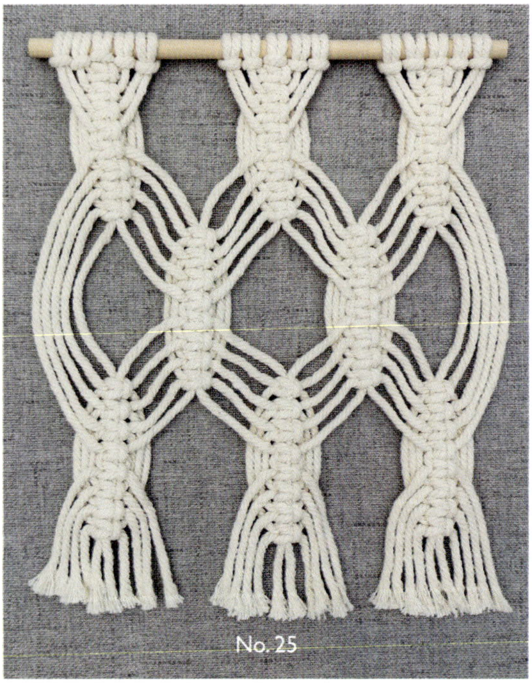

7. V-Shaped Patterns with Square Knots

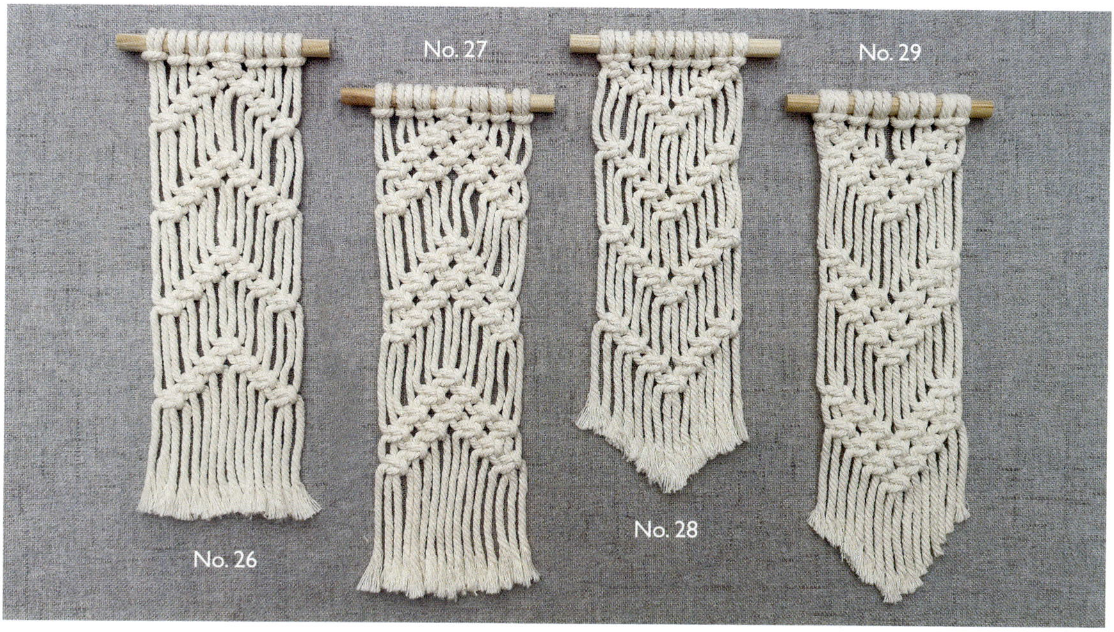

No. 26 Single-Layer Inverted V-Shaped Pattern with Square Knots (16 strands)

First Row: Use the four central cords to weave a square knot.

Second Row: Use the 5th to 8th cords and 9th to 12th cords from left to right to weave one square knot with each set.

Third Row: Use the 3rd to 6th cords and 11th to 14th cords from left to right to weave one square knot with each set.

Fourth Row: Use the four cords on the far left and right sides to weave one square knot with each set, completing the first inverted V-shaped pattern.

After a certain distance from the first inverted V-shaped pattern, repeat steps 1–4 to weave the second inverted V-shaped pattern. Ensure that the spacing between corresponding square knots is consistent.

No. 27 Double-Layer Inverted V-Shaped Pattern with Square Knots (16 strands)

Refer to No. 26. Weave the second layer of the inverted V-shaped pattern directly below the first layer.

No. 28 Single-Layer V-Shaped Pattern with Square Knots (16 strands)

First Row: Use the four cords on each side to weave one square knot with each set.

Second Row: Use the 3rd to 6th cords and 11th to 14th cords from left to right to weave one square knot with each set.

Third Row: Use the 5th to 8th cords and 9th to 12th cords from left to right to weave one square knot with each set.

Fourth Row: Use the four central cords to weave a square knot, completing the first V-shaped pattern.

After leaving a space from the first V-shaped pattern, repeat steps 1–4 to weave the second V-shaped pattern. Make sure to maintain the same spacing between the corresponding square knots.

No. 29 Double-Layer V-Shaped Pattern with Square Knots (16 strands)

Refer to No. 28. Weave the second layer of the V-shaped pattern directly beneath the first layer.

No. 30 Double-Layer V-Shaped Pattern Combination with Square Knots (40 strands)

No. 30

Step 1 Refer to No. 28. Use the 12 central cords to weave an upside down triangle.

Step 2 After a short interval, refer to No. 29 and use 40 cords to weave a double-layer V-shaped pattern.

Step 3 After another short interval, refer to No. 29 and use the 32 central cords to weave a double-layer V-shaped pattern.

Step 4 After another short interval, refer to No. 29 and use the 16 central cords to weave a double-layer V-shaped pattern.

8. Patterns of Increasing or Decreasing Alternating Square Knots

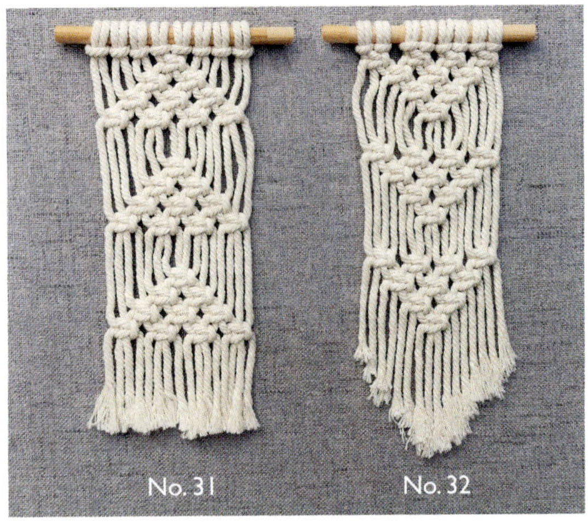

No. 31 Upright Triangle Pattern with Square Knots (16 strands)

First Row: Weave the four central cords into a square knot.

Second Row: Use the 5th to 8th cords and 9th to 12th cords from left to right to weave one square knot with each set.

Third Row: Use the 3rd to 6th, 7th to 10th, and 11th to 14th cords from left to right to weave one square knot with each set.

Fourth Row: Weave each group of four cords into one square knot, completing an upright triangle.

No. 32 Upside Down Triangle Pattern with Square Knots (16 strands)

First Row: Weave one square knot with each group of four cords.

Second Row: Use the 3rd to 6th, 7th to 10th, and 11th to 14th cords from left to right to weave one square knot with each set.

Third Row: Use the 5th to 8th, and 9th to 12th cords from left to right to weave one square knot with each set.

Fourth Row: Weave the four central cords into a square knot, completing an upside down triangle.

No. 33 Triangle Combination Pattern with Square Knots, Style A (24 strands)

Refer to No. 1. Group the cords in sets of four and weave two rows of alternating square knots.

Divide the 24 cords into left and right sections. On the left side, weave alternating square knots in the following sequence from top to bottom: three knots, two knots, two knots, one knot, one knot, forming a right-angled triangle.

On the right side, repeat step 2 to create a similar right-angled triangle.

After a short distance, refer to No. 31 and weave an upright triangle.

No. 34 Triangle Combination Pattern with Square Knots, Style B (24 strands)

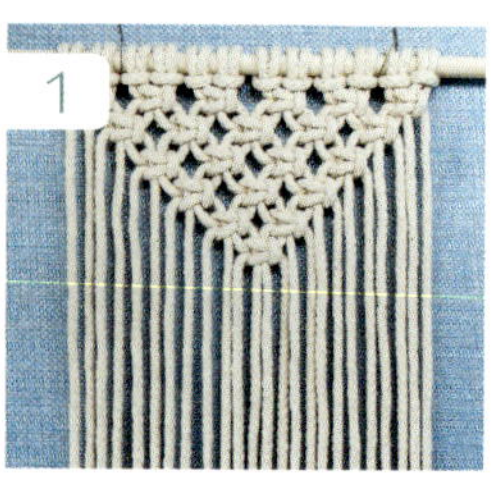

Refer to No. 32. Use 24 cords to weave an upside down triangle.

After a short distance, refer to No. 32 and weave a V-shaped pattern.

Below the left side of the V-shaped pattern, weave alternating square knots in the following sequence from top to bottom: one knot, one knot, two knots, two knots, and three knots, forming a right-angled triangle.

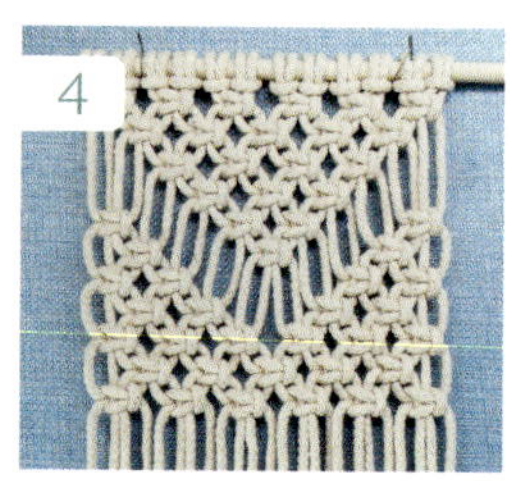

Below the right side of the V-shaped pattern, repeat step 3 to create a similar right-angled triangle.

9. Diamond Patterns with Square Knots

No. 35 Solid Diamond Pattern with Square Knots (20 strands)

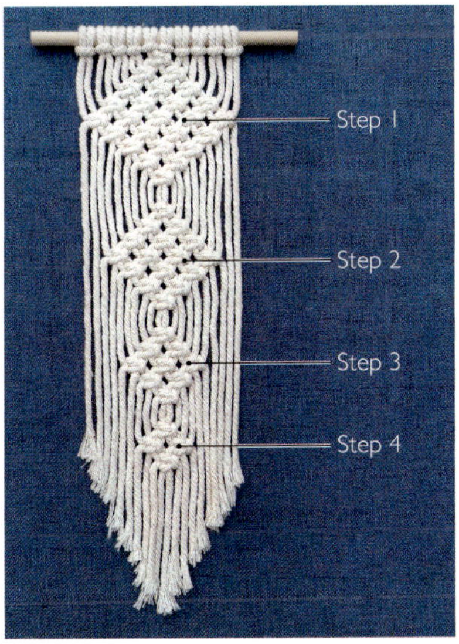

Step 1 With 20 cords, weave nine rows of alternating square knots, forming a diamond shape.

Step 2 Weave the 16 central cords into seven rows of alternating square knots, forming a diamond shape.

Step 3 Weave the 12 central cords into five rows of alternating square knots, forming a diamond shape.

Step 4 Weave the eight central cords into three rows of alternating square knots, forming a diamond shape.

No. 36 Diamond Pattern with Alternating Square Knots (32 strands)

Refer to No. 35. Arrange the eight-strand square knot diamond shapes in a staggered pattern.

No. 37 Hollow Diamond Pattern with Square Knots (16 strands)

Refer to No. 26, use 16 cords to weave an inverted V-shaped pattern.

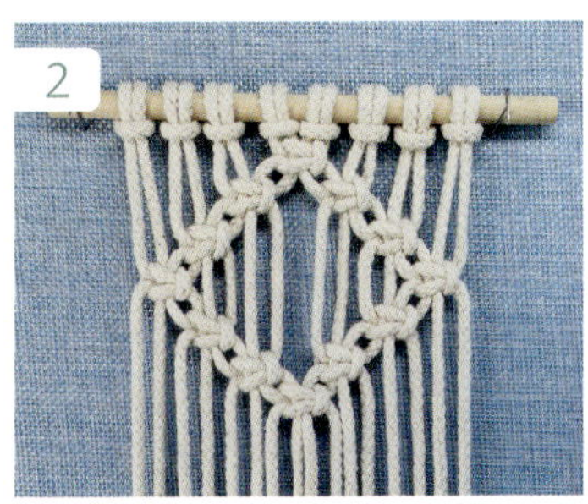

Refer to No. 28. Weave the 12 central cords into a V shape, forming a hollow diamond shape.

No. 38 Hollow Diamond Pattern with Double Square Knots (12 strands)

Refer to No. 37. Simply replace single square knots with double square knots to create the pattern.

No. 39 Diamond Pattern Embedded with Square Knots, Style A (Add cord 16 strands)

No. 39

No. 38

1

Start by weaving three square knots. Use the diagonal cord-adding technique on both sides (see P 63) to add three cords to each side.

2

Use the six central cords to weave a square knot, with the four central cords as the holding cords.

3

Refer to No. 28. Use the 12 central cords to weave a V-shaped pattern, closing the diamond shape.

No. 40 Diamond Pattern Embedded with Square Knots, Style B (16 strands)

Refer to No. 137. Use eight cords within the diamond shape to create a double-line interlacing weave.

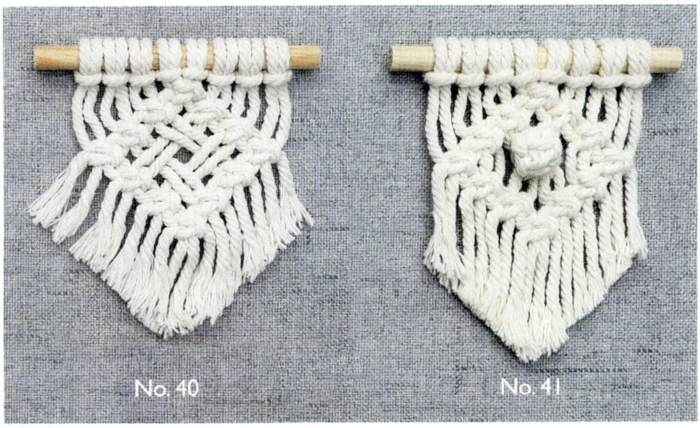

No. 41 Diamond Pattern Embedded with Square Knots, Style C (16 strands)

Refer to No. 37. Weave the four central cords within the diamond shape into a square knot button (see P 39).

No. 42 Diamond Pattern Embedded with Square Knots, Style D (20 strands)

Refer to No. 26. Use 20 cords to weave an inverted V-shaped pattern.

Weave the eight central cords into a small diamond shape. Ensure that the apex of the small diamond aligns horizontally with the fourth row of square knots in the inverted V-shaped pattern, centering the small diamond shape within the pattern.

Refer to No. 28. Weave a V-shaped pattern to close the diamond shape.

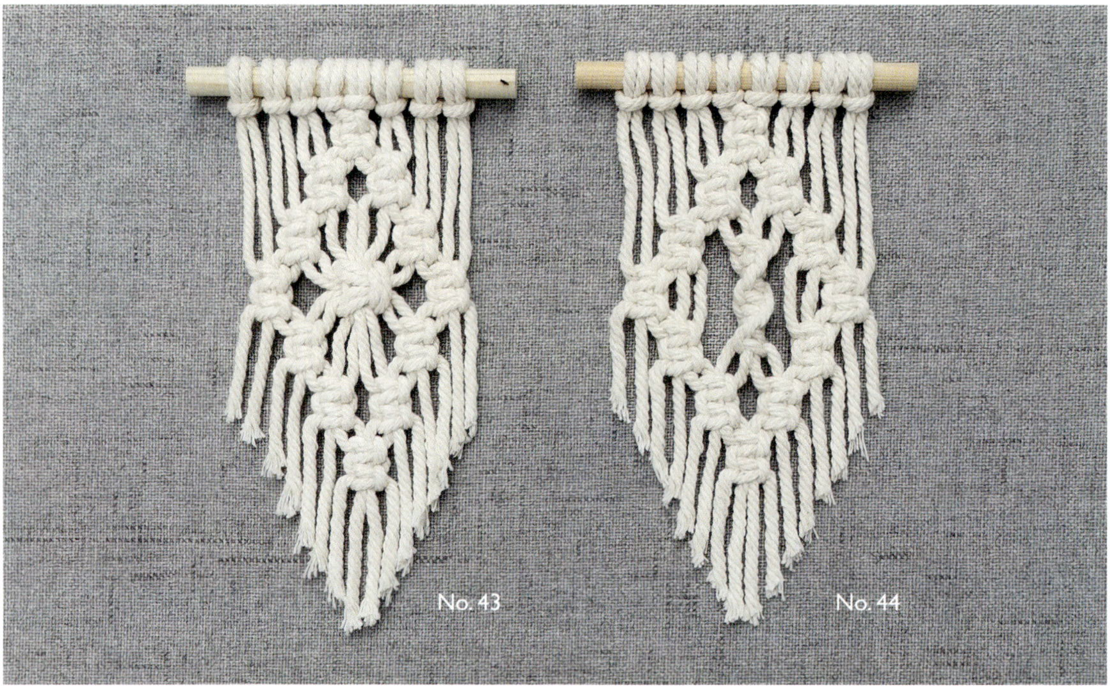

No. 43 Diamond Pattern Embedded with Double Square Knots, Style A (16 strands)

Weave 16 cords into a double square knot inverted V-shaped pattern.

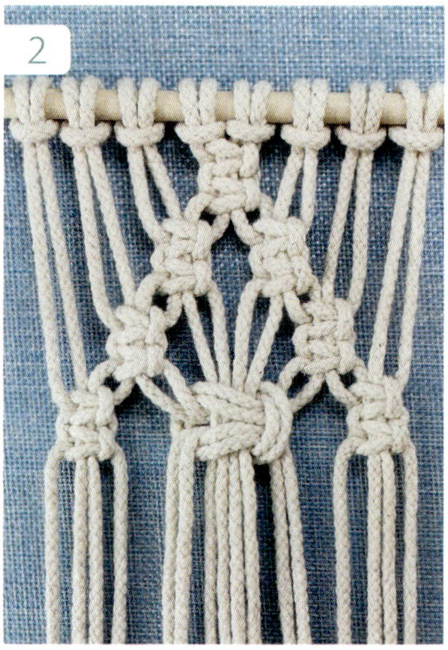

Weave the eight central cords into a large square knot, with the four central cords as the holding cords and two cords on each side as the working cords.

Weave a double square knot V-shaped pattern to close the diamond shape.

No. 44 Diamond Pattern Embedded with Double Square Knots, Style B (16 strands)

Refer to No. 43. Use the four central cords within the diamond shape to weave a segment of spiral knots (see P 40).

No. 45 Double-Layer Diamond Pattern with Square Knots (24 strands)

Refer to No. 26 and use 24 strands of cord to weave an inverted V-shaped pattern.

Use the middle 16 strands of cord, positioned directly below the first layer of the inverted V-shaped pattern, to weave the second layer of the inverted V-shaped pattern.

Refer to No. 28 to weave the V-shaped pattern corresponding to the second layer of the inverted V-shaped pattern, completing the small diamond shape inside.

Weave the second layer of the V-shaped pattern closely aligned with the first layer of the V-shaped pattern to complete the large diamond shape on the outside.

No. 46 Embedded Diamond Pattern with Square Knots, Style A (28 strands)

Refer to No. 33 and weave according to the pattern shown in the illustration.

Using the 12 strands of cord inside the diamond shape, refer to No. 137 to create a double-line interlacing weave. Secure the strands with pins.

Refer to No. 28, use the middle 16 strands of cord to weave a V-shaped pattern.

Fill in the blank areas on both sides of the V-shaped pattern with alternating square knots.

No. 47 Embedded Diamond Pattern with Square Knots, Style B (32 strands)

Referring to No. 19 and No. 46, use the 20 strands of cord in the center of the diamond shape to weave a fishbone pattern.

No. 47

No. 48 Diamond Pattern Combination with Square Knots (32 strands)

1

Refer to No. 28. Use the middle 16 strands of cord to weave V-shaped pattern.

2

At a certain distance from the first V-shaped pattern, use all the strands of cord to weave a second V-shaped pattern.

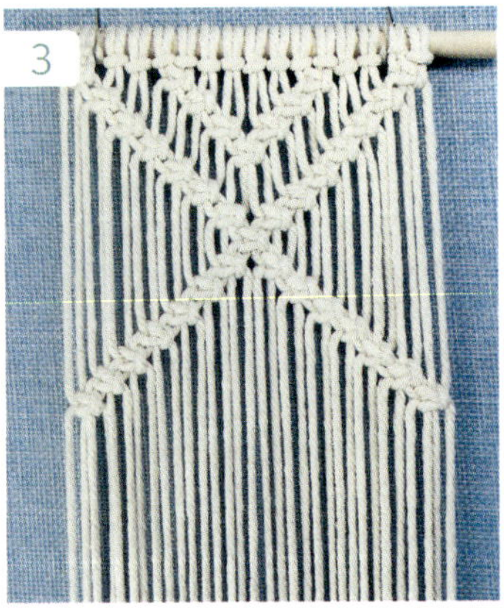

3

Using the lowest point of the V as the vertex, refer to No. 26 and use all the strands of cord to weave an inverted V-shaped pattern.

4

At a certain distance from the inverted V-shaped pattern, use the middle 24 strands of cord to weave another inverted V-shaped pattern, forming the upper half of the diamond shape. Then, use eight strands inside the diamond to weave a large square knot, with the middle four strands as the holding cords and two strands on each side as the working cords.

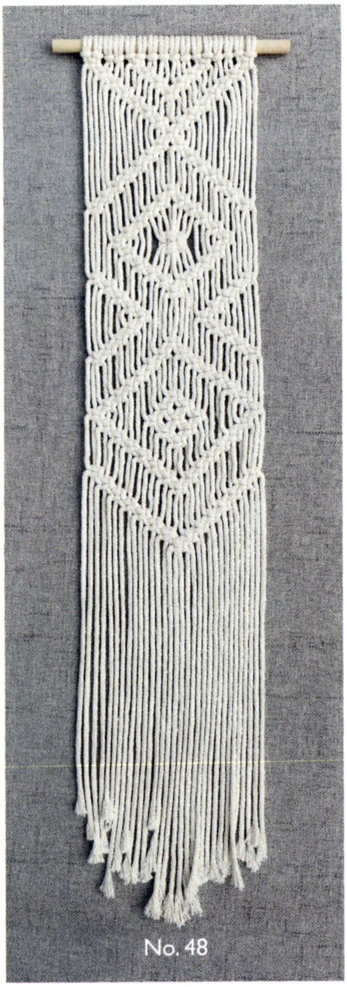

No. 48

Weave a V-shaped pattern to form the lower half of the diamond shape.

At a certain distance from the diamond, start weaving half of a diamond shape on each side, leaving the middle eight strands unwoven.

Use all the strands to weave an inverted V-shaped pattern, forming the upper half of the large diamond shape.

Refer to No. 35. Use the middle 12 strands of cord to weave a solid diamond shape.

Weave a V-shaped pattern to complete the lower half of the large diamond shape.

At a certain distance from the large diamond shape, weave a V-shaped pattern.

10. Interlaced Weaving Pattern with Square Knots

No. 49 Interlaced Weaving with Square Knots (24 strands)

No. 49

Use eight strands of cord as a group to weave a large square knot, with the middle four strands as the holding cords and the two strands on each side as the working cords.

For the eight strands of cord between adjacent square knots, refer to No. 136 to create a single-line interlacing weave. On each side, braid a segment of four-strand simple braid (see P 46).

Use eight strands of cord as a group to weave a large square knot, with the middle four strands as the holding cords and the two strands on each side as the working cords.

Repeat steps 2 and 3 until you reach the desired length.

11. Square Knot Combination Patterns

No. 50 Diamond Wave Patterns (48 strands)

Refer to No. 32. Use every 16 strands of cord as a group to weave an upside down triangle.

No. 50

Parallel to the sides of the triangle, refer to No. 28 and use every 16 strands of cord as a group to weave three V-shaped patterns in a wave pattern. Create two waves in total.

Use the second wave as the upper half of the diamond shape. For the center of the diamond, use eight strands of cord to weave a large square knot, with the middle four strands as the holding cords and the two strands on each side as the working cords. For the two sides of the half-diamond, use four strands of cord to weave square knots. Then, weave three corresponding inverted V-shaped patterns to close the diamond shape.

Parallel to step 3, weave three more groups of inverted V-shaped patterns to create a wave pattern.

Take a length of decorative cord (slightly more than twice the width of the tapestry) and refer to No. 137 to create a double-line interlacing weave. After completing the interlacing, lift the cord slightly to create a textured, raised effect with the decorative cord.

Thread the decorative cord through the space between the two layers of inverted V-shaped patterns. Flip to the back, tie a knot to secure the cord, apply glue, and trim any excess ends.

No. 51 Diagonal Stripes Pattern (28 strands)

Refer to the double-layer inverted V-shaped pattern in No. 27. Select one side of the inverted V-shaped pattern and weave the pattern shown in the illustration, creating a diagonal pattern extending to the left and right downward.

No. 52 Hexagon Pattern (48 strands)

Refer to No. 32. Use every 16 strands of cord as a group to weave an upside down triangle. Under the vertex of each upside down triangle, weave four square knots.

Use the 12 strands of cord between adjacent square knots in two groups of upside down triangles to weave a large square knot, with the middle eight strands as the holding cords and the two strands on each side as the working cords. For the sides, use six strands of cord to weave square knots, with the middle two strands as the holding cords and the two strands on each side as the working cords.

Using the last square knot woven downward in step 1 as the vertex, weave three groups of inverted V shapes to form a hexagon pattern.

Below the square knots connecting the two inverted V shapes, weave an additional four square knots.

Refer to No. 35. Use 12 strands of cord on each side of the square knots to weave a solid diamond shape.

Weave three groups of V shapes to form a hexagon pattern.

Repeat steps 2 to 4 to create an additional layer of the hexagon pattern.

Fill in the blank areas between the V-shaped patterns with alternating square knots, forming three triangles.

12. Patterns with Square Knot Buttons

No. 53 Upside Down Triangles with Square Knot Buttons (16 strands)

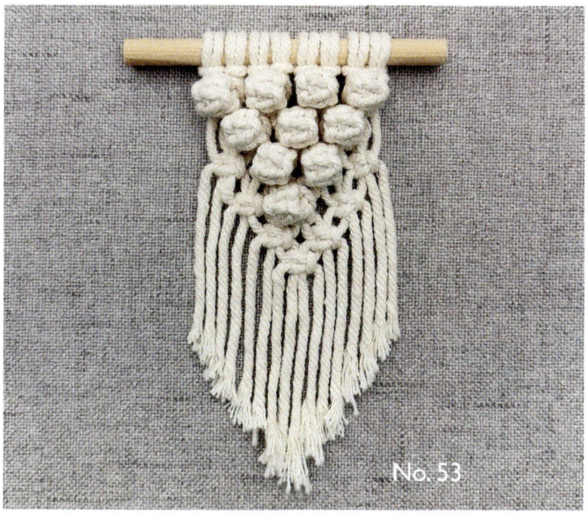

Group four strands at a time to weave four square knots, creating four square knot buttons (see P 39). Below these knots, weave an additional square knot to secure the square knot buttons in place.

Interlace three square knot buttons in a staggered arrangement.

Stagger and weave downwards two square knot buttons followed by one square knot button to form an upside down triangle. Below the square knot buttons, weave a V-shaped pattern. Ensure the distance between the square knot buttons and the V matches the distance shown in the illustration.

Patterns with Spiral Knots

Below are two patterns created by spiral knots. No. 54 showcases a finished product using 24 strands of cord, while the steps are demonstrated with 16 strands as an example.

No. 54 Upside Down Triangle with Spiral Knots (16 strands)

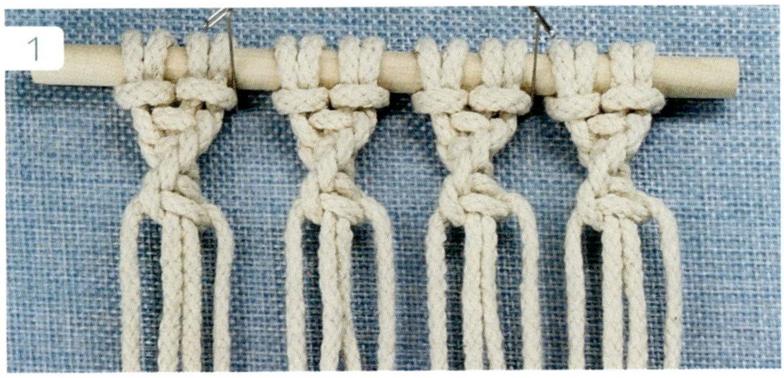

Group four strands at a time and weave five half-square knots to weave a spiral knot (see P 40). Form a row consisting of four groups of spiral knots in total.

Stagger and weave three groups, two groups, and one group of spiral knots downward to form an upside down triangle.

No. 55 Diamond Pattern Embedded with Spiral Knots (28 strands)

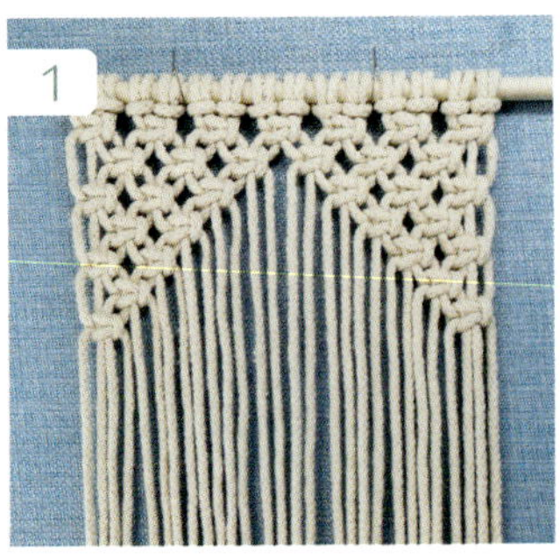

Refer to No. 33 and weave a right angled triangle on each side.

Using the middle four strands of cord, weave a segment of spiral knots, approximately twice the length of the right angled side of the triangle, down to the bottom vertex of the diamond shape.

On each side of the central spiral knot, use four strands of cord to weave two segments of spiral knots, with the length extending approximately to the edges of the lower half of the diamond shape. Weave a V-shaped pattern below the spiral knots to form a closed diamond shape.

Below the V-shaped pattern, weave two additional right triangles to fill in the blank areas.

Pattern with Sailor Knots

Here's a description of a pattern made up of sailor knots, which is relatively simple.

No. 56 Sailor Knots Combination Pattern (4 strands)

Using four strands of cord, weave a square knot. Then, use the cords on each side of the square knot to weave a sailor knot (see P 50).

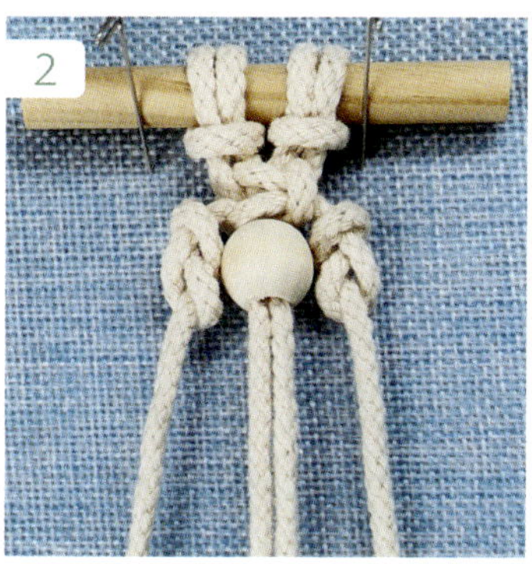

Thread a wooden bead onto the central holding cord.

Weave a square knot below the wooden bead to secure it in place.

Repeat steps 2 and 3 until the desired length is achieved.

Patterns with Reverse Lark's Head Knots Plus a Half Hitch

Here are two patterns composed of reverse lark's head knots plus a half hitch knot with each cord, which can form petal-like shapes.

No. 57 Vertical Stripes Pattern with Reverse Lark's Head Knots Plus a Half Hitch (4 strands)

Use the two strands of cord in the center as the holding cords to weave one vertical reverse lark's head knot plus a half hitch (see P 35), with the working cords on each side.

Leaving the same distance, use the right working cord to weave a vertical reverse lark's head knot plus a half hitch, then push it upwards to form a fringe. Repeat the above steps until the desired length is achieved.

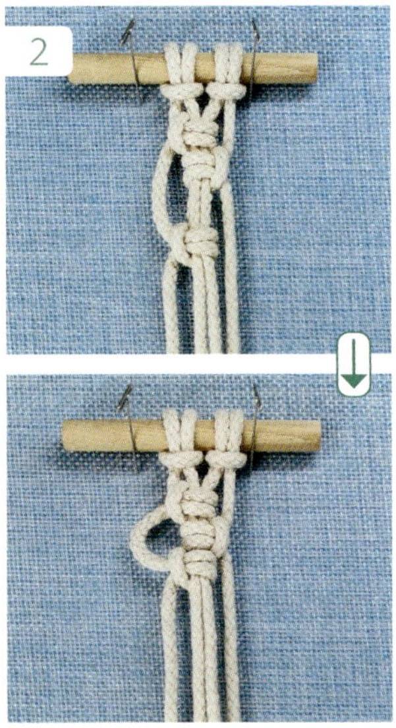

Leaving a small gap, with the left working cord, create a vertical reverse lark's head knot plus a half hitch, then push the knot upwards to form a picot.

No. 58 Reverse Lark's Head Knots Plus a Half Hitch Combination Pattern (6 strands)

Weave a square knot from the four strands of cord in the center. Referring to No. 57, use the two strands of cord on the left to continuously weave four reverse lark's head knot plus a half hitch picots.

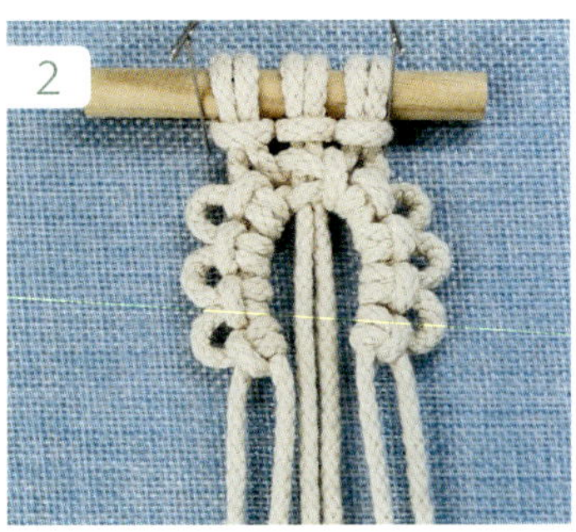

Weave the two strands of cord on the right to continuously weave four reverse lark's head knot plus a half hitch picots.

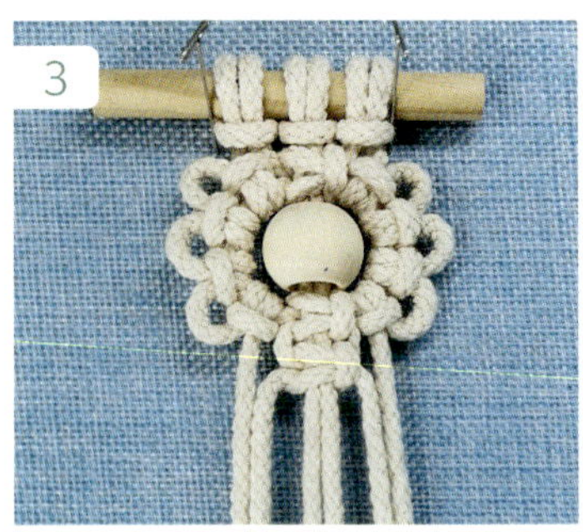

Thread a wooden bead onto the two central holding cords, then weave two square knots to secure it. Repeat the above steps until the desired length is achieved.

Patterns with Double Half Hitch Knots

The structure of double half hitch knots allows for diverse streamlined designs depending on the direction of the holding cord. These knots can also withstand significant tension. Patterns formed by combining double half hitch knots can be used to weave various home decor items.

1. Patterns with Horizontal Double Half Hitch Knots/Vertical Double Half Hitch Knots

No. 59 Horizontal Double Half Hitch Knot Waves (4 strands)

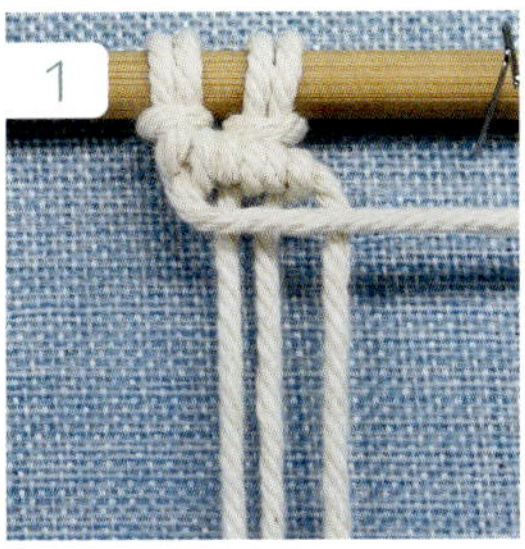

For each row, bend the leftmost cord to the right to serve as the holding cord, and then weave four rows of horizontal double half hitch knots (see P 42).

Change the direction of the holding cord for the fourth row, using the rightmost cord in each row as the holding cord, and weave four rows of horizontal double half hitch knots. Repeat the process until the desired length is achieved.

No. 60 Two-Tone Combination Pattern with Double Half Hitch Knots (10 strands)

Place a white cord horizontally across ten green cords. Use the white cord as the holding cord and weave horizontal double half hitch knots using the five green cords on the left side.

Use the white cord as the working cord and weave vertical double half hitch knots (see P 42) on the five green cords on the right side.

Add four more white cords and repeat steps 1 and 2 to form blocks of green and white colors.

Add five more white cords horizontally. On the left side, use the five green cords to weave vertical double half hitch knots, and on the right side, use the five green cords to weave horizontal double half hitch knots. This will create blocks of white and green colors.

2. Diagonal Double Half Hitch Knot Patterns

No. 61 Vertical Stripe Pattern with Diagonal Double Half Hitch Knots (6 strands)

Bend the rightmost cord to the left and downward to serve as the holding cord. Use the remaining five cords as the working cords to weave diagonal double half hitch knots (see P 43).

Use the rightmost cord of each row as the holding cord and weave diagonal double half hitch knots close to the first row.

Repeat the above steps until the desired length is achieved, ensuring that each row of diagonal double half hitch knots is closely aligned with the previous row.

No. 62 Two-Tone Vertical Stripe Pattern with Diagonal Double Half Hitch Knots (6 strands)

Place the colored cord on the far right. Bend the leftmost cord to the right and downward to serve as the holding cord, and then weave diagonal double half hitch knots.

Use the leftmost cord of each row as the holding cord, and weave diagonal double half hitch knots closely aligned with the previous row. The direction of the colored pattern runs opposite to the direction of the diagonal double half hitch knots.

No. 63 Triangle Pattern by Joining Diagonal Half Hitch Knots (6 strands)

Bend the rightmost cord to the left and downward to serve as the holding cord. Use the remaining five cords to weave five diagonal double half hitch knots along the holding cord.

Use the rightmost cord of each row as the holding cord. Starting from the second row, create one fewer diagonal double half hitch knot in each subsequent row, continuing this pattern for a total of five rows.

Bend the leftmost cord to the right and downward to serve as the holding cord. Use the remaining five cords to weave five diagonal double half hitch knots along the holding cord.

Use the leftmost cord of each row as the holding cord. Starting from the second row, weave one fewer diagonal double half hitch knot in each subsequent row, continuing this pattern for a total of five rows. Repeat the above operations until the desired length is achieved.

No. 64 3D Spiral Pattern with Diagonal Double Half Hitch Knots (8 strands)

Bend the leftmost cord to the right to serve as the holding cord. Weave seven horizontal double half hitch knots (see P 42).

Bend the leftmost cord to the right and downward, maintaining an angled spacing from the previous row. Weave seven diagonal double half hitch knots

Repeat step 2, paying attention to the direction of each row of holding cords.

During the weaving process, the pattern will naturally twist into a spiral shape.

No. 65 Inverted V-Shaped Pattern with Diagonal Double Half Hitch Knots (6 strands)

Use the middle two cords to weave a reverse double half hitch knot (see P 44). This knot will serve as the tip of the inverted V-shaped pattern. Use these two cords as the holding cords.

On the holding cords on the left and right, weave two diagonal double half hitch knots each to form the sides of an inverted V-shaped pattern.

Repeat steps 1 and 2 to continue weaving inverted V-shaped patterns until you reach the desired length. Ensure that each row of diagonal double half hitch knots is closely aligned with the previous row.

No. 65

No. 66 V-Shaped Pattern with Diagonal Double Half Hitch Knots (12 strands)

Refer to No. 65. Weave diagonal double half hitch knots from both sides toward the center to form a V-shaped pattern. Use the two outermost cords on each side as the holding cords. On the left side, bend the holding cord to the right downward, and weave five diagonal double half hitch knots (refer to No. 62) until you reach the center. On the right side, bend the holding cord to the left and downward. Weave five diagonal double half hitch knots (refer to No. 61) until you reach the center. When the holding cords on both sides meet at the center, weave a reverse diagonal double half hitch knot to form the tip of the V shape.

No. 66

No. 67 Adding Cord V-Shaped Pattern with Diagonal Double Half Hitch Knots (add cord 12 strands)

Starting with four cords, use the leftmost cord as the holding cord. Weave one double half hitch knot to the right.

Using the diagonal double half hitch knot adding cord method (see P 63), add four cords to the left holding cord.

Similarly, add four cords to the right holding cord. When the two holding cords meet, weave a reverse double half hitch knot to form a V shape.

Repeat the above steps until you reach the desired length, ensuring that each row of double half hitch knots is closely aligned with the previous row.

No. 68 Two-Tone Adding Cord V-Shaped Pattern with Diagonal Half Hitch Knots (add cord 12 strands)

Refer to No. 67 to add cords and weave a V-shaped pattern. Prepare two colored cords for the next step.

Using the colored cord, weave a row of reverse double half hitch knots on the left side.

Using the other colored cord, weave a row of reverse double half hitch knots on the right side, forming a V-shaped pattern. Trim the ends of the cords, and apply a small amount of glue at the ends. Avoid using too much.

Use the leftmost and rightmost white cords as holding cords, and weave diagonal double half hitch knots to form a V shape.

No. 69 Two-Tone Inverted V-Shaped Pattern with Diagonal Double Half Hitch Knots (8 strands)

Refer to No. 65. Place the green cord in the center and the white cords on both sides. Weave diagonal double half hitch knots to form an inverted V, resulting in a visual effect of alternating white and green V-shaped pattern.

No. 70 Two-Tone V-Shaped Pattern with Diagonal Double Half Hitch Knots (8 strands)

Refer to No. 66. Place the white cord in the center and the green cords on both sides. Weave diagonal double half hitch knots to form a V-shaped pattern, resulting in a visual effect of alternating white and green inverted V-shaped pattern.

No. 69 No. 70

No. 71 Three-Layer V-Shaped Pattern Plane Extension with Diagonal Double Half Hitch Knots (30 strands)

Refer to No. 66. Use ten cords per group and alternate the weaving to form three layers of V shapes. Repeat this process until the desired length is achieved.

No. 71

No. 72 V-Shaped Combination Pattern with Diagonal Double Half Hitch Knots, Style A (20 strands)

As shown in the diagram, first use the 16 cords in the middle to weave a square knot triangle (refer to No. 32). Then weave two rows of diagonal double half hitch knots to form a V-shaped pattern (refer to No. 66).

No. 72

No. 73 V Combination Pattern with Diagonal Double Half Hitch Knots, Style B (20 strands)

First weave a diagonal half hitch knot V-shaped pattern (refer to No. 66). Then, closely following the diagonal double half hitch knot V-shaped pattern, weave a square knot V-shaped pattern (refer to No. 28). Finally, weave another diagonal half hitch knot V-shaped pattern, creating a combined V-shaped pattern.

No. 74 V Combination Pattern with Diagonal Double Half Hitch Knots, Style C (16 strands)

Weave the eight strands in the center into three alternating square knot buttons, forming an inverted triangle (refer to No. 53). Then, weave three rows of diagonal double half hitch knots (refer to No. 66) to form a V-shaped pattern.

No. 75 V Combination Pattern with Diagonal Double Half Hitch Knots, Style D (16 strands)

Using all the cords, weave a diagonal double half hitch knot V-shaped pattern (refer to No. 66).

On both the left and right sides, skip the outermost cord on each side and use the second cord as the holding cord to weave a V-shaped pattern.

On both the left and right sides, skip the two outermost cords on each side and use the third cord as the holding cord and weave a V-shaped pattern.

On both the left and right sides, skip the three outermost cords on each side and use the fourth cord as the holding cord and weave a V-shaped pattern, ensuring that each row of diagonal double half hitch knots is closely aligned with the previous row.

No. 76 V Combination Pattern with Diagonal Double Half Hitch Knots, Style E (28 strands)

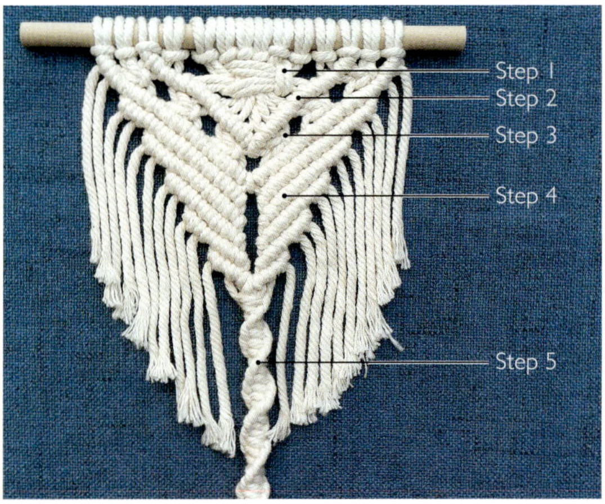

Step 1 Use the middle 12 cords to weave a large square knot, with the middle eight cords as the holding cords and two cords on each side as the working cords.

Step 2 Use the fifth cord on both the left and right sides as the holding cords, and weave diagonal double half hitch knots (refer to No. 66) to form a V-shaped pattern.

Step 3 Using the 3rd to 6th, 7th to 10th, and 11th to 14th cords from the left, weave square knots closely along the V-shaped pattern. Repeat the same on the right side.

Step 4 Refer to No. 75. Gradually decrease two working cords per row and weave a V-shaped pattern. Weave a total of six rows. Do not weave reverse double half hitch knots on the central holding cords for the 2nd to 6th rows.

Step 5 Use the middle six cords to weave spiral knots (see P 40). Finish by closing the end with a wrapping knot (see P 53).

No. 77 Cross Diagonal Double Half Hitch Knots (8 strands)

Use the leftmost cord as the holding cord and weave two rows of diagonal double half hitch knots with the four cords on the left side.

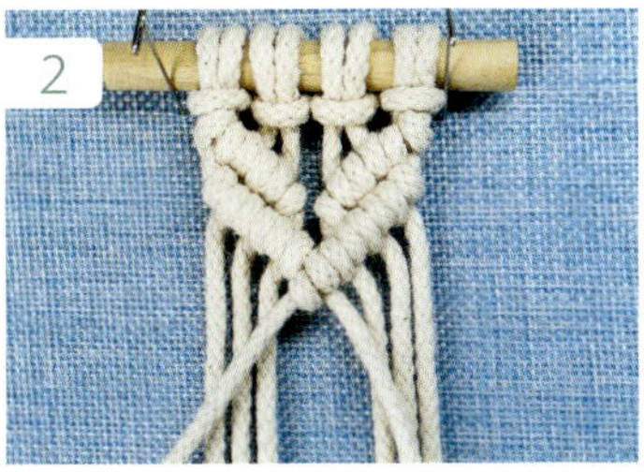

Refer to step 1. Weave the four cords on the right side into two rows of diagonal double half hitch knots. When the holding cords of the second row meet, use the right-side cord as the holding cord and the left-side cord as the working cord to weave a diagonal double half hitch knot, with the holding cord extending towards the left side.

Using the two middle cords as the holding cords on each side, weave two rows of diagonal double half hitch knots with the four cords on the left side. The first row of diagonal double half hitch knots should extend from the diagonal double half hitch knot made in step 2.

Refer to step 3. Use the four cords on the right side to weave two rows of diagonal double half hitch knots, completing a cross diagonal double half hitch knot pattern.

No. 78. Two-Tone Cross Diagonal Double Half Hitch Knots (10 strands)

Refer to No.77. Place colored cords on both sides to form a pattern where the crossing points are in color.

No. 79 Cross Diagonal Double Half Hitch Knots Plane Extension, Style A (24 strands)

Group every eight cords, and repeat the cross diagonal double half hitch knot pattern. After completing the first row, repeat steps 2 to 4 from No.77.

No. 80 Cross Diagonal Double Half Hitch Knots Plane Extension, Style B (32 strands)

Group every eight cords. Weave the rightmost cord as the holding cord into two rows of diagonal double half hitch knots, with three knots in the first row and two knots in the second row.

Weave the leftmost cord as the holding cord into two rows of diagonal double half hitch knots toward the lower right, with seven knots in the first row and six knots in the second row.

Use the third and fourth cords from each group and the seventh and eighth cords from the fourth group as holding cords. Weave two rows of diagonal double half hitch knots towards the lower left.

Repeat steps 2 and 3 until the desired length is achieved.

No. 81 Cross Diagonal Double Half Hitch Knots Plane Extension, Style C (36 strands)

For each group of 12 cords, use the four central cords in the group to weave a square knot. Each group of cords will be woven with two rows of diagonal double half hitch knots from the sides toward the center, and at the intersecting points, weave a reverse double half hitch knot.

Using the eight strands of cord between the two groups, weave a large square knot. Use four strands of cord on each side to make square knots.

Refer to No. 77. Complete the cross diagonal double half hitch knot pattern for each group.

Use the middle eight strands of cord from each group to tie a large square knot. Repeat this process until the desired length is achieved.

No. 82 Two-Tone Shell Flower Pattern with Diagonal Double Half Hitch Knots (16 strands)

Use four strands of green cord on each side to make a square knot. With the fourth green cord from each side as the holding cord, weave four diagonal double half hitch knots to the lower right on each side.

Using the four white cords as the holding cords and the second and third green cords as the working cords, weave four rows of vertical double half hitch knots. Then, using the leftmost green cord as the holding cord and the four white cords as the working cords, weave four diagonal double half hitch knots.

Repeat the same process on the right side. Then, use the green cords on both sides to weave one square knot each.

Weave the four central green cords into a square knot button. Then, use four green cords on each side to weave two square knots.

Repeat steps 1 to 3 on both sides, ensuring the directions are opposite, to complete a shell flower pattern.

No. 83 Shell Flower Pattern with Diagonal Double Half Hitch Knots (16 strands)

Refer to No. 82. Weave the four strands of cord on each side as the holding cords into diagonal double half hitch knots, and weave the eight central strands into a large square knot.

No. 84 Shell Flower Pattern Plane Extension with Diagonal Double Half Hitch Knots (48 strands)

For each group of 16 strands of cord, weave the four green strands on each side into a square knot. Using the four green strands on the left side of each group as the holding cords, weave four rows of diagonal double half hitch knots slanting down to the right.

For each group, repeat the same process on the right side, weaving four rows of diagonal double half hitch knots slanting down to the left. Weave four green cords on each side into a square knot.

Using eight green cords, weave a large square knot with the middle four cords as the holding cords.

With the green cords on each side, weave an additional square knot. Between each group, use eight white cords to weave a large square knot. Following steps 1 and 2, for each group, use four green cords on each side as the holding cords and four white cords as the working cords to weave diagonal double half hitch knots. Repeat the process until the desired length is achieved.

No. 85 Wave Pattern with Diagonal Double Half Hitch Knots, Style A (6 strands)

Use the left-side cord as the holding cord and weave five diagonal double half hitch knots toward the lower right.

Turn the same holding cord to the lower left and weave five diagonal double half hitch knots.

Repeat steps 1 and 2 with the same holding cord until the desired length is achieved.

No. 86 Wave Pattern with Diagonal Double Half Hitch Knots, Style B (6 strands)

Refer to No. 85. Weave the cord on the right side as the starting holding cord into diagonal double half hitch knots.

No. 87 Two-Layer Two-Tone Wave Pattern with Diagonal Double Half Hitch Knots (6 strands)

Using the two green cords on the right side as the starting holding cords for the first and second rows, weave two rows of diagonal double half hitch knots.

Turning the holding cord from the previous row to the right, weave two rows of diagonal double half hitch knots. Repeat the above steps until the desired length is achieved.

No. 88 Wave Interlaced Woven Pattern with Diagonal Double Half Hitch Knots (10 strands)

Refer to No. 85 and No. 86. Weave two opposing diagonal double half hitch wave knots. Use the cords between the two wave patterns for double-line interlacing weaving (refer to No. 137).

No. 88

No. 89 Multiple Waves Pattern with Diagonal Double Half Hitch Knots (14 strands)

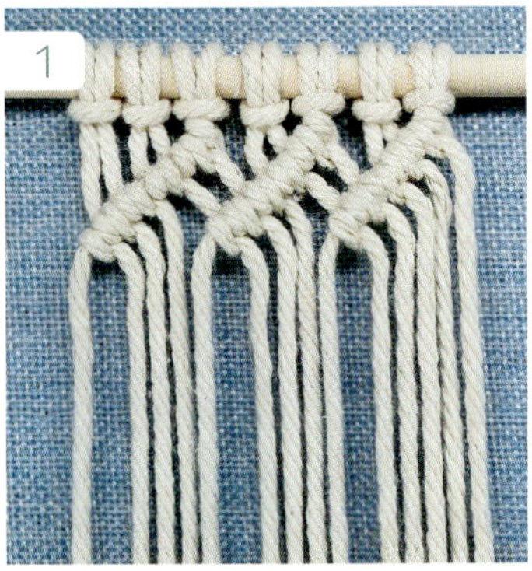

Take the 6th, 10th, and 14th cords from the left towards the right and use them as holding cords. Weave five diagonal double half hitch knots to the left and downwards for each of these holding cords.

No. 89

Bend the holding cords from step 1 to the right and weave separately, five diagonal double half hitch knots to the right and downwards.

Repeat the above steps until the desired length is achieved.

No. 90 Wave Combination Pattern with Diagonal Double Half Hitch Knots, Style A (24 strands)

For each group of eight strands of cord, use the 4th and 5th strands of each group as the holding cords, and weave three diagonal double half hitch knots on either side.

Within each group, use the middle four strands of cord to weave a square knot.

Use the 1st and 8th strands of cord from each group as the holding cords and weave three diagonal double half hitch knots inward on each side. Then, weave a square knot using four strands of cord between each group.

Repeat steps 1 to 3 until the desired length is achieved.

No. 91 Wave Combination Pattern with Diagonal Double Half Hitch Knots, Style B (36 strands)

Refer to No. 90. For every group of 12 strands of cord, weave diagonal double half hitch knots. Between the diagonal double half hitch knot waves, weave eight strands of cord into diamond-shaped square knots (refer to No. 35).

No. 92 Two-Tone Diamond Pattern with Diagonal Double Half Hitch Knots (6 strands)

Using the central green cord as the holding cord, weave diagonal double half hitch knots to form an inverted V-shaped pattern (refer to No. 69).

Form the green cords on both sides as holding cords to weave diagonal double half hitch knots into a V-shaped pattern (refer to No. 70), creating a diamond shape.

Repeat the above steps until the desired length is achieved.

No. 93 Diamond Pattern with Diagonal Double Half Hitch Knots Plane Extension, Style A (24 strands)

For each group of four strands of cord, weave a diamond pattern.

Weave the four strands of cord between adjacent diamonds into additional diamonds, creating an alternating pattern. Repeat the above steps until the desired length is achieved.

No. 94 Diamond Pattern with Diagonal Double Half Hitch Knots Plane Extension, Style B (48 strands)

Refer to No. 93. Weave diamonds using 16 strands of cord per group, connecting the diamonds with diagonal double half hitch knots. Make sure that the diagonal double half hitch knots at the intersections of the diamonds are consistently either left-leaning or right-leaning to achieve a neater pattern.

No. 94

No. 95 Diamond Pattern with Diagonal Double Half Hitch Knots Part Extension (6 strands)

No. 95

1

Use the four strands of cord on the left to weave wave patterns (refer to No. 86).

2

When weaving the wave pattern on the right side, make sure the holding cord extends all the way to the far left.

3

Use the rightmost cord as the holding cord to weave wave patterns.

4

Repeat step 2 to complete a full pattern. Repeat the above steps until the desired length is achieved.

No. 96 Embedded Diamond Pattern with Diagonal Double Half Hitch Knots, Style A (8 strands)

Use diagonal double half-hitch knots (refer to No. 65) to weave an inverted V-shaped pattern. Use the middle four cords to weave double-line alternating half hitch knots (see P 34).

Use diagonal double half-hitch knots to weave a V-shaped pattern (refer to No. 66), forming a diamond shape. Repeat the steps above until you reach the desired length.

No. 97 Embedded Diamond Pattern with Diagonal Double Half Hitch Knots, Style B (8 strands)

Refer to No. 96. Use the four cords in the middle of the diamond shape to weave a square knot button (see P 39).

No. 98 Embedded Diamond Pattern with Diagonal Double Half Hitch Knots, Style C (12 strands)

Use diagonal double half hitch knots to weave an inverted V-shaped pattern (refer to No. 65). Use the middle eight cords to weave square knots, forming a diamond pattern (refer to No. 35).

Use diagonal double half-hitch knots to weave a V-shaped pattern (refer to No. 66) to close the diamond shape.

No. 99 Embedded Diamond Pattern with Diagonal Double Half Hitch Knots, Style D (12 strands)

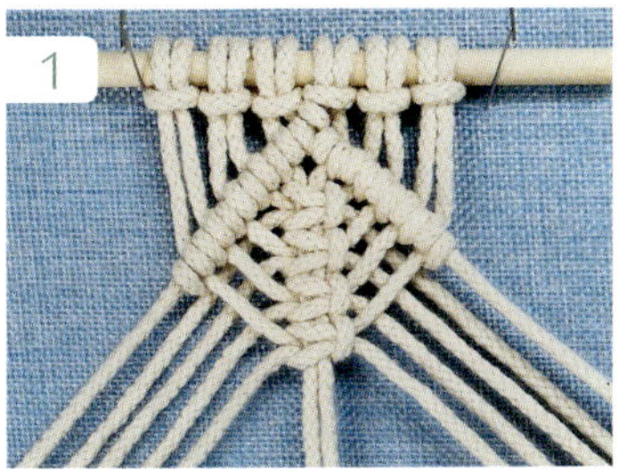

Use diagonal double half-hitch knots to weave an inverted V-shaped pattern (refer to No. 65). Use the middle ten strands of cord to weave a fishbone pattern with square knots (refer to No. 19).

Use diagonal double half hitch knots to weave a V-shaped pattern (refer to No. 66) to close the diamond shape.

No. 100 Embedded Diamond Pattern with Diagonal Double Half Hitch Knots, Style E (12 strands)

Use diagonal double half hitch knots to weave an inverted V-shaped pattern. Use the middle four strands of cord to weave a section of spiral knots (see P 40).

Use diagonal double half hitch knots to weave a V-shaped pattern (refer to No. 66), closing the diamond shape.

No. 101 Embedded Diamond Pattern with Diagonal Double Half Hitch Knots, Style F (12 strands)

Use diagonal double half hitch knots to weave an inverted V-shaped pattern (refer to No. 65). Use the middle four strands of cord to weave a diagonal double half hitch knot diamond shape (refer to No. 93).

Use diagonal double half hitch knots to weave a V-shaped pattern (refer to No. 66) and close the diamond shape.

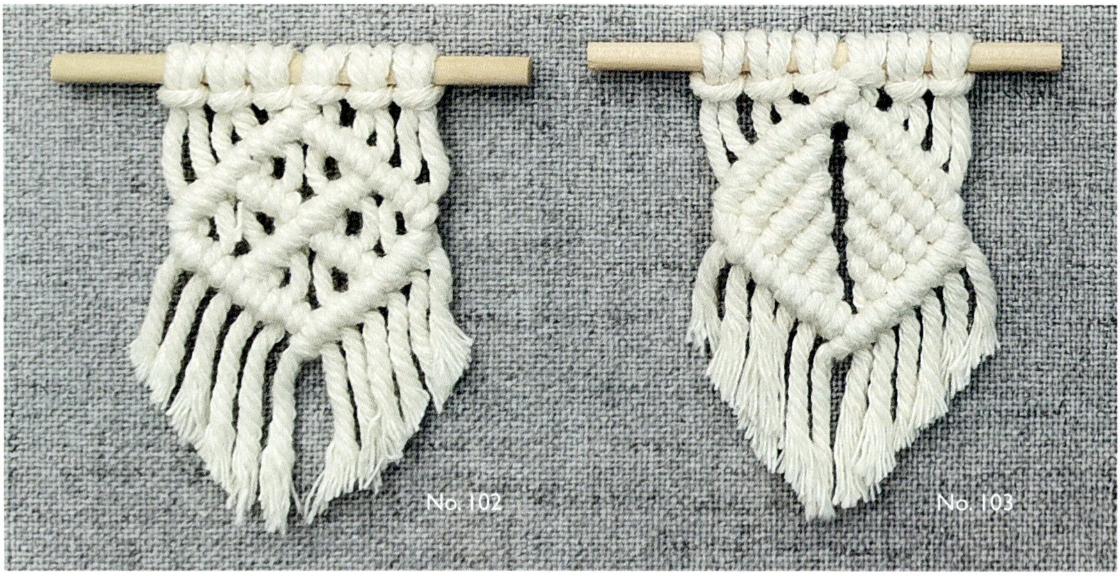

No. 102 Embedded Diamond Pattern with Diagonal Double Half Hitch Knots, Style G (12 strands)

Use diagonal double half hitch knots to weave an inverted V-shaped pattern (refer to No. 65). Use the six strands of cord in the middle to weave a cross diagonal double half hitch knot pattern (refer to No. 77).

Use diagonal double half hitch knots to form a V-shaped pattern (refer to No. 66), closing the diamond shape.

No. 103 Embedded Diamond Pattern with Diagonal Double Half Hitch Knots, Style H (12 strands)

Use diagonal double half hitch knots to weave an inverted V-shaped pattern. Use the middle ten cords to weave two diagonal double half hitch knot triangles on both sides (refer to No. 63).

Use diagonal double half hitch knots to weave a V-shaped pattern (refer to No. 66) to close the diamond shape.

No. 104 Diamond Interwoven Pattern with Diagonal Double Half Hitch Knots (12 strands)

Use diagonal double half hitch knots to weave an inverted V-shaped pattern (refer to No. 65).

Using the green cords on the left side, weave diagonal double half hitch knots sequentially from inside to outside on the leftmost holding cord (white cord), making a total of five knots.

Repeat the same process on the right side to close the diamond shape. Ensure even tension throughout the weaving process to maintain the structure of the diamond.

No. 105 Diamond Single Line Interwoven Pattern with Diagonal Double Half Hitch Knots (12 strands)

Weave diagonal double half hitch knots with the left green cords, working from the inside out on the right-side holding cord (green cord).

Use diagonal double half hitch knots to weave an inverted V-shaped pattern (refer to No. 65).

The right white cords are threaded through the green cords in sequence (refer to No. 136).

Weave the white cords into diagonal double half hitch knots from the outside in along the white holding cord. When the two holding cords meet, weave a diagonal double half hitch knot in the same direction as the initial diagonal double half hitch knot to close the diamond shape.

No. 106 Diamond Combination Pattern with Diagonal Double Half Hitch Knots, Style A (20 strands)

Step 1 Weave the square knots into right angled triangles on both sides (refer to No. 33).

Step 2 Weave the middle 14 strands of cord into diagonal double half hitch knots to form an inverted V-shaped pattern (refer to No. 65), which will serve as the upper part of the diamond shape.

Step 3 Use the middle 12 strands of cord in the diamond shape to perform three-line interweaving.

Step 4 From both sides, weave diagonal double half hitch knots V-shaped patterns (refer to No. 66) towards the center, closing the diamond shape.

Step 5 Use square knots to weave right angled triangles on both sides to complete the pattern.

No. 107 Diamond Combination Pattern with Diagonal Double Half Hitch Knots, Style B (30 strands)

Refer to No. 94. Weave intersecting diagonal double half hitch knot diamonds with embedded large square knots. Use the middle six strands of cord below the adjacent diamonds to weave a large square knot.

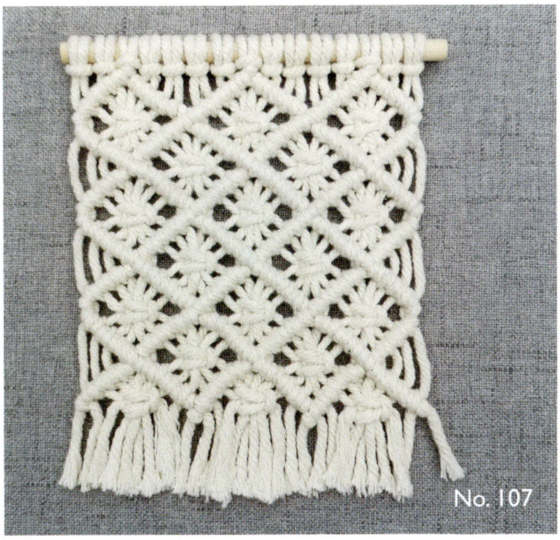

No. 107

No. 108 Diamond Combination Pattern with Diagonal Double Half Hitch Knots, Style C (24 strands)

Refer to No. 96. Weave diagonal double half hitch knot diamonds with embedded double-cord alternating half hitch knots. Use two strands of cord on the leftmost and rightmost sides to respectively weave half of a diagonal double half hitch knot diamond and alternating half hitch knots.

No. 108

No. 109 Diamond Combination Pattern with Diagonal Double Half Hitch Knots, Style D (24 strands)

Refer to No. 96. For each group of eight strands of cord, weave a diagonal double half hitch knot diamond pattern embedded with square knots. For each group, the eight strands of cord between the diamond shapes are used to weave square knots to connect them.

No. 109

No. 110 Diamond Combination Pattern with Diagonal Double Half Hitch Knots, Style E (36 strands)

For each group of 12 strands of cord, weave an inverted V-shaped pattern using diagonal double half hitch knots (refer to No. 65). Each group of inverted V-shaped patterns is connected using reverse double half hitch knots (see P 44).

No. 110

Refer to No. 99 and use the 10 strands of cord within the diamond to weave a square knot fishbone pattern (refer to No. 19). Weave diagonal double half hitch knots to form a V-shaped pattern (refer to No. 66) and close the diamond shape.

Refer to No. 104. Use the central cords as the holding cords and the cords arranged from the outside to the inside as the working cords to weave a diagonal double half hitch knot inverted V-shaped pattern. Repeat the above steps until the desired length is achieved.

No. 111 Diamond Combination Pattern with Diagonal Double Half Hitch Knots, Style F (48 strands)

In this demonstration using 16 strands of cord, be mindful of controlling the angle of the holding cord while weaving to ensure that the diamond takes on an oval shape. When using 48 strands, as shown in the diagram, the holding cords for the third square knot on both the left and right sides consists of eight strands.

No. 111

Divide the strands into groups of six, four, and six strands, and weave three square knots.

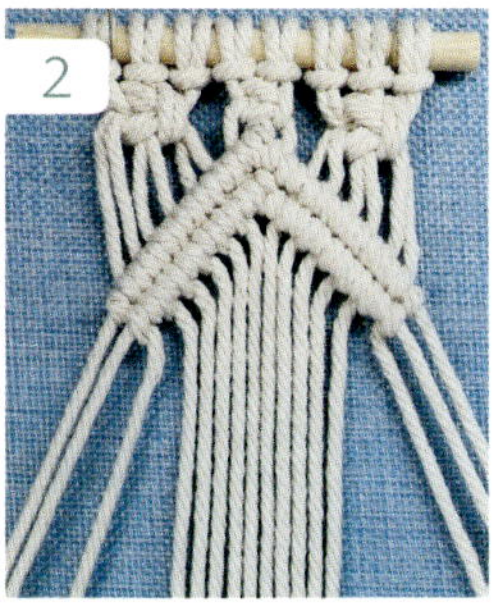

Use the two central strands as the holding cords and weave two rows of diagonal double half hitch knots to form an inverted V-shaped pattern, which will serve as the upper half of the diamond. For the second row of the inverted V-shaped pattern, leave one strand on each side unwoven.

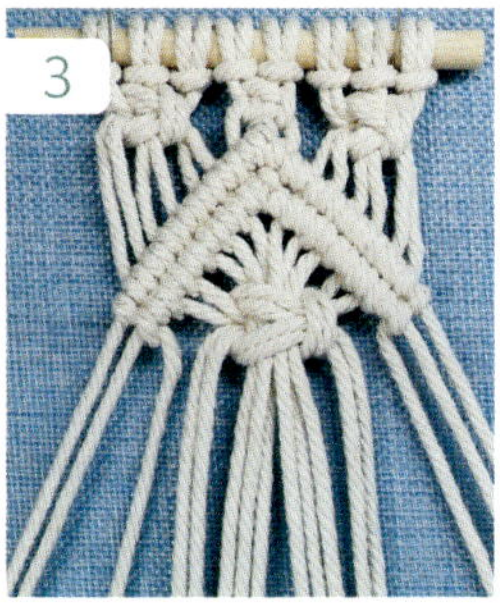

Inside the diamond, use ten strands to weave a large square knot, with the central six strands as the holding cords.

From the outer sides toward the center, weave two rows of diagonal double half hitch knots forming a V-shaped pattern, closing the diamond shape.

No. 112 Diamond Combination Pattern with Diagonal Double Half Hitch Knots, Style G (48 strands)

Step 1 For each group of 12 strands, weave a square knot forming a V-shaped pattern (refer to No. 28).

Step 2 Between each group of V-shaped patterns, use 12 strands to weave a diagonal double half hitch knot diamond with an embedded large square knot. The sides feature half-diamonds and square knots.

Step 3 Between each group of diagonal double half hitch knot diamonds, weave a square knot diamond (refer to No. 35).

Step 4 Repeat step 2.

Step 5 Between each group of diamonds, weave eight strands into a diagonal double half hitch knot diamond and finish with a hitch knot (see P 32).

Step 6 At the lower end of the large diamond, weave four strands into a section of spiral knots (see P 40). On both sides, use the spiral knot cord adding method (see P 62) to add two strands and continue weaving spiral knots, then finish with a hitch knot.

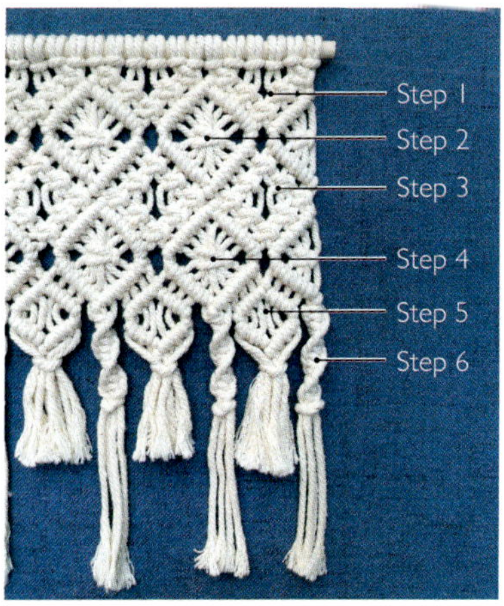

No. 113 Diamond Combination Pattern with Diagonal Double Half Hitch Knots, Style H (32 strands)

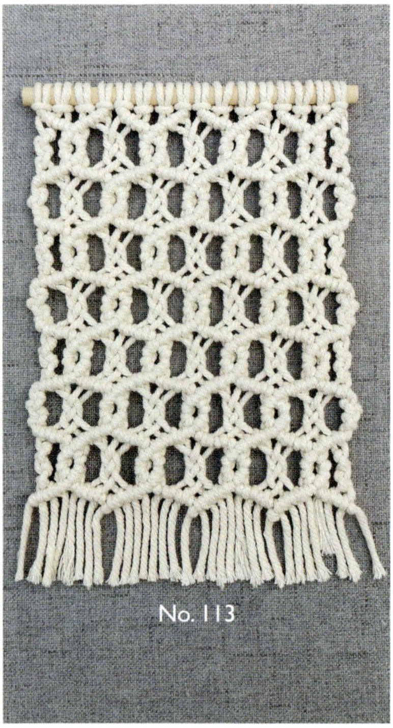

Step 1 For each group of eight strands, use diagonal double half hitch knots to weave V-shaped patterns (refer to No. 66). Then, use the four strands below the V-shaped pattern to weave a diagonal double half hitch knot diamond pattern.

Step 2 Between adjacent diamonds, use four strands of cord to weave a four-strand simple braid (see P 46). On the far left and right sides, use two strands of cord each to weave alternating half hitch knots (see P 34).

Step 3 At the bottom of the diamonds, use eight strands of cord to weave diagonal double half hitch knot inverted V-shaped patterns (refer to No. 65). Connect adjacent sets of inverted V-shaped patterns with four-strand diagonal double half hitch knot diamonds. Use the four strands of cord below the inverted V-shaped patterns to weave a four-strand continuous weave braid. On the far left and right sides, use two strands of cord each to weave alternating half hitch knots.

Step 4 Repeat the above steps until the desired length is achieved.

No. 114 Diamond Combination Pattern with Diagonal Double Half Hitch Knots, Style I (40 strands)

Step 1 Alternately weave four-strand diagonal double half hitch knot diamonds and eight-strand large square knots.

Step 2 From the bottom end of each pair of small diamonds, weave diagonal double half hitch knot V-shaped patterns (refer to No. 66).

Step 3 Below the top points of the V-shaped patterns, weave two four-strand diagonal double half hitch knot diamonds. Between adjacent V-shaped patterns, use eight strands of cord to weave a large square knot. On the left and right sides, use six strands of cord to weave square knots.

Step 4 From the bottom of the small diamonds, weave diagonal double half hitch knot inverted V-shaped patterns (refer to No. 65) toward the sides, closing the hexagon. Repeat the above steps until the desired length is achieved.

No. 115 Leaf Pattern with Diagonal Double Half Hitch Knots (6 strands)

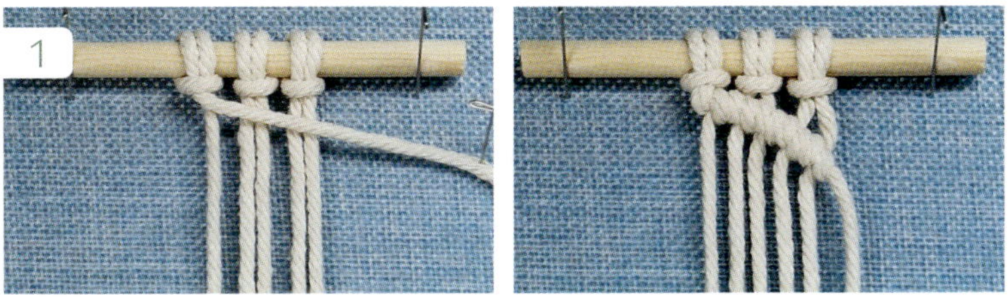

Use the leftmost cord as the holding cord and weave five diagonal double half hitch knots toward the lower right, forming the arc as depicted in the diagram.

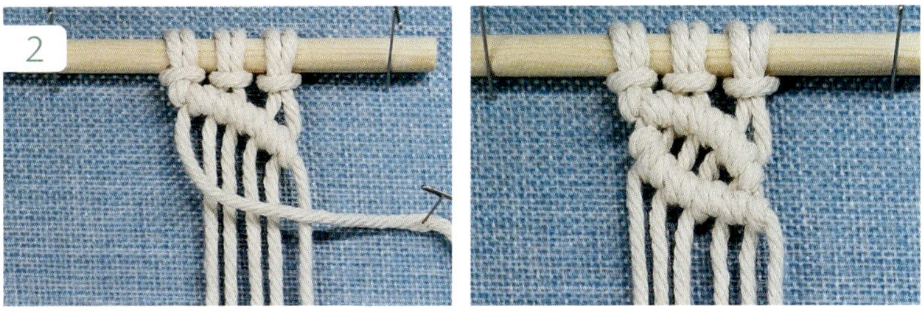

Use the leftmost cord again as the holding cord and weave five diagonal double half hitch knots towards the lower right, forming an arc as shown in the diagram. This will combine with the diagonal double half hitch knots from the previous row to create a leaf shape.

No. 116 Butterfly Pattern with Diagonal Double Half Hitch Knots, Style A (16 strands)

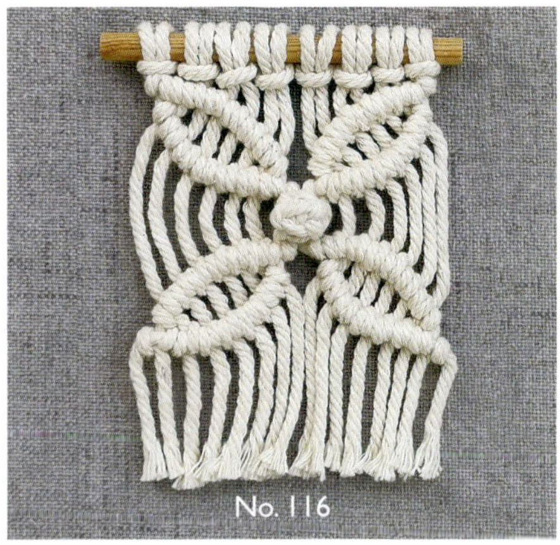

Divide the 16 cords into two equal parts left and right. Use the eight cords on each side to weave a leaf shape (refer to No. 115), with the weaving direction being opposite on each side.

Weave the middle four cords into a square knot button (see P 39).

Continuing downward, weave two more leaves, creating a butterfly shape.

No. 117 Butterfly Pattern with Diagonal Double Half Hitch Knots, Style B (20 strands)

Divide the 20 strands of cord into two equal parts left and right. From each side, weave two rows of diagonal double half hitch knots towards the center.

Below the diagonal double half hitch knots on each side, use the four middle cords to weave a square knot and a row of diagonal double half hitch knots, closing the leaf shape. Keep in mind the goal of creating a smooth curve.

From the center, weave two rows of diagonal double half hitch knots toward each side to form a curved shape.

Under each of the diagonal double half hitch knots on the left and right, weave the middle four strands of cord into a square knot and a row of diagonal double half hitch knots to close the leaf shape. Ensure that the two leaves at the bottom are symmetrical with the ones at the top.

Weave the four strands of cord on each side into a diagonal double half hitch knot diamond shape, creating the butterfly's tail.

No. 118 Butterfly Combination Pattern with Diagonal Double Half Hitch Knots, Style A (32 strands)

Here, eight strands of cord are used as a demonstration for the internal method for weaving the leaf.

First, weave a leaf (refer to No. 115).

Thread the green cord through a large-eye needle. Refer to No. 140, and weave a braided pattern inside the leaf.

No. 119 Flower Petal Pattern with Diagonal Double Half Hitch Knots, Style A (16 strands)

Step 1 Weave the middle eight strands of cord into a diagonal double half hitch knot diamond pattern.

Step 2 Refer to No. 116. Weave a butterfly pattern.

Step 3 Using the middle eight strands of cord, weave another diagonal double half hitch knot diamond to form a petal shape.

No. 120 Flower Petal Pattern with Diagonal Double Half Hitch Knots, Style B (24 strands)

Refer to No. 119. Weave small square knot diamonds inside the top and bottom diamonds. Inside the four leaves on the left and right, weave two alternating square knots.

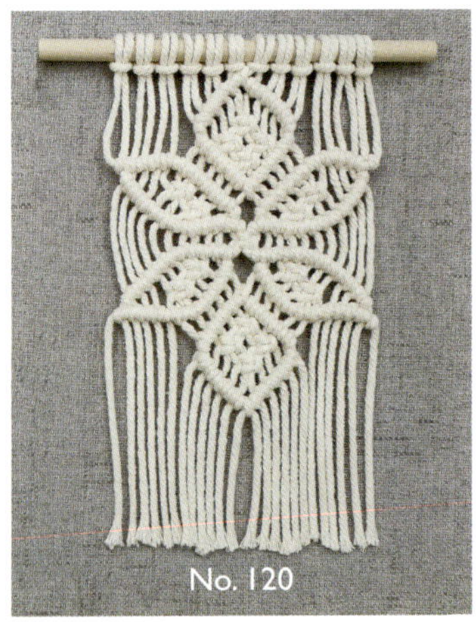

No. 121 Leaf Pattern Plane Extension with Diagonal Double Half Hitch Knots (24 strands)

Using six cords for each group, weave a leaf (refer to No. 115), making a total of four leaves.

Use the third cord from the second to fourth groups, counted from left to right, as the holding cord, and weave the leaves diagonally to the left in an alternating pattern. Repeat the above steps until the desired length is achieved.

No. 122 Leaf Pattern with Diagonal Half Hitch Knots, Style A (24 strands)

No. 122

Divide the 24 cords into two parts, left and right, and weave two consecutive leaves from the inside out (refer to No. 115).

Use the 12 middle cords to weave a solid square knot diamond shape.

On both sides, weave two leaves continuously from the outer edges toward the center.

No. 123 Leaf Pattern with Diagonal Half Hitch Knots, Style B (36 strands)

No. 123

For each group of 12 strands, weave a set of leaves in opposite directions.

Use the six central strands and the three strands on each side from each set of leaves to weave a square knot.

Weave another set of leaves in the opposite direction to form a butterfly shape.

Use the six strands of cord below the butterfly to weave a square knot. Repeat the above steps until the desired length is achieved.

No. 124 Leaf Pattern with Diagonal Half Hitch Knots, Style C (20 strands)

No. 124

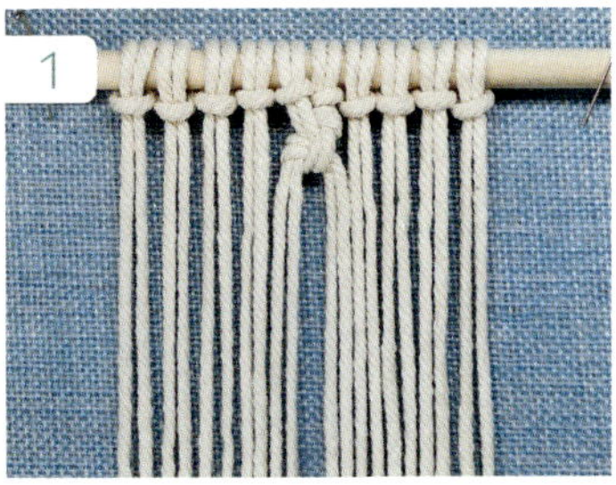

1

Use the four central strands of cord to weave two double-line alternating half hitch knots (see P 34).

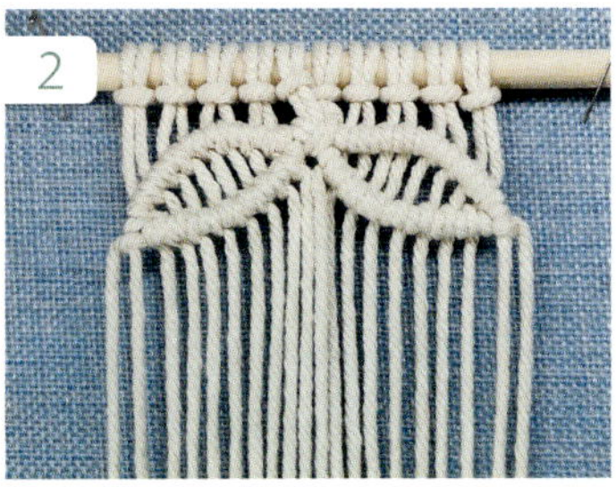

2

From the inside out, weave two leaf shapes (refer to No. 115).

3

Use the four central cords to make three double-line alternating half hitch knots, and from the inside out, weave two leaf shapes.

4

Repeat the above steps, and finally finish with double-line alternating half hitch knots and diagonal double half hitch knot diamonds.

No. 125 Leaf Pattern with Diagonal Half Hitch Knots, Style D (12 strands)

No. 125

1

Use the third cord from the left as the holding cord, and weave seven diagonal double half hitch knots to the lower right.

2

Use the sixth cord from the left as the holding cord, and weave one leaf to the left.

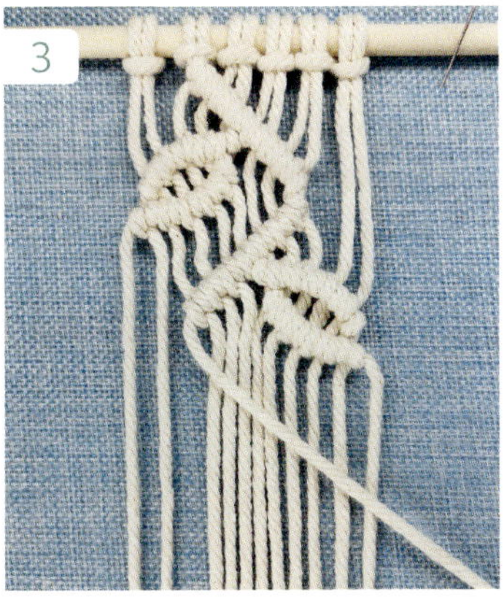

Reverse the direction of the holding cord used in step 1, and weave seven diagonal double half hitch knots to the lower left. And use the sixth strand of cord from the right as the holding cord, weaving a leaf shape to the right.

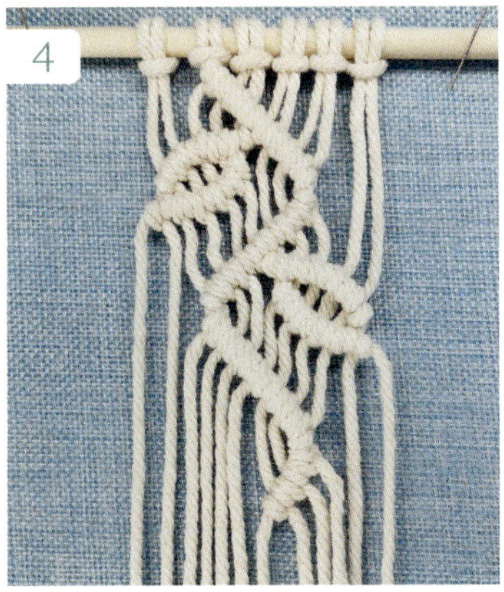

Repeat steps 1 to 3 to weave several leaves until the desired length is achieved. Then, reverse the direction of the holding cord and weave seven diagonal double half hitch knots toward the bottom right. After that, switch direction and weave three diagonal double half hitch knots toward the bottom left.

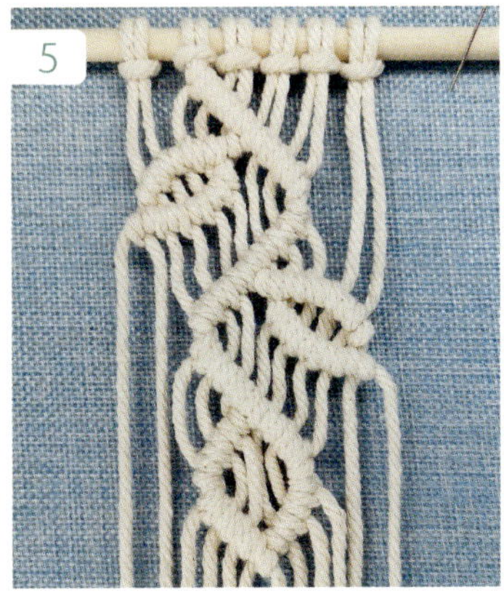

Using the sixth strand of cord from the left as the holding cord, close the diagonal double half hitch knot diamond pattern to form a group of leaves with branches.

No. 126 Leaf Pattern with Diagonal Half Hitch Knots, Style E (44 strands)

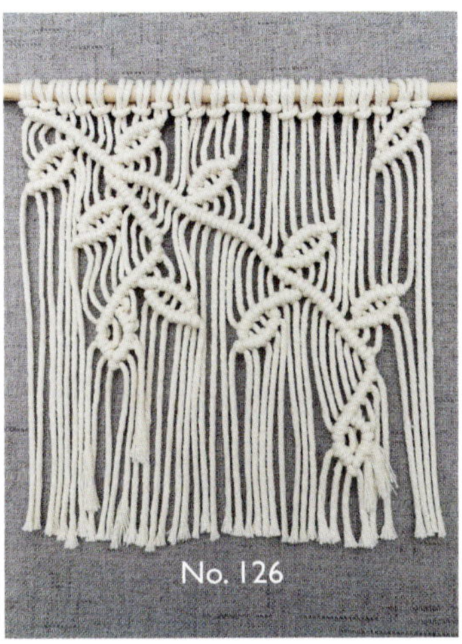

Starting from the left, weave ten diagonal double half hitch knots downward to the right as the branch, and use the 11th to 16th strands of cord to form a leaf.

Use the first to sixth strands of cord to weave a leaf below the branch. Weave diagonal double half hitch knots in different directions at appropriate points to form branching stems. First, weave the upper branch, then the lower one, weaving leaves on both sides of the branches.

Continue weaving the branches and leaves, ensuring that they intersect at specific points.

Weave the six strands of cord on the right into a leaf in the upper-right corner, then continue extending the branch, weaving leaves on both sides of the branch.

Finally, finish with a leaf. You can either follow the illustrated pattern or create your own design freely.

Flower/Feather/Tassel Patterns

Flower, feather, and tassel patterns are the highlights in macramé pieces, showcasing the beauty of nature. Flower patterns are full of vitality, feather patterns are ethereal and light, and tassel patterns are lively and graceful. Together, they bring a sense of vibrancy to the macramé pieces.

No. 127 Flower, Style A (square knot weaving method)

Weave two square knots side by side and position them accordingly. For the second row, add two extra cords to each side using the square knot cord-adding method (see P 61), and weave square knots.

Follow the diagram to weave alternating square knots (refer to No. 1).

Use the leftmost cord as the holding cord and weave a diagonal double half hitch knot inward.

Combine the working cord with the previous holding cord to use as the new holding cord and weave a diagonal double half hitch knot inward.

Similarly, continue to merge the working cords with the holding cords to use as the new holding cord until all the cords are gathered in the center.

Repeat steps 3 to 5 on the right side until all the cords are gathered in the center, completing one petal.

Make a total of five petals and five leaf knots (see P 49) as the flower center.

Place the petals around the outer edge and the flower center in the middle. Secure everything with a wrapping knot (see P 53).

Adjust the length and angle of the petals and flower center. Trim any very short cord ends. Alternatively, select 30 to 40 cords to create various lengths of leaf knots and barrel knots as the finishing touches. Cut off the ends of the cords (use glue if necessary). Your piece is complete.

No. 128 Flower, Style B (diagonal double half hitch knot weaving method)

Pin the middle of the holding cord. Below the pin on the holding cord, add four strands of cord and weave one double half hitch knot with each. These four double half hitch knots will serve as the starting point.

Bend the holding cord downward to the right, and with the four newly added strands of cord, weave four more double half hitch knots.

Use the cords on each side as the holding cords and weave a row of double half hitch knots on each side. Then, join the two holding cords together with a reverse double half hitch knot.

Repeat step 3, weaving two more rows of diagonal double half hitch knots.

Refer to steps 3 to 5 from No. 127. Gather the cords on both sides together and complete a petal.

Make a total of five petals, and weave one monkey's fist knot (see P 52) and six overhand knots (see P 31) to form the flower's center.

Place the petals on the outer side and the flower center in the middle, then use a wrapping knot to tie them together securely.

Adjust the length and angle of the petals and the flower center. The cord ends can be finished in various styles according to personal preference.

No. 129 Leaves and Branches

Fold three cords in half and secure them using a lark's head knot, creating a total of six strands. Select any one strand as the working cord, and leave the rest as holding cords to weave a double half hitch knot.

Next, select any one strand as the working cord and use the remaining cords as holding cords to weave double half hitch knots until only one holding cord remains.

Use the fifth strand from the top as the holding cord and the remaining four strands as working cords. Weave four double half hitch knots upward.

Following the same method as in step 3, use the fourth strand from the top as the holding cord and weave three double half hitch knots. Then in the fourth row, weave one double half hitch knot to form half a leaf.

Using the outermost cord as the holding cord, weave one, two, three, and four double half hitch knots to the left, creating a leaf.

Repeat steps 1 and 2 to gather all the cords together. Continue weaving the leaves until the desired length is reached.

No. 130 Feather, Style A

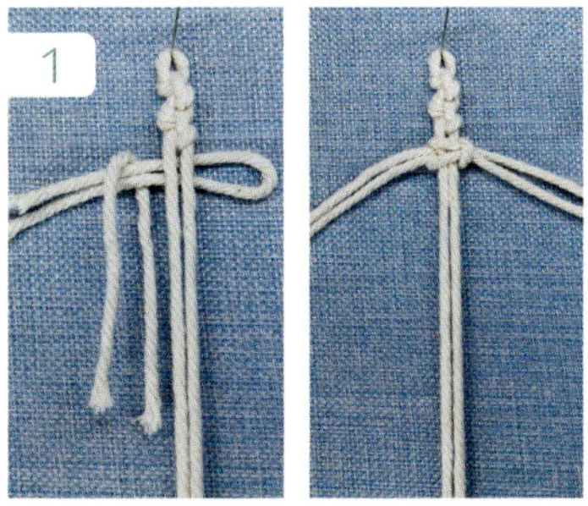

Fold one cord in half and weave four alternating half hitch knots (see P 34). Take a short piece of cord, fold it in half, and place it horizontally under the alternating half hitch knots. Then, take another short piece of cord, fold it in half, and loop it around the end of the previous short cord, passing the end through the loop from front to back to form a square knot.

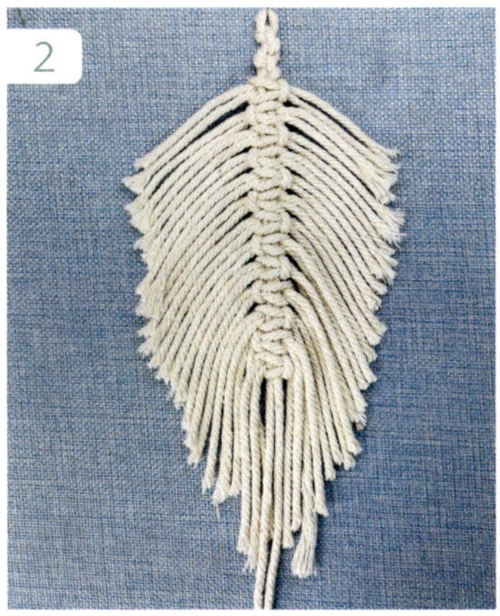

Take a short piece of cord and repeat the square knot weaving process until the desired length is achieved.

Use a comb to separate the cotton threads, trim the edges neatly, and shape them into a feather-like appearance.

No. 131 Feather, Style B

Weave eight strands of cord into two diagonal double half hitch knot diamond shapes with embedded square knots (refer to No. 96).

Secure several short cords in the gaps between the diamond shapes using lark's head knots (see PP 29–30). For the first layer of gaps, use two cords on each side. For the second layer, use three cords on each side. Then, use a comb to separate the cotton threads.

Trim the edges into a feather-like shape.

No. 132 Tassel, Style A

Prepare several short cords and a wooden bead. Fold a long cord in half and weave an overhand knot (see P 31).

Place the short cords between the two strands of the long cord below the overhand knot, and then thread a wooden bead below.

Take another cord and use a wrapping knot (see P 53) to gather all the cords together.

Adjust the cords to completely cover the wooden bead and trim the cords.

No. 133 Tassel, Style B

Wrap the cord around a piece of cardboard, with the height of the cardboard determined by the desired length of the tassel. Use another piece of cord to weave a segment of spiral knots.

Use the cord under the spiral knot to weave a knot at the midpoint of the cord loop removed from the cardboard, securing it in place.

Take another piece of cord and use a wrapping knot to gather all the cords together.

Cut the cord loop to create the tassel.

No.134 Tassel, Style C

Prepare several cords of equal length.

Take another green cord and wrap it around the middle of the white cords. Secure both sides with a hitch knot (see P 32).

Gather the white cords together as the holding cords, and use the green cords on either side as the working cords to weave a section of spiral knots (see P 40). Trim the green cords and secure them with glue.

No. 135 Tassel Combination Pattern (48 strands)

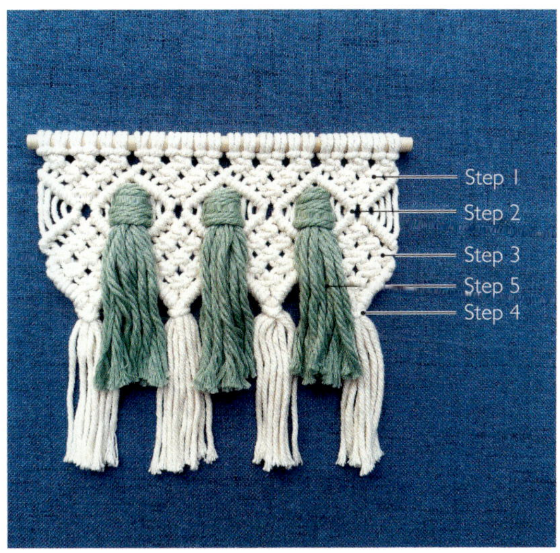

Step 1 For a group of 12 cords, weave a square knot upside down triangle (refer to No. 32).

Step 2 Weave the 12 cords between each group of triangles into diagonal double half hitch knot diamonds (refer to No. 96). On the sides, weave half a diamond shape.

Step 3 Weave the 12 cords between each group of diagonal double half hitch knot diamonds into a solid diamond pattern with square knots (refer to No. 35).

Step 4 Refer to No. 127, steps 3 to 5. Gradually gather the cords together using diagonal double half hitch knots.

Step 5 Thread green cords through the diagonal double half hitch knot diamonds to create tassels (refer to No. 141).

Weaving Patterns

Weaving patterns consist of warp threads and weft threads. First, organize the warp threads, and then use weft threads with different orientations to create various patterns. The density can be adjusted according to needs.

No. 136–141

No. 136 Single-Cord Interweaving Pattern

Single cord weft threads follow a "pick one, press one" pattern. When reaching the end, the direction of the weft thread is reversed.

No. 137 Double-Cord Interweaving Pattern

Double-cord weft threads follow a "pick two, press two" pattern. When reaching the end, the direction of the double-cord weft thread is reversed.

No. 138 Interwoven Pattern

Single-cord weft thread follow a "pick one, press three" pattern. When reaching the end, the direction of the weft thread is reversed.

No. 139 Twill Pattern

Loop a single-cord weft thread around two strands of warp thread and pass through. Then, wrap it around four strands of warp thread and pass through. Next, press it down on six strands of warp thread and pass it through behind the second strand of warp thread. Press down on another six strands of warp thread and pass it through behind the fourth strand of warp thread, and so on.

No. 140 Braid Pattern

Fold the weft thread and insert it into a large-eye needle. Pass it through behind two strands of warp thread, coming out from the left side. Then pass it through behind four strands of warp thread, coming out from the middle of two strands of warp thread, passing through behind six strands of warp thread, coming out from the middle of four strands of warp thread, and so on.

No. 141 Tassel Pattern

Insert both ends of the weft thread behind two strands of adjacent warp thread, then bring both ends out together from the middle. Alternatively, multiple strands of weft threads can be combined and used together.

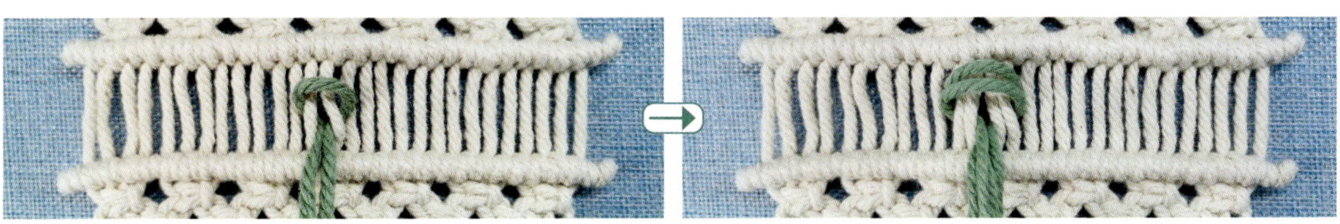

Fig. 42 *Composite Cloud Shoulder Tapestry*
The outdoor garden of the guesthouse features a mottled flower wall. When the photo was taken in late fall, only a few green leaves remained, so the entire scene came to life when the cloud shoulder tapestry was hung on it (see PP 207–209 for the project).

CHAPTER FOUR

Macramé Projects

The macramé items showcased in this book are all photographed from the homes of my friends. At the initial planning stage, I visited my friends' homes to measure dimensions and choose color schemes. I then designed different macramé items based on the settings of their homes, aiming to show readers that just a small piece of macramé design can enhance the overall aesthetic of their living space.

Cactus Tapestry

Incorporating a cactus pattern into a tapestry and pairing it with green plants can create a rich, textured home décor effect. Square knots can be used to create large, flat-patterned designs. When we want to translate a pattern into a weaving design, we can first pixelate the pattern and then arrange the positions for the square knots accordingly.

Materials

Wooden rod: length 40 cm, diameter 2 cm
Cord material: 8 mm white flat cotton

cord, green decorative cord (or other specialty threads as alternatives)

Cord Cutting Guide

White flat cotton cord: 5 m × 14 pieces (28 strands), 50 cm × 4 pieces (to be used as the holding cord for horizontal double half hitch knots)
Green decorative cord: 1.5–2 m × 1 piece (for braid pattern), 35 cm × several pieces (for tassel pattern)
Note: If the specialty cords are thin, you can combine several to make one strand.

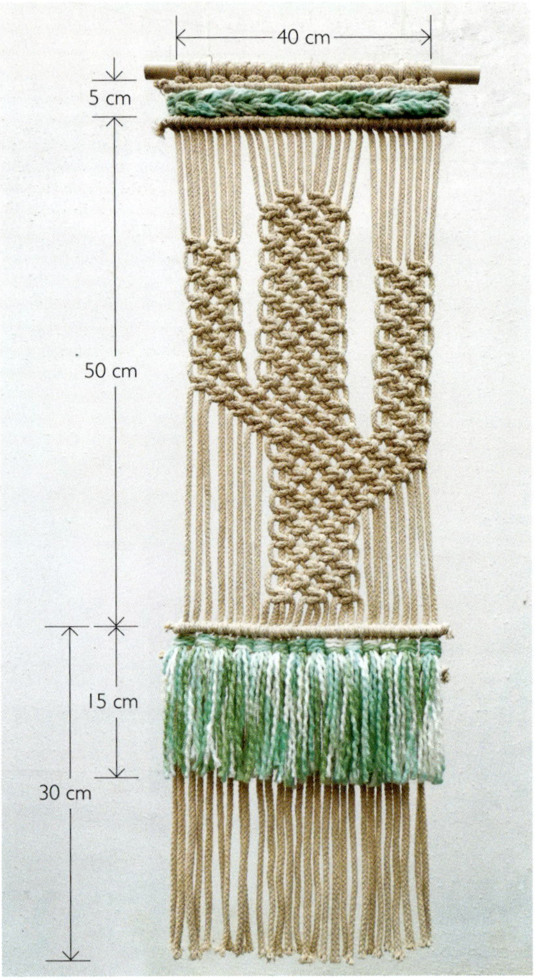

Basic Knots

Lark's head knot, square knot, horizontal double half hitch knot, overhand knot

Patterns

Alternating square knots pattern (No. 1), braid pattern (No. 140), tassel pattern (No. 141)

Starting Technique

Lark's head knot horizontal starting method

Product Dimensions

Length 85 cm, width 40 cm

Steps

Fold 14 strands of cord in half and secure them to the wooden rod using lark's head knots. Take a 50 cm long cord for the holding cord, and weave a row of horizontal double half hitch knots closely next to the lark's head knots. Secure both ends with an overhand knot. Add a new holding cord spaced 2 cm apart from the previous one and weave another row of horizontal double half hitch knots. Secure both ends with overhand knots.

Take a 1.5 m length of decorative cord and weave a braid weaving pattern between the two rows of horizontal double half hitch knots.

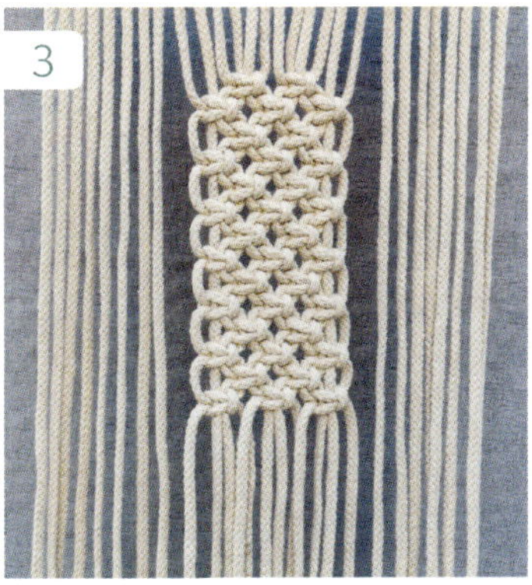

Weave the 12 central strands into 14 rows of alternating square knots, spacing them 6 cm apart.

Weave the eight strands of cord on each side into alternating square knots. On the left side, weave 11 rows, and on the right side, weave 13 rows. This will create a tiered effect with three columns of knots, as shown in the diagram.

Weave four rows of alternating square knots. Merge the left side with the center part, decreasing one square knot on the left side with each new row.

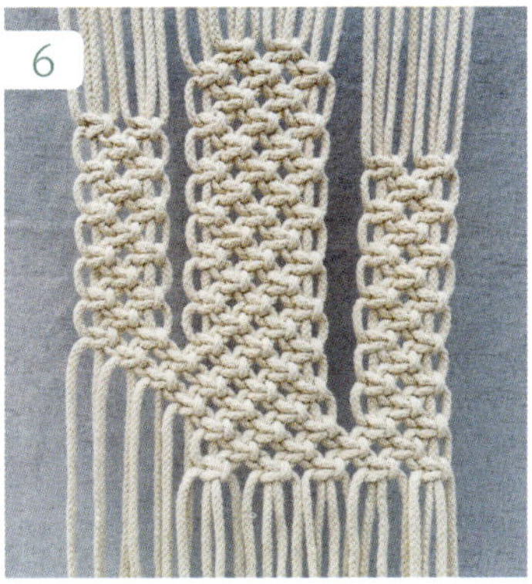

Weave two rows of alternating square knots, merging the center part with the right side.

Continue weaving four rows of alternating square knots downward, with the right side decreasing by one knot for each row.

Using the central 12 strands of cord, continue weaving six rows of alternating square knots downward.

Add two strands of holding cord 3 cm below the cactus. Weave two rows of horizontal double half hitch knots with a spacing of 2 cm between each knot.

Use the remaining decorative cord to weave a tassel weaving pattern between the horizontal double half hitch knots.

Hanging Storage Basket

Hanging the storage basket can make full use of the wall space, while the woven pattern can become an interesting decorative background. Diagonal double half hitch knots are ideal for creating linear pattern designs. In this project, the lines are designed into a lotus flower pattern, and the diagonal double half hitch knots make the design more defined and clear. When using diagonal double half hitch knots to create a pattern, it is important to follow the weaving order carefully, starting from the top and working your way down, moving from the center outward to both sides.

Materials

Storage box: length 26 cm, width 21 cm, height 11 cm
Natural branch: length 45 cm
Cord material: 3 mm white cotton cord, 3 mm dark green cotton cord

Cord Cutting Guide

White cotton cord: 1.5 m × 26 pieces (52 strands)
Dark green cotton cord: 3 m × 6 pieces (12 strands), 4 m × 6 pieces (12 strands)

Basic Knots

Lark's head knot, square knot, diagonal double half hitch knot, overhand knot, alternating half hitch knot

Patterns

Diamond pattern with alternating square knots (No. 36), diamond pattern with diagonal double half hitch knots part extension (No. 95), diamond combination pattern with diagonal double half hitch knots, style F (No. 111), leaf pattern with diagonal double half hitch knots (No. 115)

Starting Technique

Lark's head knot horizontal starting method

Product Dimensions

Length 30 cm, width 21 cm, height 30 cm

Steps

Step 1 Fold all the white cords in half and attach them to the branch using lark's head knots. Weave diamond patterns with square knots. Weave eight strands of cord on each side into two diamond patterns with square knots, skipping four strands in between and then weaving two more. Then, under the first row of diamond patterns with square knots, weave one more diamond pattern with square knots on each side, forming an alternating pattern.

Step 2 Using the 16 strands of cord in the center, weave a diamond combination pattern with diagonal double half hitch knots, style F. Inside the diamond, wrap one large square knot using eight strands. The four middle strands will serve as the holding cords, while two strands on each side will be used as the working cords.

Step 3 Use the 13th strand from the left as the holding cord. Weave a leaf pattern with diagonal double half hitch knots towards the center. On the upper edge of the leaf, weave ten diagonal double half hitch knots. On the lower edge, weave 13 diagonal double half hitch knots down to the bottom vertex of the diamond. Pay attention to the curvature of the leaf. For the right side, follow the same method as for the left side.

Step 4 Use the fifth strand from the left as the holding cord and weave a leaf pattern with diagonal double half hitch knots towards the center. On the leaf's upper edge, weave 11 diagonal double half hitch knots, and on the lower edge, weave 21 diagonal double half hitch knots down to the bottom vertex of the diamond. Pay attention to the curvature of the leaf. Follow the same method for the right side as for the left side.

Step 5 Take the 14th strand from the left as the holding cord and weave nine diagonal double half hitch knots towards the center. Pay attention to the curvature of the arc. For the right side, follow the same method as for the left side.

Step 6 Weave the eight central strands into a square knot diamond shape. Then, weave the eight strands on each side into additional diamond patterns with square knots, skipping four strands and then adding two more diamonds. In the next row, weave alternating square knot diamonds.

Step 7 Weave an overhand knot at the bottom of each strand as decoration. Trim any excessively long strands after weaving the overhand knots to the desired height.

Step 8 Secure six strands of 3 m long green cord on both sides of the main body using lark's head knots. For each side, use six strands and extend the woven section with diagonal double half hitch knot diamonds for about 30 cm.

Step 9 Secure six strands of 4 m long green cord on both sides of the section from step 8 using a lark's head knots. For each side, use six strands and extend the woven section with diagonal double half hitch knot diamonds for about 40 cm.

Step 10 Use alternating half hitch knots to secure the ends of the diamond patterns with diagonal double half hitch knots to the corners of the storage box. Ensure the box remains level. The longer excess parts can be braided into a three-strand simple braid or made into tassels according to personal preference.

Five-Panel Combination Tapestry

Multiple tapestries can be combined to create various patterns. Each tapestry can be used individually or combined to form a cohesive whole. When designing such tapestries, start by conceptualizing the overall pattern, and then consider where to split the design.

Materials

Wooden rod: length 80 cm, diameter 1 cm
Cord material: 2.5 mm cotton cord

Cord Cutting Guide

Column A: 1.5 m × 32 pieces (64 strands)
Column B: 2 m × 32 pieces (64 strands)
Column C: 2.5 m × 24 pieces (48 strands)

Basic Knots

Lark's head knot, square knot

Patterns

Inverted V-shaped pattern with square knots (No. 26–27), V-shaped pattern with square knots (No. 28–29), upside down triangle pattern with square knots (No. 32), solid diamond shape with square knots (No. 35), diamond pattern embedded with double square knots, style A (No. 43), diamond pattern combination with square knots (No. 48)

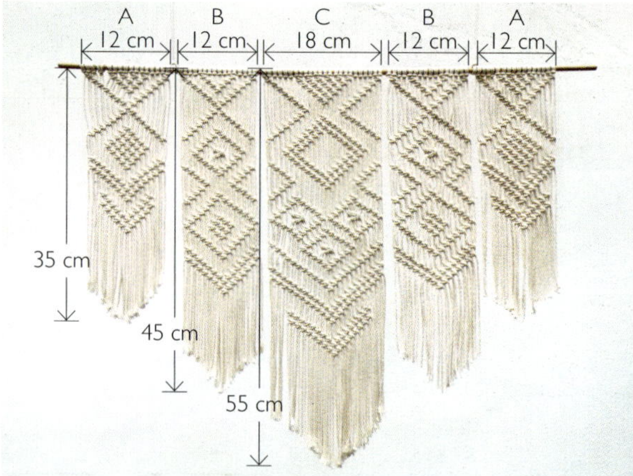

Starting Technique

Lark's head horizontal starting method

Product Dimensions

Length 55 cm, width 66 cm

Steps

Step 1 Starting from the middle column C makes it easier to manage the overall design. Attach 24 pieces of 2.5 m long cotton cords to the center of the wooden rod using lark's head knots. Then, use the 24 central cords to weave an upside down triangle pattern with square knots.

Step 2 Use the 18 cords on each side to weave half of a diamond shape with square knots inward, making sure they are parallel to the sides of the upside down triangle.

Step 3 Use the 36 central cords to weave a double-layer diamond pattern with square knots, ensuring it is parallel to the half-diamond shapes from step 2.

Step 4 Use the 12 cords on each side to weave half a diamond pattern with square knots inward.

Step 5 Divide the 48 cords into two groups and weave one diamond pattern with an embedded 8-strand square knots in each group. Then take the middle 24 cords and weave another diamond pattern with an embedded eight-strand square knot.

Step 6 Weave single-layer V-shaped pattern with square knots from the sides toward the center, ensuring they are parallel to the diamonds above.

Step 7 Weave double-layer V-shaped pattern with square knots from the sides toward the center.

Step 8 Skip six strands of cord on each side, then continue to weave V-shaped pattern with double-layer square knots.

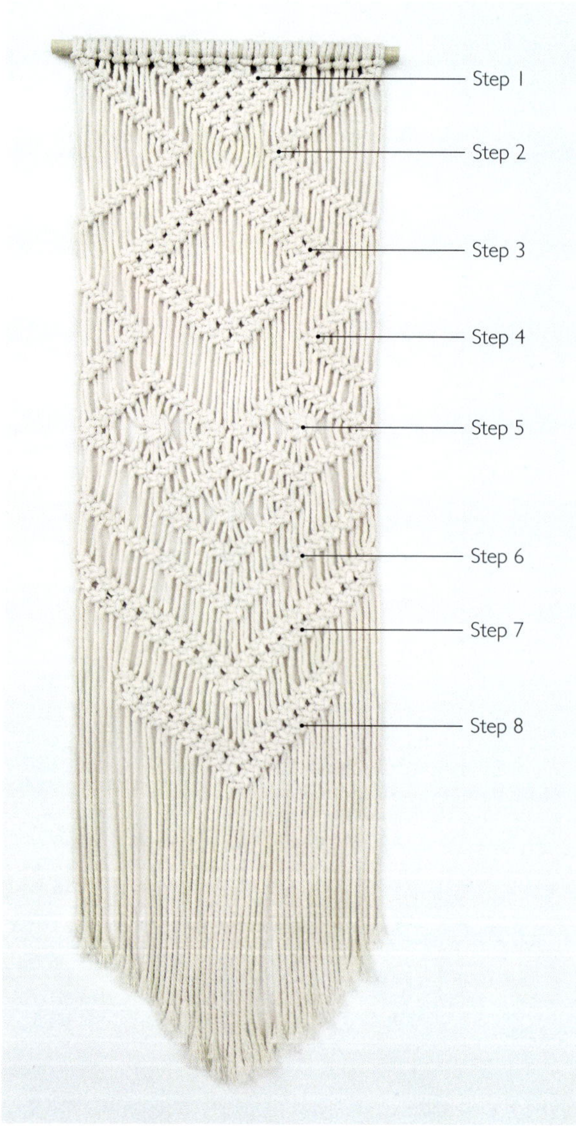

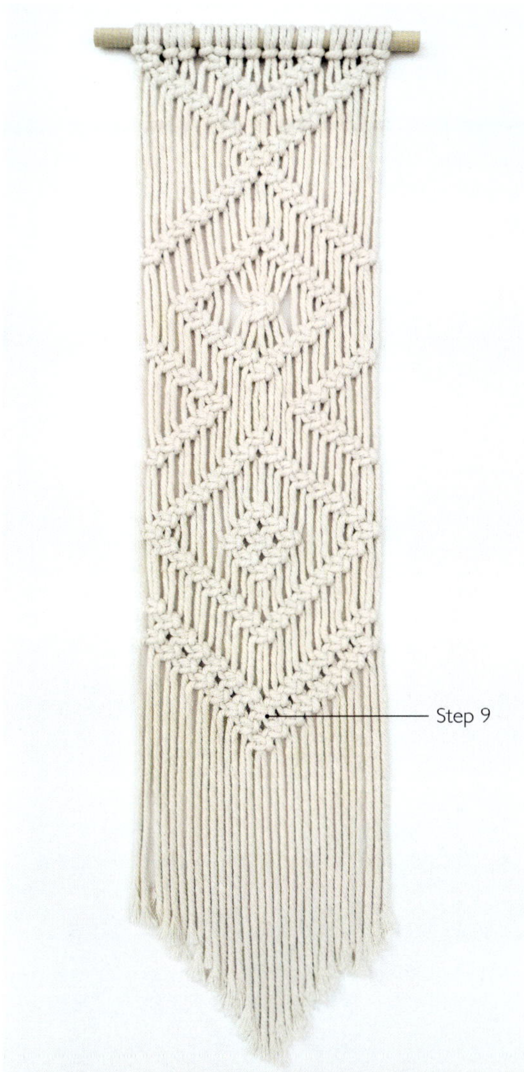

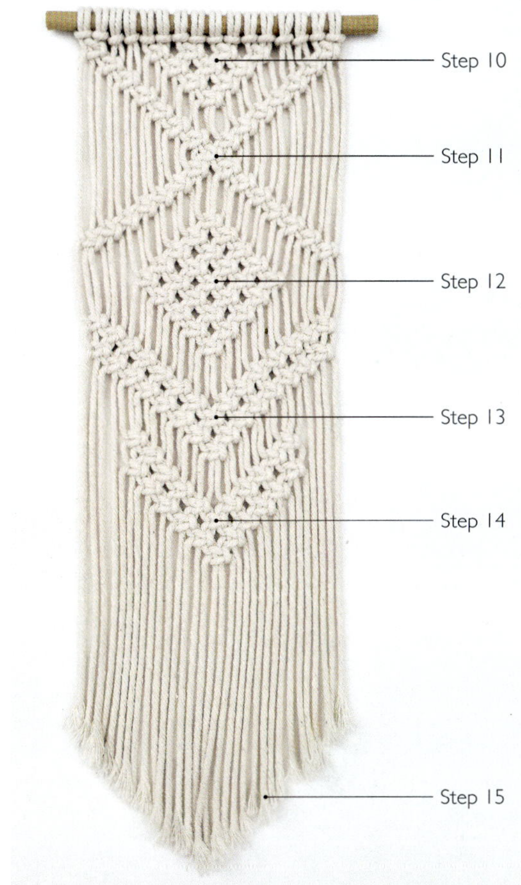

Step 9 Weave column B. Fix 32 cotton cords using lark's head knots on both sides of column C, with 16 cords on each side. Refer to the detailed steps from the diamond pattern combination with square knots (No. 48), and replace the final single-layer V-shaped pattern with a double-layer V-shaped pattern with square knots. Ensure that the slanted angles of the V patterns, diamonds, and other elements align with the angle of column C.

Step 10 Weave column A. Fix the 32 cotton cords using lark's head knots on both sides of column B, then use the middle 16 strands to weave an upside down triangle pattern with square knots.

Step 11 Weave square knots from both sides toward the center to form V patterns, followed by inverted V patterns, creating an X shape.

Step 12 Use the middle 20 strands to weave a solid diamond shape with square knots, ensuring it aligns with the V patterns above.

Step 13 From both sides, weave double-layered V-shaped patterns with square knots toward the center.

Step 14 Skip four strands on each side and continue weaving double-layered V-shaped patterns with square knots.

Step 15 Finally, trim the bottom of the five panel tapestry to the same slanted angle, creating a unified appearance.

One-Piece Square Tapestry

A one-piece design is composed of repeating one to three patterns, resulting in a clean, organized visual effect that is also easy to execute. When weaving, you can first choose a pattern that controls the overall visual effect, and then incorporate other detailed variations within that pattern.

Materials

Wooden rod: length 40 cm, diameter 1.5 cm
Cord material: 3 mm dark brown cotton cord

Cord Cutting Guide

3.2 m × 32 pieces (64 strands)

Basic Knots

Lark's head knot, square knot, diagonal double half hitch knot

Pattern

Hollow diamond pattern with square knots (No. 37)

Starting Technique

Lark's head knot horizontal starting method

Product Dimensions

Length 60 cm, width 30 cm

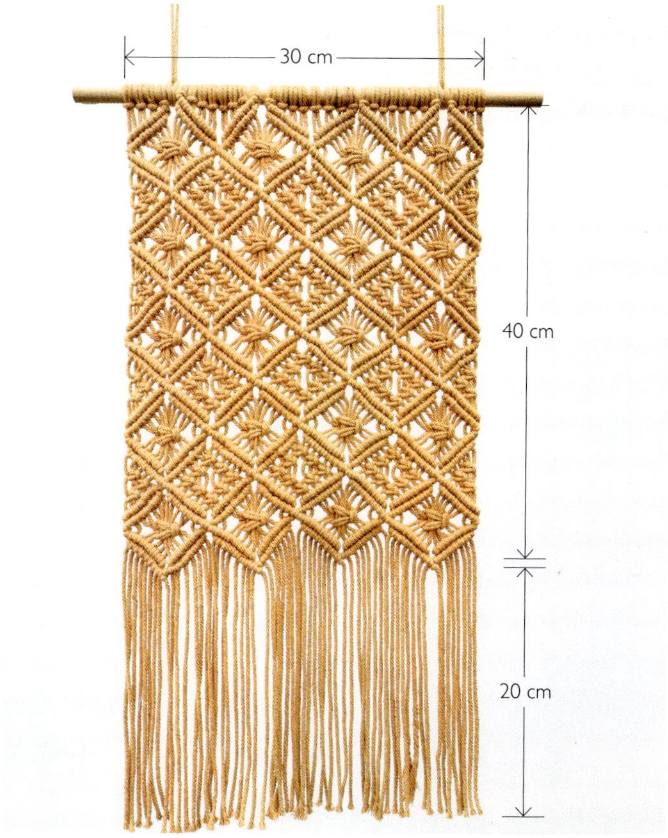

Steps

Step 1 Attach all the cords to the wooden rod using lark's head knots.

Step 2 Divide the cords into groups of 16. Take the four cords in the middle and weave double-layer diagonal double half hitch knots towards each side.

Step 3 Using the ten cords in the middle of each group, create a large square knot, with the six middle cords as the holding cords and two cords on each side as the working cords.

Step 4 In each group, work from the sides toward the center to weave double-layer diagonal double half hitch knots.

Step 5 Use the 12 cords between every two groups to weave a hollow diamond pattern with square knots.

Step 6 Repeat the above steps until the length reaches 40 cm. Then cut the cords at 60 cm, creating neat, even tassels.

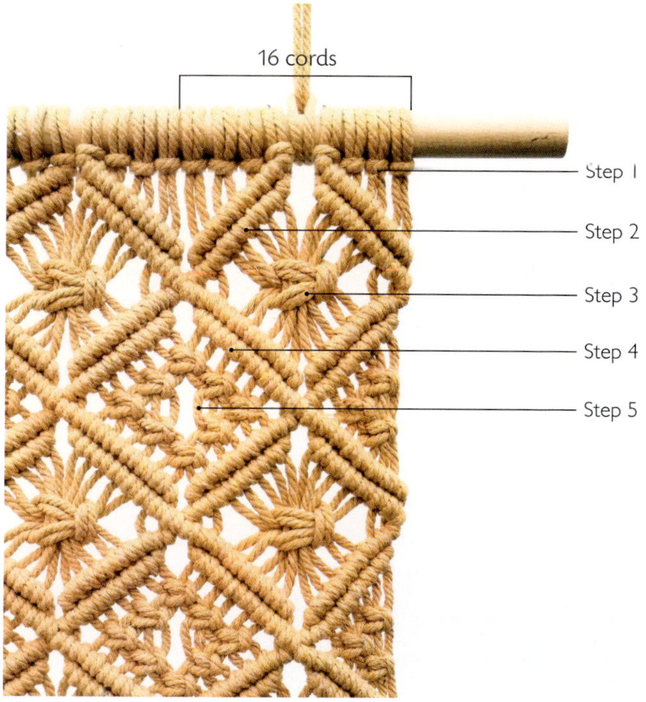

One-Piece Gradient Tapestry

In addition to the one-piece square design, you can also create patterns that gradually decrease row by row. With each row, the design on both sides is reduced by one, forming an upside down triangle shape. Please note, when using this type of weaving design, the middle section of the cords will become progressively shorter as you work down. At this point, you can use the barrel knot technique to extend the length and decorate the blank areas.

Materials

Natural branch: length 40 cm
Cord material: 3 mm cotton cord

Cord Cutting Guide

3 m × 24 pieces (48 strands)

Basic Knots

Lark's head knot, diagonal double half hitch knot, square knot, barrel knot

Patterns

Inverted V-shaped pattern with diagonal double half hitch knots (No. 65),
V-shaped pattern with diagonal double half hitch knots (No. 66)

Starting Technique

Lark's head knot horizontal starting method

Extending Cord Technique

Barrel knot extending cord method

Product Dimensions

Length 85 cm, width 33 cm

Steps

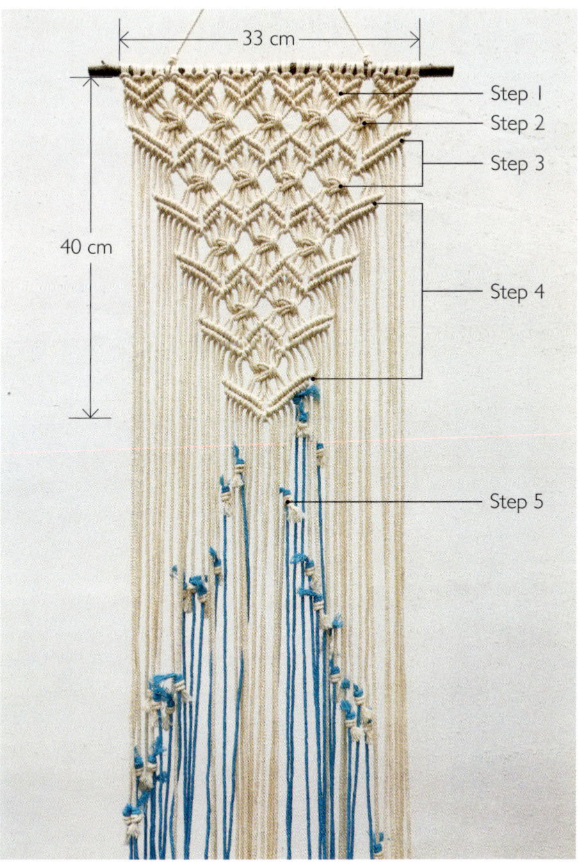

Step 1 Attach all the cords to the branch using lark's head knots. Group the cords into sets of eight, and then weave double-layer diagonal double half hitch knots to form V shapes.

Step 2 Use the eight cords between every two groups to weave a large square knot. Use the middle four cords as the holding cords and the two cords on each side as the working cords.

Step 3 On the left and right sides, use eight cords to weave double-layer diagonal double half hitch knots inward. In the center of each group, weave double-layer diagonal double half hitch knots in an inverted V-shaped pattern. Using the eight cords between every two groups, weave a large square knot. The four cords in the center serve as the holding cords, while the two cords on each side are used for braiding.

Step 4 Repeat step 3, and decrease weaving by four cords on each side per row until reaching the central pattern of the last group.

Step 5 In a typical downward triangular gradient tapestry design, the remaining cords in the middle will be shorter after weaving, which makes it difficult to trim the shape. At this point, you can use the barrel knot technique to extend the cords. The blue cords in the image represent the extended sections, while the other blank areas are decorated with barrel knots.

Segmented Small Tapestry

Segmented design involves dividing the tapestry into several blocks for knotting. For a small tapestry, you can simply add holding cords and weave horizontal double half hitch knots along them to create the division lines. Then, weave the same pattern within each block. To enhance visual appeal, alternate between dense and sparse patterns, creating a striking contrast in texture and density.

Materials

Wooden stick: length 30 cm, diameter 1.5 cm
Cord material: 3 mm cotton cord

Cord Cutting Guide

3.5 m × 20 pieces (40 strands), 35 cm × 2 pieces (to be used as division lines)

Basic Knots

Reverse lark's head knot, square knot, horizontal double half hitch knot, diagonal double half hitch knot, overhand knot

Patterns

Alternating double square knots pattern (No. 4), V-shaped pattern with diagonal double half hitch knots (No. 66), diamond pattern with diagonal double half hitch knots plane extension, style B (No. 94)

Starting Technique

Reverse lark's head knot horizontal starting method

Product Dimensions

Length 65 cm, width 24 cm

Steps

Step 1 Secure all cotton cords to the wooden stick using reverse lark's head knots. Weave three rows of alternating double square knots, approximately 7 cm in length.

Step 2 Add a 35 cm division line as the holding cord. Weave horizontal double half hitch knots with all cotton cords on this holding cord. Secure both ends with overhand knots.

Step 3 Divide into groups of eight strands each. Weave diamond patterns with diagonal double half hitch knots, approximately 10 cm in length.

Step 4 Add a 35 cm division line as the holding cord. Weave horizontal double half hitch knots with all cotton cords on this holding cord. Secure both ends with overhand knots.

Step 5 Divide into groups of eight strands each. Interlace and weave five layers of V-shaped pattern with diagonal double half hitch knots, approximately 24 cm in length.

Step 6 At a 24 cm interval, weave a row of evenly spaced overhand knots. Trim and finish once completed.

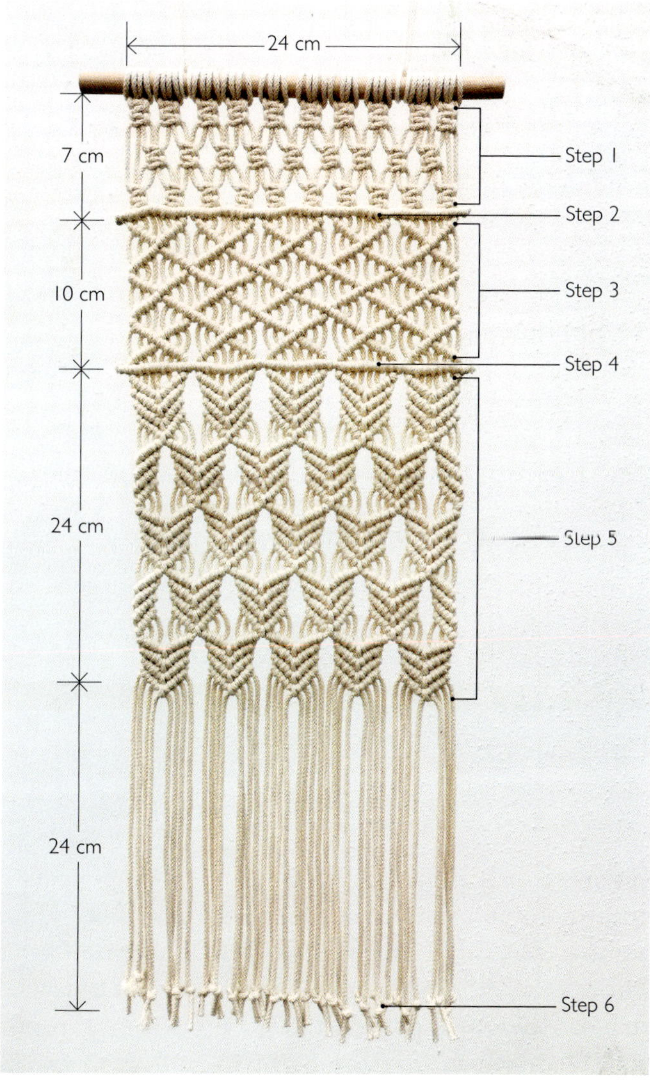

Segmented Large Tapestry

Whether small tapestries or large tapestries, the approach to segmentation is the same. However, for large tapestries, the division lines should be changed to thin wooden rods or stiffer materials, because if you use cotton cords as division lines after each segment of the pattern is woven, it may result in uneven or crooked lines. When selecting weaving patterns for large tapestries, besides large lines and blocks, you can also incorporate some weaving patterns.

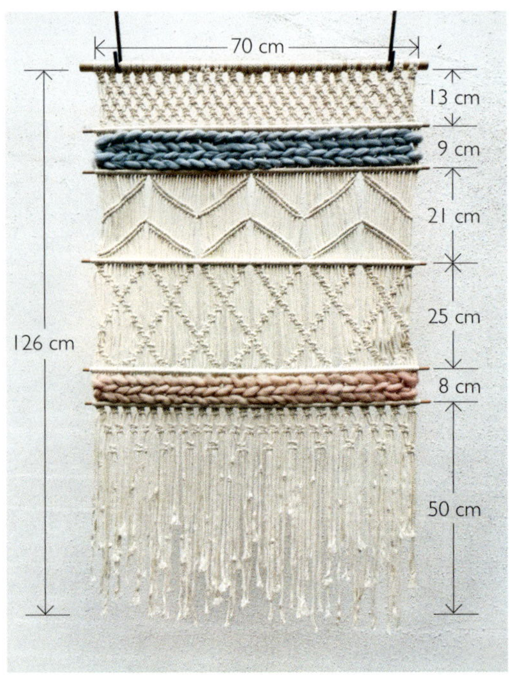

Materials

Wooden rod: length 1 m with diameter 2 cm × 1, length 0.9 m with diameter 6 mm × 5 (as division lines)
Cord material: 4 mm white cotton cord, gray coarse yarn, khaki coarse yarn

Cord Cutting Guide

White cotton cord: 6 m × 48 pieces (96 strands). For making large tapestries, it is best to prepare enough cord. If you run out of cord in the latter part of the project, you can also use extension techniques flexibly.
Blue coarse yarn: 6 m. It is advisable to divide the cord into manageable sections. Using very long lengths at once can cause friction and pilling during the process. When working with weaving patterns in segments, simply tie the ends of the cords into secure knots on the back of the tapestry.
Khaki course yarn: 4 m

Basic Knots

Lark's head knot, square knot, horizontal double half hitch knot, diagonal double half hitch knot, barrel knot

Patterns

Alternating double square knots pattern (No. 4), hollow diamond pattern with double square knots (No. 38), inverted V-shaped pattern with diagonal double half hitch knots (No. 65), braid pattern (No. 140)

Starting Technique

Lark's head knot horizontal starting method

Product Dimensions

Length 126 cm, width 70 cm

Steps

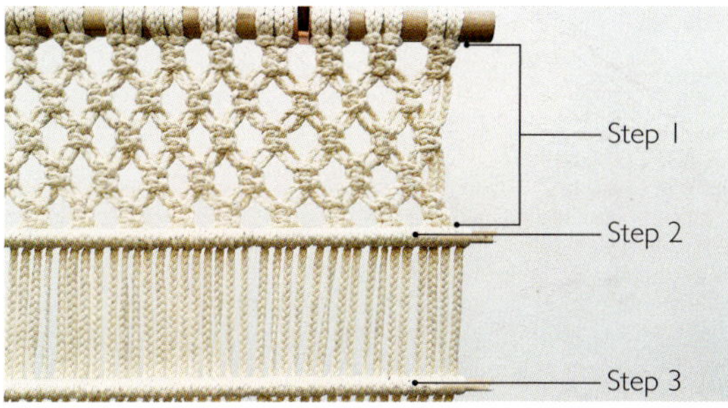

Step 1 Fold 48 cotton cords in half and fix them onto a wooden rod using lark's head knots. Group them into sets of four cords each, and weave five rows of alternating double square knots.

Step 2 Use all the cotton cords to weave horizontal double half hitch knots on the thin wooden rod as a division line and tighten the knots.

Step 3 At a 9 cm interval, use all the cotton cords to weave horizontal double half hitch knots on the second thin wooden rod as a division line.

Step 4 Use gray coarse yarn to create braid pattern.

Step 5 Group every 32 strands and weave two rows of double-layer inverted V-shaped patterns with diagonal double half hitch knots, with a spacing of 9 cm.

Step 6 Use all the cotton cords to weave horizontal double half hitch knots on the third wooden rod.

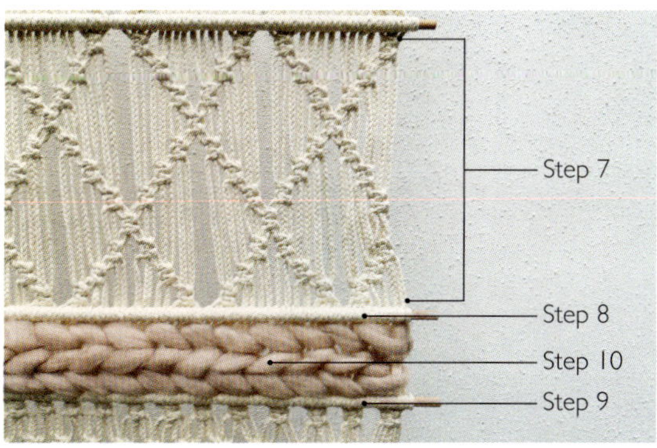

Step 7 Group every 16 strands and weave hollow diamond patterns with double square knots.

Step 8 Use all the cotton strands to weave horizontal double half hitch knots on the fourth thin rod.

Step 9 At an interval of 8 cm, use all the cotton cords to weave horizontal double half hitch knots on the fifth thin rod as a division line.

Step 10 Use khaki coarse yarn to create braid pattern.

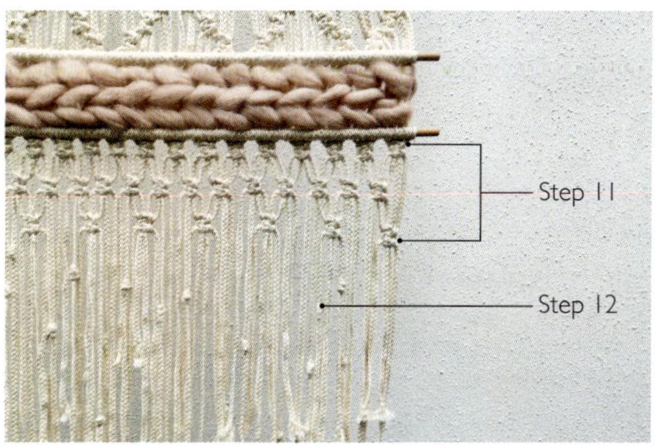

Step 11 For every four strands, weave two rows of alternating double square knots. In the third row, skip four strands and weave one double square knot.

Step 12 Tie barrel knots on some of the cotton cords. Leave most of the cords untrimmed to maintain the overall effect, but trim excessively long ones as needed.

Segmented Irregular Tapestry

This project combines knots and weaving patterns to create a patchwork visual effect. Besides horizontal dividing sections used in the first two designs, the tapestry can also be divided into irregular areas using diagonal double half hitch knots. Some areas should leave warp threads exposed to prepare for weaving patterns.

Materials

Natural branch: length 35 cm
Cord material: 2.5 mm white cotton cord, various specialty cords

Tool

Large-eye needle

Cord Cutting Guide

White cotton cord: 2.5 m × 26 pieces (52 strands), 50 cm × 1 piece (used as the holding cord)
The length of specialty cords is decided according to the design in different sections, and extension techniques can be used as needed.

Basic Knots

Lark's head knot, square knot, diagonal double half hitch knot

Patterns

Alternating square knots pattern (No. 1), weaving patterns (No. 136–141)

Starting Technique

Lark's head knot horizontal starting method

Product Dimensions

Length 50 cm, width 30 cm

Steps

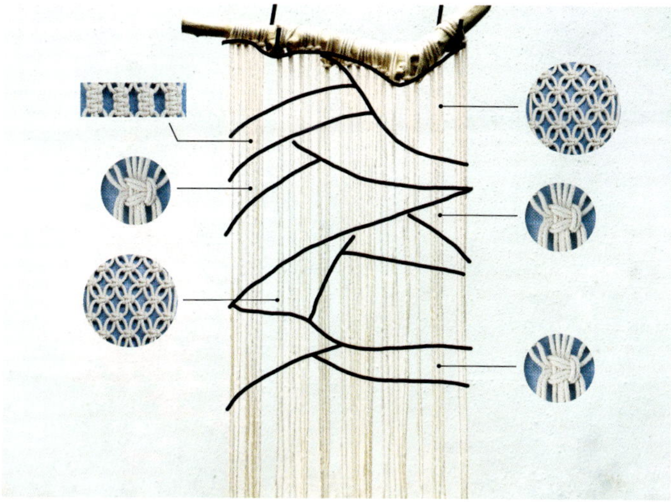

Step 1 Determine the placement angle of the branch. In this project, the branch is placed as shown in the diagram. Use lark's head knots to attach 26 cords to the branch. You can roughly draw a partition diagram and arrange the weaving patterns for some sections.

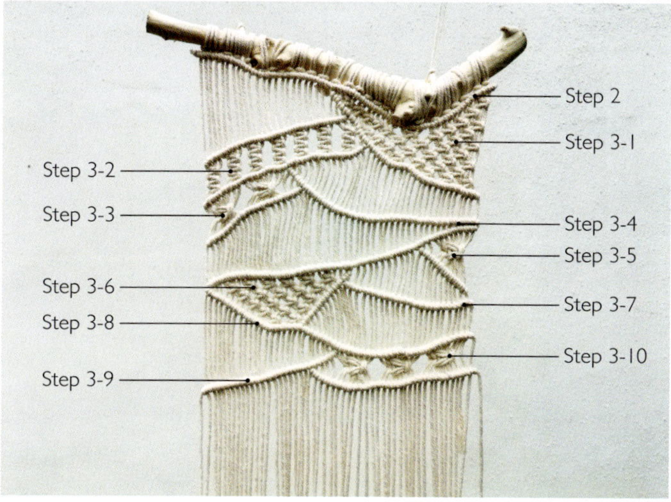

Step 2 Add a 50 cm cord as the holding cord, and closely follow the branch to weave a row of double half hitch knots. The curved branch causes the cotton cords to be distributed unevenly, but this row of double half hitch knots can help align the cotton cords neatly.

Step 3 Follow the diagram drawn in step 1 and weave according to the numbered sequence. The principle is to work from top to bottom and from the center to the sides. After weaving the square knot patterns (alternating square knots or large square knots) in each section, use diagonal double half hitch knots to close off the area.

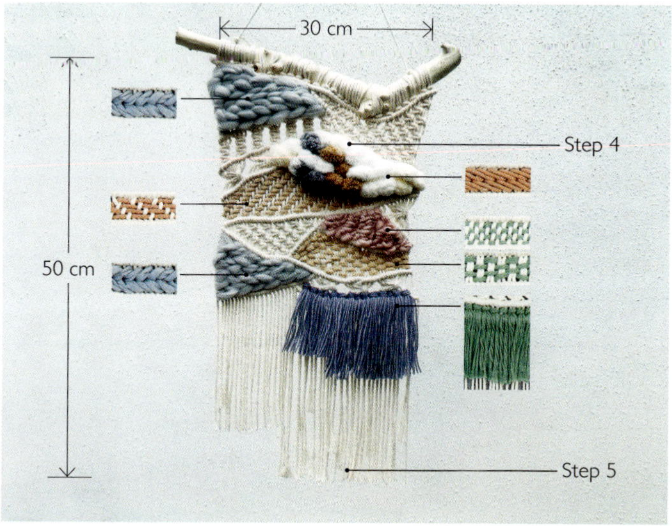

Step 4 Select various specialty cords, and fill the six blank areas created in step 3 with different weaving patterns.

Step 5 Make final adjustments and trim the cords as needed.

Square Throw Pillow

The square throw pillow in this example uses a one-piece design approach. This type of design which doesn't finish with tassels requires addressing the issue of loose ends. Using the double half hitch knot for finishing makes trimming easier but requires tight securing to prevent unraveling. If you use a square knot for finishing, you will need to tuck the loose ends of the cord into the knot before trimming them. For woven items like pillows, cushions, and blankets that come into direct contact with skin, use materials such as cloth strips or other non-shedding cords for weaving.

Materials

Square pillowcase, pillow core: length 40 cm, width 40 cm
Cord Material: two bundles of lake blue cloth strip, two bundles of off-white cloth strip, one bundle of bright yellow cloth strip.

Tools

Thin wooden sticks (length 40–50 cm), sewing needles, sewing thread.

Cord Cutting Guide

Lake blue cloth strip: 2.8 m × 16 pieces (32 strands), 70 cm × 2 pieces (add holding cords), 20 cm × 1 piece (tassels)
Off-white cloth strip: 2.8 m × 16 pieces (32 strands)
Bright yellow cloth strip: 2.8 m × 8 pieces (16 strands), 20 cm × 11 pieces (tassels)

Basic Knots

Lark's head knot, diagonal double half hitch knot, square knot, horizontal double half hitch knot, hitch knot, barrel knot

Patterns

Diamond combination pattern with diagonal double half hitch knots, style F (No. 111), tassel, style A (No. 132)

Starting Technique

Lark's head knot horizontal starting method

Product Dimensions

Length 40 cm, width 40 cm

Steps

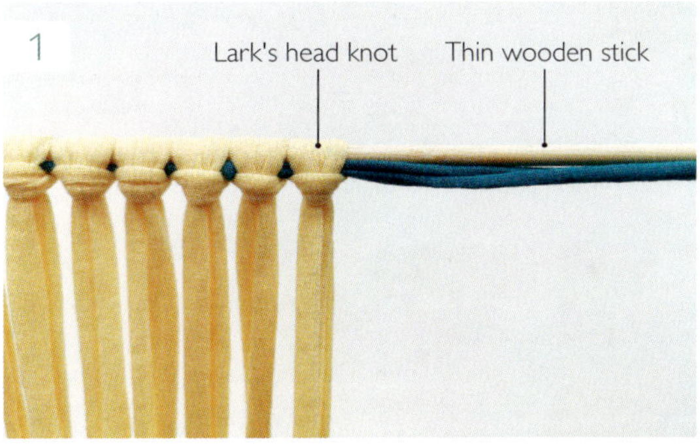

Fold all 2.8 m long cloth strips in half and secure them to a 70 cm long lake blue holding cord using the lark's head knots. Arrange them in the following order: eight lake blue, eight off-white, eight bright yellow, eight off-white, and eight lake blue. If securing the strips to the cloth line initially does not provide enough support for further weaving, there are two solutions. First, you can use pins to fix the holding cord to a corkboard; or second, you can add a thin wooden stick to the holding cord for extra support during weaving, which can be removed after the piece is completed. In this example, we're using a thin wooden stick for support.

Weave four rows of diamond combination pattern with diagonal double half hitch knots style F as the main design, then weave four tassels.

Add a 70 cm long lake blue cloth strip as the holding cord. Weave all cloth strips sequentially onto the holding cord using horizontal double half hitch knots, then trim all remaining ends. Ensure that the horizontal double half hitch knots are pulled tight to prevent them from coming undone.

Take sewing thread that matches the color of the pillowcase and use a sewing needle to stitch the woven piece onto the pillowcase.

Thread the cloth strips from the corners of the pillowcase through the tassels and tie them securely with a hitch knot or a barrel knot, securing the loose ends.

Butterfly-Shaped Pillow

Using a segmented design approach to add an additional pattern based on the main motif of a cushion cover can create a striking visual highlight.

Materials

Square pillow case, pillow insert: length 40 cm, width 40 cm
Cord material: khaki fabric strips × 2 balls, coffee-colored fabric strips × 1 ball, ginger-yellow fabric strips × 1 ball, bright red fabric strips × 1 ball

Tools

Thin wooden rod: length 40–50 cm, sewing needle, sewing thread

Cord Cutting Guide

Khaki fabric strips: 2.4 m × 24 pieces (48 strands), 50 cm × 3 pieces (added holding cord)
Coffee-colored fabric strips: 2.4 m × 3 pieces (6 strands), 50 cm × 3 pieces (added working cord)
Ginger-yellow fabric strips: 2.4 m × 3 pieces (6 strands), 50 cm × 3 pieces (added working cord)
Bright red fabric strips: 2.4 m × 2 pieces (4 strands), 50 cm × 4 pieces (added working cord)

Basic Knots

Reverse lark's head knot, square knot, diagonal double half hitch knot, square knot button, horizontal double half hitch knot, spiral knot, alternating half hitch knot

Pattern

Butterfly pattern with diagonal double half hitch knots, style A (No. 116)

Adding Cord Technique

Square knot adding cord method

Starting Technique

Reverse lark's head knot horizontal starting method

Product Dimensions

Length 40 cm, width 40 cm

Steps

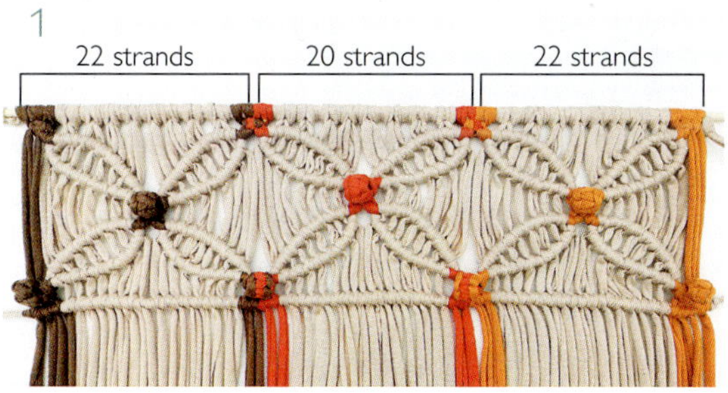

Fold all the 2.4 m long fabric strips in half, then use reverse lark's head knots to secure them onto a 50 cm long khaki holding cord in this order: coffee colored (two strands), khaki (eight strands), coffee colored (one strand), bright red (one strand), khaki (eight strands), bright red (one strand), ginger-yellow (one strand), khaki (eight strands), ginger yellow (two strands). In this project, thin wooden rods are used as auxiliary support.

Use four groups of colored fabric strips to each weave a square knot. Skip the outermost two strands on both the left and right sides. Group every 20 strands together, then weave a butterfly pattern with diagonal double half hitch knots, style A. After that, weave four square knot buttons below.

Add a khaki holding cord. Weave horizontal double half hitch knots in a sequence with all the fabric strands on this holding cord.

Group every four fabric strips together. Using the coffee colored strip on the left side, the ginger-yellow strip on the right side, and some khaki fabric strips, weave six square knots.

Add the corresponding colored braiding strips to the other positions as shown in the diagram. In each column, weave six square knots from top to bottom.

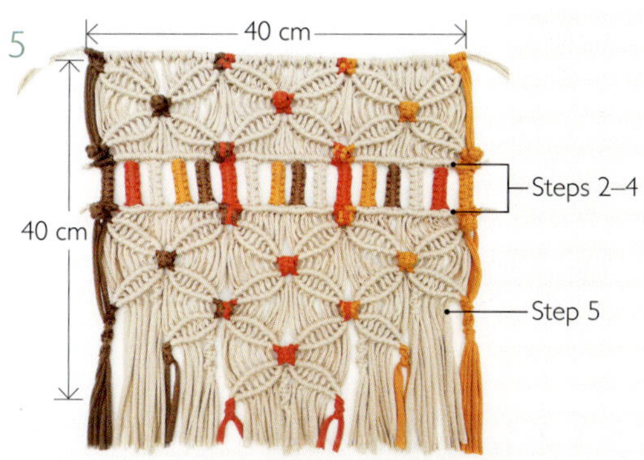

Using the original fabric strips (excluding the added cords), weave horizontal double half hitch knots along the added holding cord. Continue weaving square knot buttons and butterfly patterns downward, gradually reducing row by row. Then, weave several spiral knots and alternating half hitch knots below the butterflies.

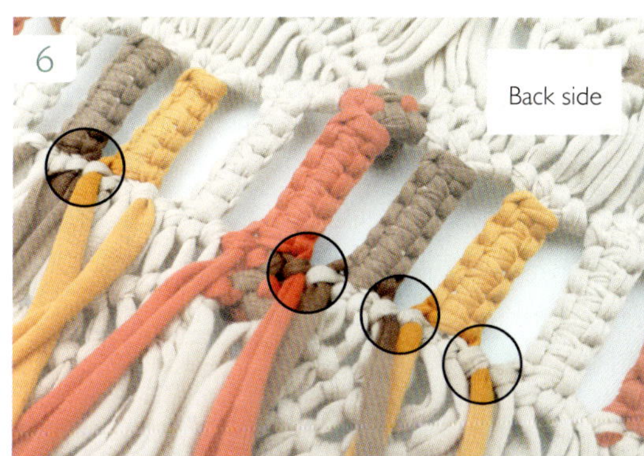

Flip to the back, tuck the ends of the added cords into the knots, apply glue, and cut off the excess ends.

Use sewing thread in a color similar to the cushion cover to stitch the woven piece to the cushion cover.

Using the same method, you can create cushions with different visual effects simply by swapping the order of the patterns or adjusting their proportions.

Coaster and Placemat

Coasters and placemats can add a sense of ritual to tea drinking. In this project, the basic square knot is sufficient. The structure is also very simple, and you can match different colors according to your home's style.

1. Coaster

Materials

3 mm white cotton cord, 3 mm mint green cotton cord

Tool

1 cm diameter auxiliary wooden rod

Cord Cutting Guide

For a single coaster, you need 80 cm × 10 pieces (20 strands) of cord. The quantity of white cotton cord and mint green cotton cord can be adjusted according to the designed color scheme.

Basic Knots

Lark's head knot, square knot

Pattern

Alternating square knots pattern (No. 1)

Starting Technique

Lark's head knot horizontal starting method

Product Dimensions

Length 10 cm, width 10 cm

Steps

Step 1 Secure the cotton cords of different colors to the wooden rod using lark's head knots, following the color scheme shown in the diagram. In this project, the wooden rod is used as a support for weaving and will be removed once the project is completed.

Step 2 Weave 11 rows of alternating square knots with all the cords. The coaster will have a unique appearance depending on the color scheme used. Here, there are five different patterns listed from A to E.

Step 3 Remove the auxiliary wooden rod, and loosen the lark's head knots, cutting each cord in the middle. Trim the ends of the cords to the same length and use a comb to fluff them up.

2. Placemat

Materials, Tool, Basic Knots, Starting Technique

The same as those for coasters.

Cord Cutting Guide

White cotton cord: 15 cm × 10 pieces (20 strands), 6 cm × 16 pieces (tassel on both sides)
Mint green cotton cord: 15 cm × 8 pieces (16 strands)

Patterns

Alternating square knots pattern (No. 1), embedded diamond pattern with square knots, style A (No. 46)

Product Dimensions

Length 20 cm, width 20 cm

Steps

Step 1 Attach 18 pieces of 15 cm long cotton cords to the auxiliary wooden rod using lark's head knots in the sequence shown in the diagram.

Step 2 Group the cords into sets of four strands each and weave three rows of alternating square knots.

Step 3 Weave a diamond shape, incorporating a large square knot in the center of the diamond. Use 12 strands in the middle as the holding cords, with two strands on each side for the working cords.

Step 4 Weave three rows of alternating square knots symmetrically above and below the pattern created in step 3.

Step 5 Remove the auxiliary wooden rod, loosen the lark's head knots, and cut each cord in the middle. Then, weave lark's head knots using 6 cm short cords through the holes on both sides of the woven piece. Finally, trim the ends of the cords around the four edges to the same length and use a comb to fluff them up.

Memo Holder

In frame design, a picture frame is a commonly used auxiliary tool. For small frames, you can weave directly onto them. For larger frames, nails are needed to help with positioning, as some patterns may become misshaped without this support, affecting the overall result. In this project, the most basic square knot is used. By widening the spacing, the pattern creates a honeycomb effect. Adding a pin turns it into a memo holder and photo frame.

Materials

Large frame: length 90 cm, width 60 cm
Cord material: 3 mm cotton cord

Tools

Nails, hammer

Cord Cutting Guide

4 m × 16 pieces (32 strands), 1 m × 14 pieces (28 strands)

Basic Knots

Square knot, horizontal double half hitch knot, alternating half hitch knot

Pattern

Square knot plane extension (No. 3)

Starting Technique

Square knot starting method

Product Dimensions

Length 120 cm, width 60 cm

Steps

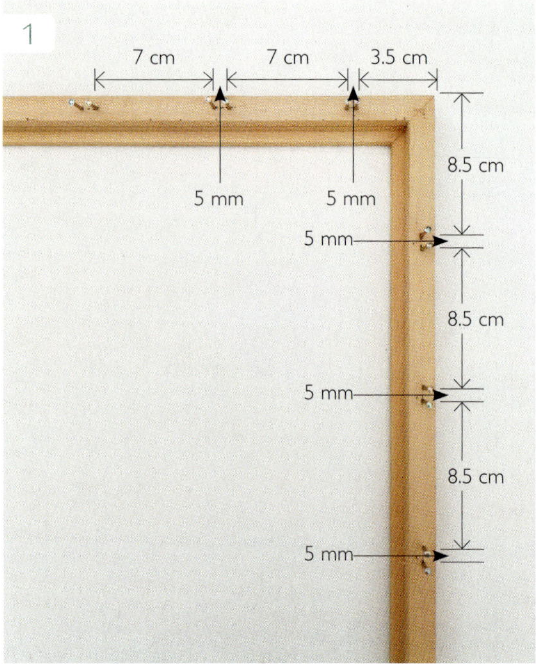

Divide the short side of the picture frame, which is 60 cm long, into nine sections. The two sections on each side should be 3.5 cm long, and the seven middle sections should be 7 cm long each. Use two nails to separate each section, with a spacing of 5 mm between the nails. Divide the long side of the picture frame, which is 90 cm, into ten sections. One side should be 9 cm long, and the remaining sections should each be 8.5 cm long. Use two nails to separate each section, with a spacing of 5 mm between the nails.

After determining the positions, gently insert the nails into the picture frame. Do not drive them all the way in. Leave about 5 mm of height to secure the cords.

Fold 16 pieces of 4 m long cotton cord in half and hang them on the nails along the short side of the frame. Group the cords into sets of four strands each, and weave eight square knots for each group.

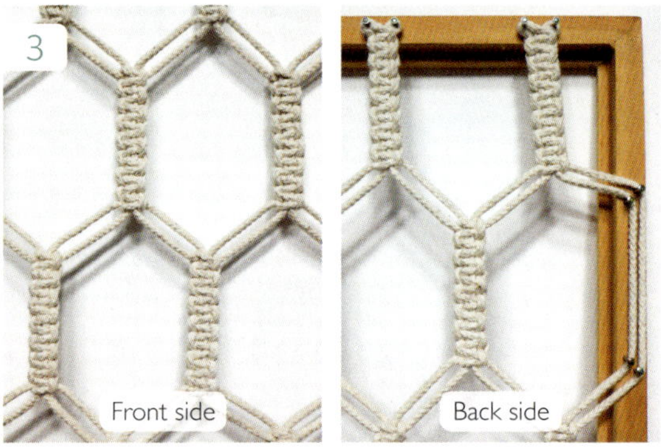

Weave alternating square knots with an approximately 3 cm spacing between each row. Each row should consist of eight square knots. Hook the cotton cords on the nails along the long sides of the frame to form a hexagon shape.

When you reach the bottom of the picture frame, imagine the frame as an holding cord. Weave horizontal double half hitch knots with the existing cotton cords along the frame. Add two pieces of 1 m long cotton cords between each set of square knots. Add one 1 m long cotton cord on each side of the square knots. Attach all added cords to the picture frame using lark's head knots. Group the cords into sets of four strands each and weave different lengths of double-strand alternating half hitch knots.

Round Mirror

Rings are often used as auxiliary frames in macramé. For this mirror, it consists of two rings of different sizes, with weaving done from the inside out. The mirror is mounted on the back of the smaller ring. The inner and outer rings have different sizes, so the amount of cord needed will also vary. It is necessary to add cords at appropriate points. Cords can be added either to the rings themselves or within the weaving pattern. In this project, the former method is used.

Materials

Metal ring: two, with diameters 20 cm and 35 cm
Mirror: diameter 20 cm
Cord material: 3 mm white cotton cord, 3 mm mint green cotton cord

Cord Cutting Guide

White cotton cord: 1 m × 80 pieces (160 strands)
Mint green cotton cord: 60 cm × 20 pieces (40 strands), 1 m × 2 pieces (used to secure mirror at the back)

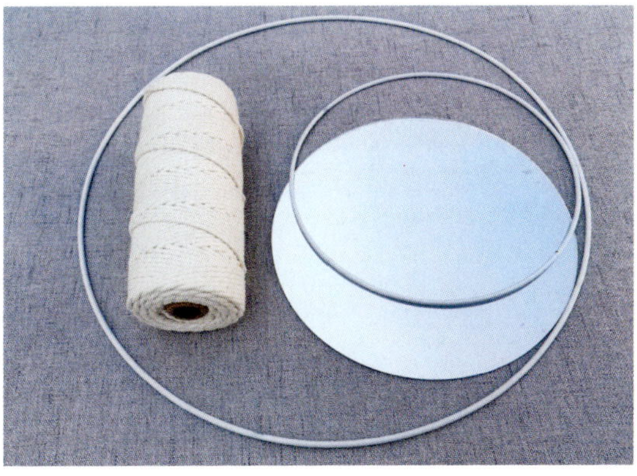

Basic Knots

Reverse lark's head knot, square knot, double half hitch knot, vertical double half hitch knot, hitch knot, reverse lark's head knot plus a half hitch

Patterns

Fishbone pattern with square knots (No. 19), upside down triangle pattern with square knot (No. 32), V-shaped pattern with diagonal double half hitch knots (No. 66)

Starting Technique

Reverse lark's head knot starting method

Product Dimension

Diameter around 50 cm

Steps

Step 1 Secure all the white cotton cords to the small ring using reverse lark's head knots.

Step 2 Group the cords into sets of 16 strands each and weave fishbone pattern with square knots. Be sure to control the tension carefully so that the woven length aligns perfectly with the large ring.

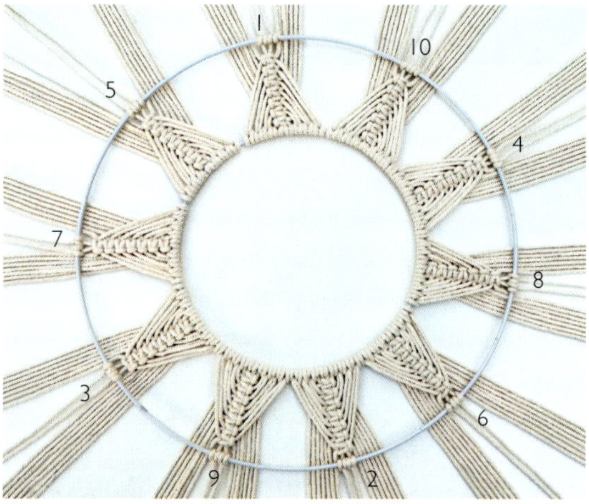

Step 3 Connect the holding cord of each fishbone pattern to the large ring using double half hitch knots in the diagonal positions indicated in the diagram. This will help tighten and align the working cord. In the diagram, first weave the holding cords to secure the position of each group. This prevents any movement during the weaving process. Then, weave all the white cotton cords with double half hitch knots around the large ring.

Step 4 Add two pieces of 60 cm long mint green cotton cords between each group, and secure them to the large ring using reverse lark's head knots.

Step 5 Weave a upside down triangle pattern with square knots using 16 strands of white cord.

Step 6 Group the cords into sets of 20 strands each (16 white cotton cords and two mint green cords on each side). Use the green cords as the holding cords and, as shown in the diagram, weave double layer diagonal double half hitch knots to create a V shape, positioned close to the upside down triangle pattern with square knots.

Step 7 Take six cords separately from between the two groups. Use the top two cords as the working cords and weave three vertical double half hitch knots on each of the two holding cords below. Finally, use a hitch knot to gather and finish the ends.

Step 8 Flip the piece to the back and place the mirror on the small ring. Using a 1 m long mint green cotton cord, secure the mirror with reverse lark's head knots plus a half hitch with each cord in a pentagram weaving pattern to hold the mirror in place. Stagger by one corner, and use another mint green cord to reinforce the structure, perfectly filling the space between the ten groups of the fishbone patterns with square knots. The specific sequence can be followed according to the numbered indicators in the diagram.

Step 9 Set aside four strands of mint green cotton cord to create a hanging loop. Trim and comb the remaining cords.

Dreamcatcher

A dreamcatcher is a hanging ornament from Native American culture, symbolizing the capture of bad dreams while allowing good dreams to come true. The design within the ring features a floral pattern, and feathers are woven using cord knots. Adding some dried flowers and leaves enhances the dreamcatcher's layers, giving it more depth and richness.

Materials

Rattan hoop: diameter 20 cm
Natural flower material: cotton, dried strawflowers, eucalyptus leaves, pinecones, and similar elements
Cord material: 3 mm cotton cord

Tools

Floral wire, hot glue

Cord Cutting Guide

Center: 1 m × 12 pieces (24 strands)
Feather section: 2 m × 2 pieces (long), 1.5 m × 4 pieces (medium), 1 m × 4 pieces (short)
Feather adding cord section: 30 cm × 40 pieces

Basic Knots

Reverse lark's head knot, lark's head knot, square knot, double half hitch knot, alternating half hitch knot, diagonal double half hitch knot

Patterns

Alternating square knots pattern (No. 1), feather, style B (No. 131)

Starting Technique

Encircling center starting method

Adding Cord Method

Diagonal double half hitch knot adding cord method

Product Dimensions

Length 60 cm, width 20 cm

Steps

1

Create the center portion. Take a 1 m long cotton cord as the holding cord (green cord is used for demonstration here), and using the surrounding center starting method, attach the remaining 11 pieces of 1 m long cotton cord to the holding cord with reverse lark's head knots. Tighten the loops.

2

Use the holding cord of the loop as the holding cord for the first square knot, and then group the remaining cords into sets of four strands each to weave five groups of square knots in sequence.

3

Continue weaving alternating square knots outward, gradually increasing the spacing as you move out. Weave a total of four rounds of square knots.

4

Place the rattan ring over the woven section. Secure six groups of cotton cords to the rattan ring using double half hitch knots. Tie the cord ends securely at the back, apply glue, and trim off the excess.

5

Create the feather section. Generally, feathers are designed in odd numbers, and in this case, five feathers are included in the design. Start by weaving the longest feather in the middle. Fold two 2 m long cords in half and secure them to the rattan ring using a lark's head knot. Weave about 24 cm of alternating half hitch knots. Next, weave three diamond patterns with diagonal double half hitch knots with embedded alternating half hitch knots. On both sides of the adjacent diamond patterns, add two 30 cm long cotton cords to each side, forming tassels.

6

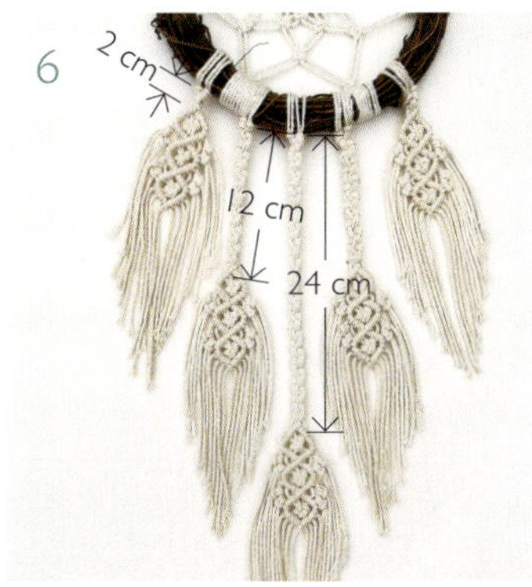

Take cords of appropriate lengths to create the remaining four feathers, with the lengths of the five feathers gradually decreasing. The tassels can be combed out or left uncombed, depending on personal preference.

7

Create the decorative elements. Eucalyptus leaves are secured to the rattan ring by wrapping floral wire around them. Various flowers, pinecones, cotton, and other materials are attached to the rattan ring with hot glue. For stiff flower stems, they can be directly inserted into the rattan ring.

Lampshade

Placing a lampshade with woven patterns in your home creates a unique romantic ambiance. When the lamp is turned on, the woven patterns will be projected onto the walls, adding a special touch. Lampshades can be purchased online in various shapes such as cylindrical, oval, square, or tapered. You can also find some with unique shapes to spark your creativity.

Materials

Lampshade dimensions: top frame diameter 20 cm, bottom frame diameter 30 cm, height 23 cm.
Cord material: 3 mm white cotton cord, 3 mm blush pink cotton cord
Lamp base, light bulb

Cord Cutting Guide

White cotton cord: 2.2 m × 60 pieces (120 strands)
Blush pink cotton cord: 2.2 m × 12 pieces (24 strands)

Basic Knots

Lark's head knot, square knot, spiral knot, diagonal double half hitch knot, horizontal double half hitch knot, barrel knot

Patterns

Alternating square knots pattern (No. 1), butterfly pattern with diagonal double half hitch knots, style A (No. 116)

Starting Technique

Lark's head knot horizontal starting method

Product Dimensions

Top frame diameter 20 cm, bottom frame diameter 30 cm, height 33 cm

Steps

Step 1 Divide all the cords into six groups, with each group consisting of ten white cotton cords and two blush pink cotton cords. Use lark's head knots to secure the cords to the top frame of the lampshade according to each group.

Step 2 Weave three rows of alternating square knots, using the vertical frame of the lampshade as the holding cord for the weaving.

Step 3 Use the blush pink cords as the holding cords and weave butterfly patterns with diagonal double half hitch knots on either side. In the center of each butterfly, weave a square knot. Incorporate the vertical frame of the lampshade into the weaving to help secure the positions. Between adjacent butterflies, weave a large square knot using 14 strands of cord. Use the ten middle strands as the holding cords and the remaining two strands on each side as the working cords.

Step 4 Starting with the blush pink cords, group four strands together and weave spiral knots. When you reach the bottom frame of the lampshade, switch to horizontal double half hitch knots. Make sure to weave tightly. When weaving spiral knots, ensure that the vertical frame of the lampshade is included as part of the holding cord in the weaving.

Step 5 Gather every eight strands together and use one of the strands to tie a barrel knot. Finally, trim the ends evenly for a clean finish.

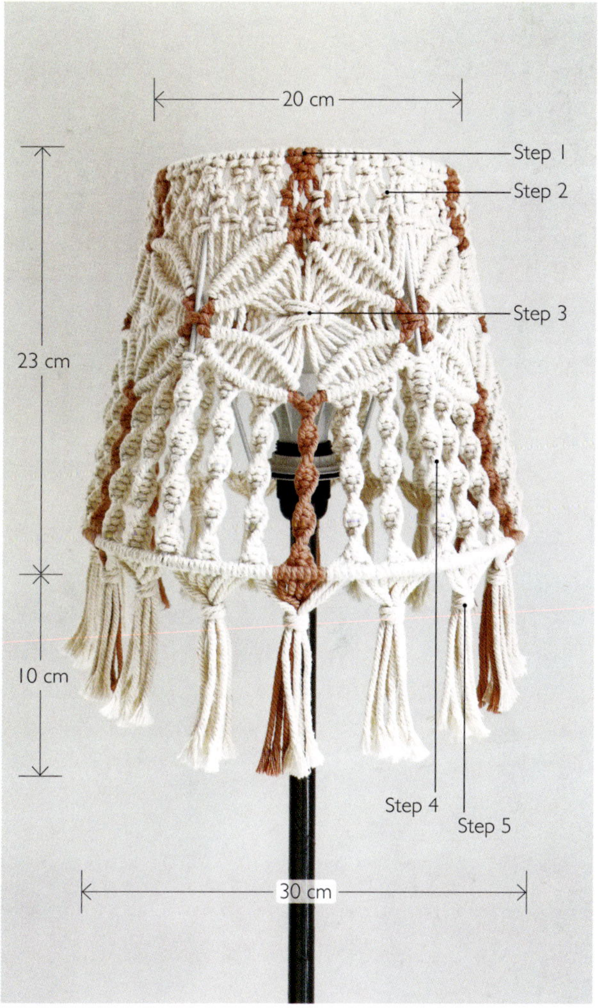

Twig Pendant Light

Pendant lights offer more design flexibility than lampshades. Metal rings of different sizes and shapes can be combined into cylindrical, square, drum-shaped, multi-layered tassel forms, or other creative shapes. When choosing closed shapes like cylindrical designs, and if the woven pattern involves repeating motifs, it is important to carefully arrange everything to ensure the pattern remains complete and cohesive. The spacing of knots, as well as adding or reducing cords, will impact the pattern. Experimenting with different techniques is key to achieving the desired style.

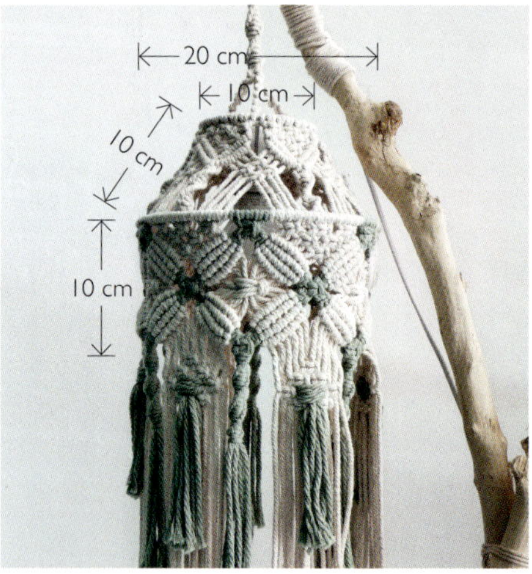

Materials

Pendant light fixture: diameter 10 cm
Large ring: diameter 20 cm
Cord material: 3 mm white cotton cord, 3 mm mint green cotton cord
Lamp base, light bulb

Cord Cutting Guide

White cotton cord: 3 m × 39 pieces (78 strands, of which three are used to make the pendant light hanging cord)
Mint green cotton cord: 2 m × 24 pieces (48 strands), 30 cm × 24 pieces (tassel section)

Basic Knots

Reverse lark's head knot, square knot, spiral knot, diagonal double half hitch knot, horizontal double half hitch knot

Patterns

Upside down triangle pattern with square knots (No. 32), hollow diamond pattern with square knots (No. 37), V-shaped pattern with diagonal double half hitch knots (No. 66), shell flower pattern plane extension with diagonal double half hitch knots (No. 84), tassel pattern (No. 141)

Starting Technique

Reverse lark's head knot horizontal starting method

Product Dimensions

Top frame diameter 10 cm, bottom frame diameter 20 cm, height 44 cm

Steps

Step 1 Fold 36 strands of 3 m long white cord in half and attach them to the pendant light frame using reverse lark's head knots. Divide the cords into groups of 12 strands each and weave an upside down triangle pattern with square knots.

Step 2 Along the upside down triangle, weave a double-layer V-shaped pattern with diagonal double half hitch knots.

Step 3 Between every two groups, use eight strands of cord to weave a diamond pattern with square knots.

Step 4 Use the four strands of cord beneath the V-shaped pattern with diagonal double half hitch knots to weave a section of spiral knots. The length from the light fixture to the spiral knots is approximately 10 cm.

Step 5 First, weave horizontal double half hitch knots with the four strands of cotton cord used for the spiral knot onto the large ring to secure their position. Next, divide the eight strands of cotton cord used for the diamond patterns with square knots into two equal parts and weave horizontal double half hitch knots near the spiral knots separately.

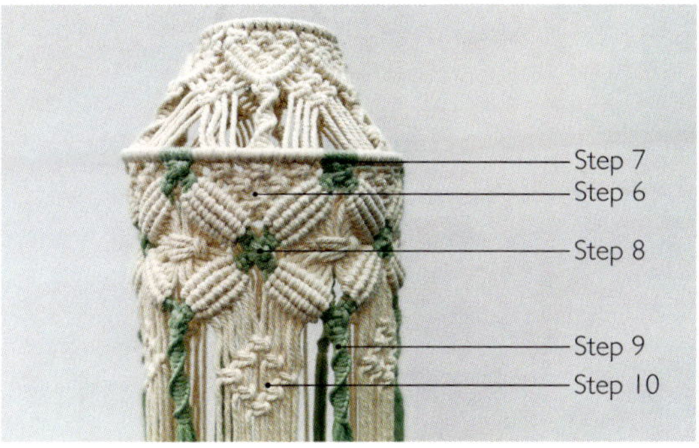

Step 6 Group the cords into sets of 12 strands each and weave an upside down triangle pattern with square knots.

Step 7 Between each group, add four strands of 2 m mint green cord using reverse lark's head knots. Use eight strands of the mint green cord to weave a large square knot, with four strands in the middle as the holding cords and two strands on each side as the working cords.

Step 8 Weave four strands of mint green cord as the holding cords into a shell flower pattern with diagonal double half hitch knots. Between each flower, use the 12 strands of white cord to weave a large square knot, with eight strands in the middle as the holding cords and two strands on each side as the working cords.

Step 9 Weave the eight strands of green cord between the adjacent petals into a large square knot, with four strands in the middle as the holding cords and two strands on each side as the working cords. Then, take two of the longer strands as the working cords, and weave the remaining six strands as the holding cords into a section of spiral knots.

Step 10 Weave the 12 white strands below the shell flower into a hollow diamond pattern with square knots. Take four 30 cm long green cords, thread them through the hollow diamond pattern with square knots, and create tassels. Then, trim all the cord ends.

Step 11 Create the hanging cord for the pendant lamp. Based on the structure of the pendant lamp frame, add three folded white cords, and weave a section of alternating half hitch knots for each.

Step 12 After inserting the light bulb, take two strands of cotton cord as the working cords and use the remaining cotton cords and electrical wire as the holding cords. Weave spiral knots until you reach the desired length.

Vase Sleeves

Having too many vases at home can become a bit monotonous. Using macramé to weave a unique cover for the vase can bring a fresh look, as if you have a new vase, and it can lift your mood. Vase sleeves can be divided into two types, removable and non-removable. This example belongs to the latter. The vase sleeve is designed in a columnar shape and requires a repeatable pattern for weaving.

1. Type A

Materials

Glass vase: diameter 7cm, height 11 cm
Cord material: 3 mm cotton cord

Cord Cutting Guide

70 cm × 1 piece, 45 cm × 31 pieces (following the diameter of the neck of the vase)

Basic Knots

Lark's head knot, square knot

Pattern

Upside down triangle pattern with square knots (No. 32)

Starting Technique

Lark's head knot horizontal starting method

Product Dimensions

Diameter 7 cm, height 10 cm

Steps

Step 1 Secure all 45 cm long cotton cords to a 70 cm long holding cord using the lark's head knots. Tighten the holding cord around the neck of the vase and connect using diagonal double half hitch knots.

Step 2 Using the lines from the lark's head knots in step 1 as the new holding cords, weave a round of square knots.

Step 3 Group the ropes into sets of 12 strands each and weave upside down triangle patterns with square knots.

Step 4 Use eight strands from the adjacent two upside down triangle pattern groups to weave a large square knot. Use the middle four strands as the holding cords, and the two strands on each side as the working cords.

Step 5 Trim all the cords evenly along the bottom of the vase.

2. Type B

Materials

Glass vase: diameter 7 cm, height 18 cm
Cord material: 3 mm cotton cord

Cord Cutting Guide

1.1 m × 1 piece, 0.8 m × 29 pieces (following the diameter of the neck of the vase)

Basic Knots

Lark's head knot, square knot, diagonal double half hitch knot, hitch knot

Patterns

Diamond pattern with square knots (No. 35), leaf pattern with diagonal double half hitch knots (No. 115)

Starting Technique

Lark's head knot horizontal starting method

Product Dimensions

Diameter 7 cm, height 17 cm

Steps

Step 1 Secure all 0.8 m long cotton cords to a 1.1 m long holding cord using the lark's head knots. Tighten the holding cord around the neck of the vase and connect using diagonal double half hitch knots.

Step 2 Using the lines from the lark's head knots in step 1 as the new holding cords, group the ropes into sets of six strands each, and weave leaf patterns with diagonal half hitch knots.

Step 3 Using the four strands of cord from below two adjacent leaf patterns, weave six square knots, then secure with a hitch knot.

Step 4 Using the eight strands of cord between two adjacent leaves, weave a diamond pattern with square knots. Gather the ends using diagonal double half hitch knots and secure them with a hitch knot.

Step 5 Trim all the cords evenly to ensure a neat finish.

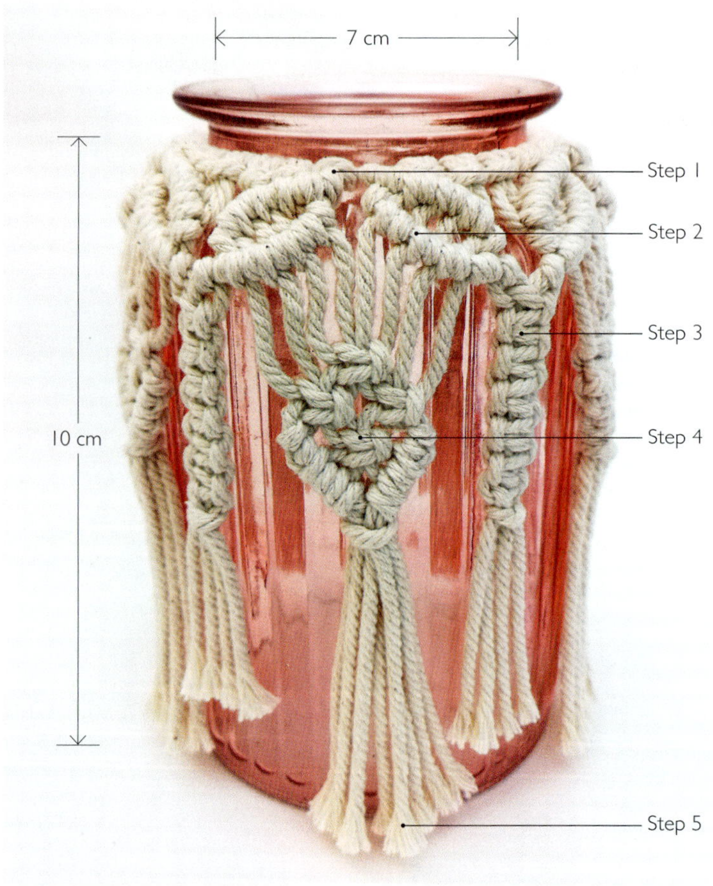

Pennant

Pennants give a lively decorative feel. In weaving design, pennants are commonly used small items that can be extended into many different designs. They can also be used with various colors to create playful effects.

Materials

Wooden bead: 11, hole diameter 1 cm
Cord material: 3 mm white cotton cord, 3 mm mint green cotton cord

Cord Cutting Guide

White cotton cord: 2 m × 1 piece (as the holding cord), 80 cm × 8 pieces (16 strands) × 5 flaps
Mint green cotton cord: 80 cm × 8 pieces (16 strands) × 5 flaps

Basic Knots

Lark's head knot, square knot, diagonal double half hitch knot

Patterns

Alternating square knots pattern (No. 1), upside down triangle pattern with square knots (No. 32)

Starting Technique

Lark's head knot horizontal starting method

Product Dimensions

Length 22 cm, width 81 cm

Steps

Step 1 Thread a wooden bead onto the long holding cord, then wrap the end of the cord around and through the bead again to secure it in place.

Step 2 Fold eight strands of white cotton cord in half and attach them to the long holding cord using lark's head knots. Weave three rows of alternating square knots with 16 strands of cord, and then weave an upside down triangle pattern using square knots.

Step 3 Use the cords on either side as the holding cords to weave diagonal double half hitch knots along the upside down triangle. Then, thread a wooden bead onto the long holding cord.

Step 4 Repeat steps 2 and 3. After completing each pennant, thread a wooden bead.

Spinning Rainbow

Rainbows always evoke a sense of hope and longing. In this example, several rainbow-shaped woven elements are combined into a hanging arrangement. Additionally, three-dimensional spiral patterns are included to enhance the dreamy visual effect.

Materials

Bamboo ring: diameter 25 cm
Pom-poms: 7
Cord Material: 3 mm white cotton cord, a variety of colored cotton cords, like purple, blue, pink, yellow and others

Tools

Corkboard, beading needles, sewing needle, sewing thread, comb, hot glue

Cord Cutting Guide

White cotton cord: 3.5 m × 5 pieces (hanging cord), 4 m × 1 piece, 3 m × 6 pieces (spiral pattern adding cords), 40 cm × 3 pieces.

For the rainbow part, look at the table below. The colors can be randomly paired.

	White Holding Cord	Colored Holding Cord
Inner part	25 cm × 9 pieces	1 m × 3 pieces
Middle part	30 cm × 9 pieces	1.5 m × 3 pieces
Outer part	35 cm × 9 pieces	2 m × 3 pieces

Basic Knots

Reverse lark's head knot plus a half hitch, spiral knot, diagonal double half hitch knot, hitch knot, square knot

Pattern

3D spiral pattern with diagonal double half hitch knots (No. 64)

Starting Technique

Reverse lark's head knot plus a half hitch, spiral knot hanging starting technique

Adding Cord Techniques

Diagonal double half hitch knot adding cord technique, square knot adding cord technique

Product Dimensions

Diameter 25 cm, height 50 cm

Steps

1

Take five pieces of 3.5 m long white cotton cord as the initial holding cord. Take one piece of 4 m long white cotton cord (demonstrated here with green cord) as the working cord. Weave a reverse lark's head knot plus a half hitch in the middle of the holding cord, approximately 10–12 cm long.

Fold the reverse lark's head knot plus a half hitch in half and secure it with a beading needle on a corkboard for easier weaving.

Gather all the white cords together as the holding cord, and use the green cord as the working cord to create a section of spiral knot, which serves as the suspension point for hanging.

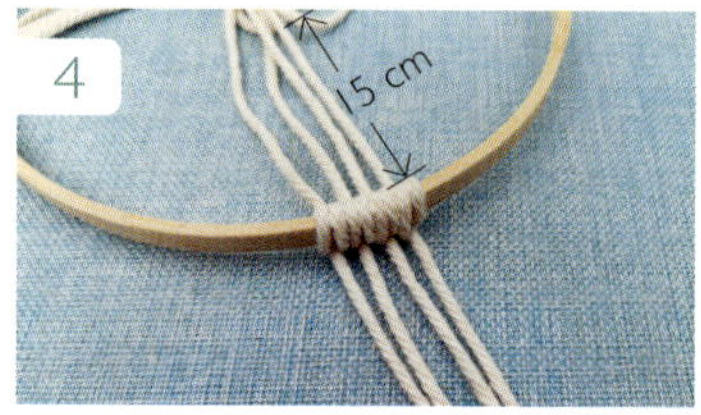

Divide the bamboo ring into three equal parts and mark them. Divide the 12 strands of cord from step 3 into three groups, and use horizontal double half hitch knots to connect them to the marked divisions on the ring.

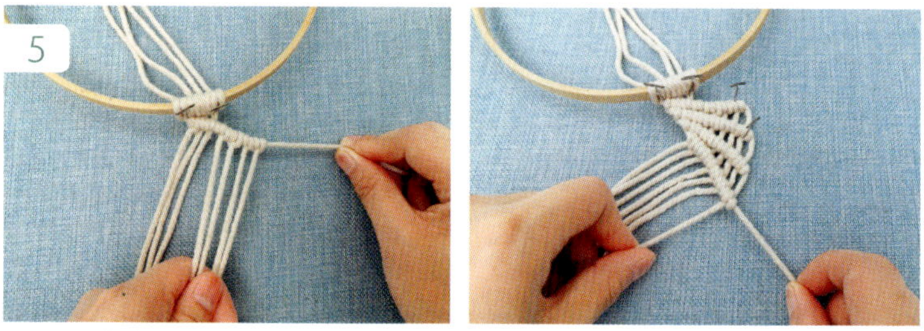

Start with the leftmost strand as the holding cord. Weave three diagonal double half hitch knots to the right. Then, on the same holding cord, use the diagonal double half hitch knot adding cord technique to add two strands of 3 m long working cords (folded to make four strands). Continue weaving a three-dimensional spiral with diagonal double half hitch knots.

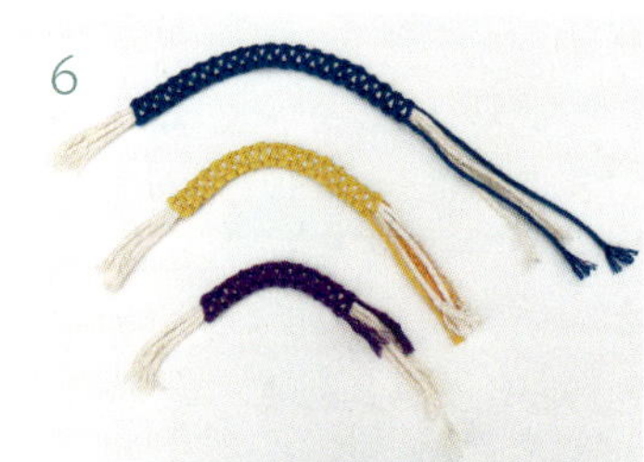

Choose your favorite color, and weave square knots according to the holding and working cords corresponding to the inner, middle, and outer parts.

Arrange the three layers of colorful square knots neatly and sew them together with needle and thread. Pay attention to the curvature and length of each layer while sewing, and trim the lengths of both ends of the threads evenly.

Use a comb to fluff up the white cotton cord.

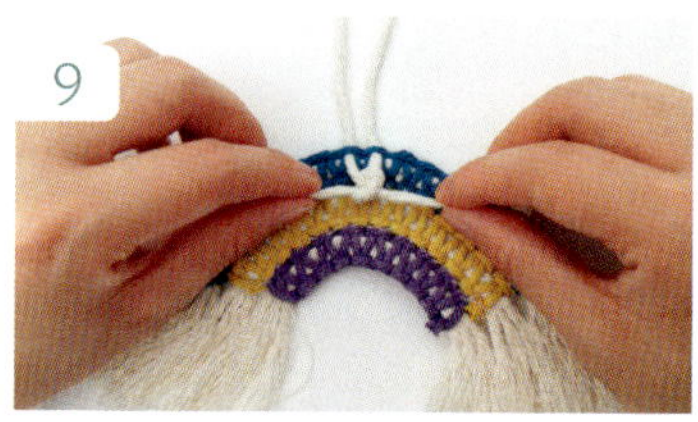

Take a 40 cm long white cotton cord, pass it through the midpoint of the outer edge of the rainbow, secure it with a hitch knot around multiple cords, and cut off the loose ends of the cords.

Repeat the same process to complete three rainbows, then hang them on the bamboo ring.

Use hot glue to attach the prepared pom-poms onto the bamboo ring

Hanging Planter

A hanging planter is a classic suspended design, with one support point at the top and three to six vertical woven patterns evenly distributed below. Using hanging planters, you can create an aerial garden and add a sense of layering to the distribution of indoor plants.

1. Style A

Materials

Wooden ring: diameter 3 cm
Wooden bead: hole diameter 1 cm × 1, hole diameter 5 mm × 3
Cord material: 3 mm white cotton cord, 3 mm grass green cotton cord

Cord Cutting Guide

White cotton cord: 3.5 m × 6 pieces (12 strands)
Grass green cotton cord: 50 cm × 1 piece (1 strand)

Basic Knot

Square knot

Patterns

Square knot with exchanging holding cords and working cords (No. 6), pattern with square knot picots, style B (No. 15)

Product Dimension

Length 70 cm

Steps

Step 1 Fold six strands of white cord in half and thread them through the wooden ring and wooden bead with a large hole.

Step 2 Group the cords into sets of four strands each and weave eight square knots.

Step 3 Exchange the holding and working cords. Weave two square knots and two patterns with square knot picots. Then thread a small wooden bead onto the holding cord, and symmetrically weave two more square knot picot patterns and two square knots.

Step 4 Exchange the holding and working cords, and then weave eight square knots.

Step 5 At a certain distance apart, weave three patterns with square knot picots in an alternating pattern, positioning them in the middle of the planter.

Step 6 Gather all the cords and place them into the planter. Leave a length of cord below the patterns with square knot picots from step 5, approximately one-third of the planter's height. Weave around the edge of the planter to the center of the bottom, making about four to five square knots.

Step 7 Gather all the cords and use a 50 cm length of grass green cotton cord to weave a wrapping knot.

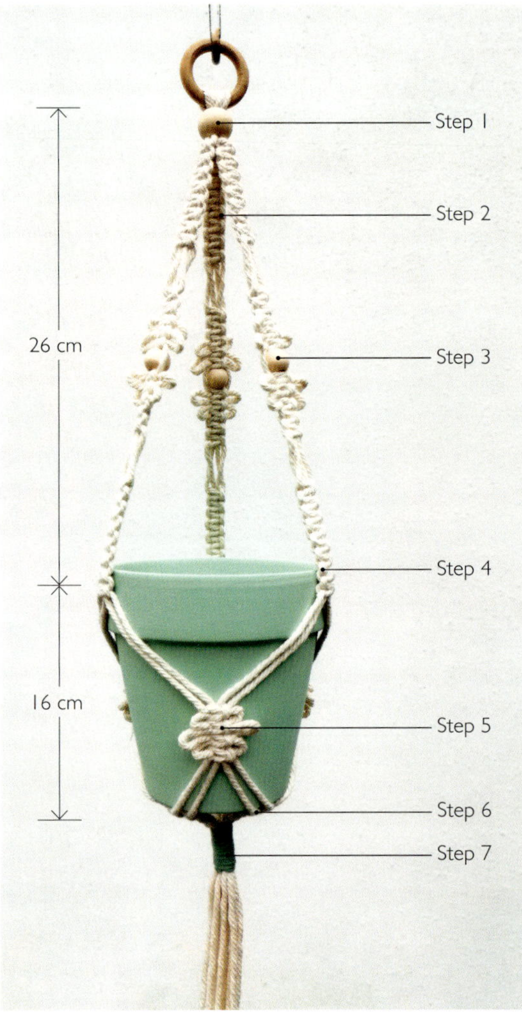

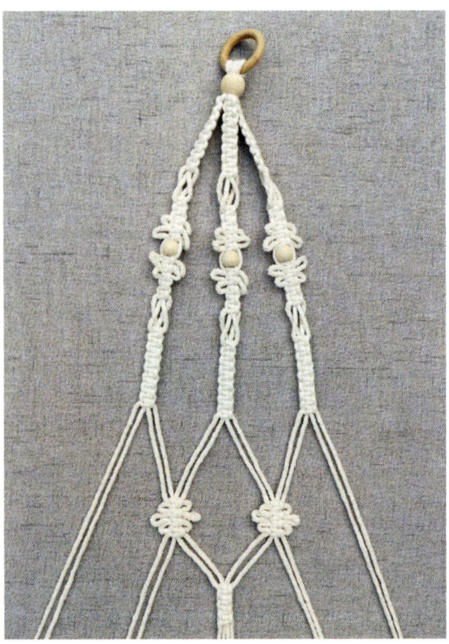

2. Style B

Materials

Wooden ring: diameter 3 cm
Cord Material: 3 mm white cotton cord, 3 mm gray cotton cord

Cord Cutting Guide

White cotton cord: 2.2 m × 4 pieces (8 strands), 50 cm × 2 pieces (to make wrapping knots)
Gray cotton cord: 3.8 m × 4 pieces (8 strands)

Basic Knots

Wrapping knot, spiral knot, square knot

Pattern

Square knot with exchanging holding cords and working cords (No. 6)

Starting Technique

Wrapping knot suspension starting method

Product Dimension

Length 67 cm

Steps

Step 1 Fold four white cords and four gray cords in half and thread them through the wooden ring.

Step 2 Using the wrapping knot suspension starting method, secure the 16 strands of cord with a 50 cm length of white cord by weaving a wrapping knot.

Step 3 Pair two white cords with two gray cords, using the white cords as the holding cords and the gray cords as the working cords. Weave an approximately 20 cm length of spiral knots. Then, switch the holding and working cords. Use the gray cords as the holding cords and the white cords as the working cords, and weave an approximately 3 cm length of spiral knots. Next, switch the holding and working cords again, and weave an approximately 3 cm length of spiral knots.

Step 4 At an interval of approximately 10 cm, switch the holding and working cords, and weave three alternating square knots.

Step 5 Gather all the cords and place them into the flower pot. Measure the position at the bottom of the pot, and weave a 50 cm length of white cord into a wrapping knot at the center of the pot's bottom.

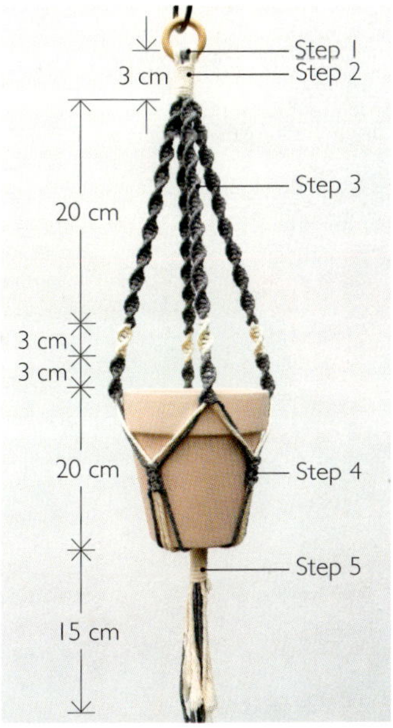

3. Style C

Materials

Wooden ring: diameter 3 cm
Cord material: 3 mm white cotton cord

Cord Cutting Guide

3.5 m × 8 pieces (16 strands), 50 cm × 1 piece (to make wrapping knot)

Basic Knots

Square knot, cylindrical knot, diagonal double half hitch knot

Patterns

Square knot pattern with exchanging holding cords and working cords (No. 6), embedded diamond pattern with diagonal double half hitch knots (No. 96)

Product Dimension

Length 80 cm

Steps

Step 1 Fold eight cords in half and thread them through the wooden ring. Then, weave approximately 5 cm of cylindrical knots.

Step 2 Group every four strands together and weave two square knots. After a certain distance, exchange the holding and working cords, and weave another two square knots. Repeat the above steps to weave approximately 35 cm in total.

Step 3 Immediately follow by weaving three embedded diamond patterns with diagonal double half hitch knots.

Step 4 After some distance, weave one embedded diamond pattern with diagonal double half hitch knots in an alternating pattern.

Step 5 Gather all the cords and place them into the flowerpot. Measure the position of the flowerpot's bottom. Leave a length of cord equal to half the height of the flowerpot below the embedded diamond pattern with diagonal double half hitch knots from step 4. Then, in the center of the pot's bottom, alternate and weave two square knots, making a total of four groups.

Step 6 Gather all the cords and use a 50 cm long cotton cord to weave a wrapping knot.

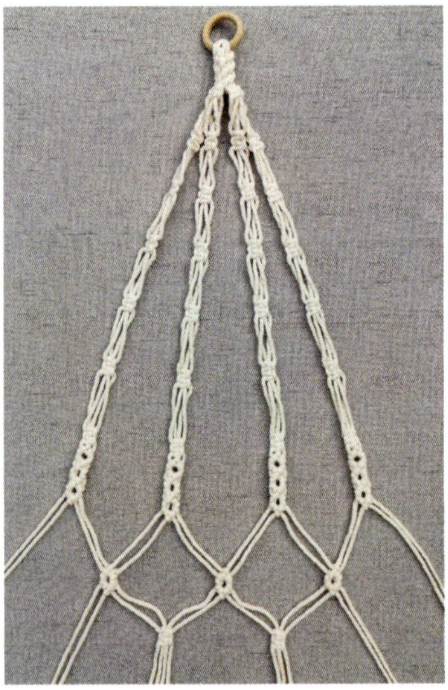

Tapestry-Style Hanging Planter

This project is different from the previous hanging planter designs. It is a combination of a tapestry and a hanging basket in a single woven design. Side-by-side hanging baskets are perfect for placing small flower pots or vases with simple greenery or fresh flowers.

Materials

Natural branch: length 40 cm
Cord material: 3 mm cotton cord

Cord Cutting Guide

3 m × 30 pieces (60 strands), 50 cm × 3 pieces (for making wrapping knots)

Basic Knots

Lark's head knot, square knot, spiral knot, diagonal double half hitch knot, wrapping knot

Patterns

Inverted V-shaped pattern with square knots (No. 26), V-shaped pattern with square knots (No. 28), diamond pattern embedded with square knots (No. 40), V-shaped pattern with diagonal double half hitch knots (No. 66), embedded diamond pattern with diagonal double half hitch knots (No. 96)

Starting Technique

Lark's head knot horizontal starting method

Product Dimensions

Length 55 cm, width 32 cm

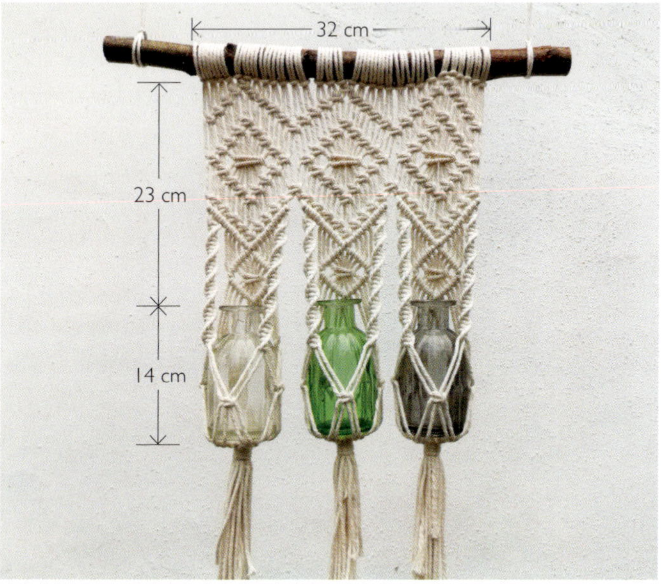

Steps

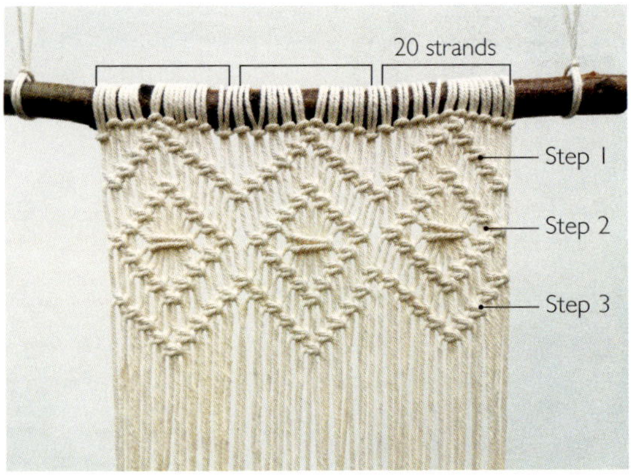

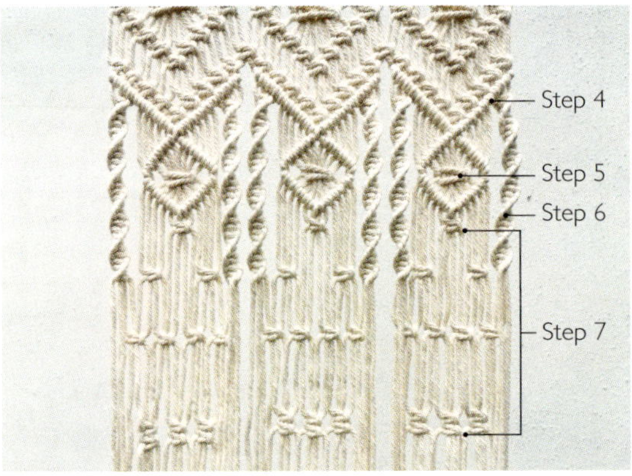

Step 1 Fold all the cotton cords and fix them to the branch using lark's head knots. For each group of 20 strands, weave three inverted V-shaped patterns with square knots, connecting the V-shaped patterns with additional square knots.

Step 2 Weave three diamond patterns embedded with square knots, with each diamond center wrapped with a large square knot. Use eight strands in the center as holding cords and one strand on each side as the working cord. Ensure that the diamonds remain parallel to the V-shaped patterns.

Step 3 Weave a square knot with the four strands between adjacent diamonds, and then weave three V-shaped patterns with square knots. Ensure that the diamonds remain parallel to the V-shaped patterns.

Step 4 Directly adjacent to the square knots from step 3, weave a V-shaped pattern with diagonal double half hitch knots.

Step 5 Use the 12 strands of cord below the V-shaped to weave a embedded diamond pattern with diagonal double half hitch knots. In the center of the diamond, wrap a large square knot, with eight strands in the middle as the holding cords and one strand on each side as the working cord.

Step 6 On each side of the embedded diamond pattern with diagonal double half hitch knots, weave a segment of spiral knots, with a length approximately twice that of the diamond pattern.

Step 7 Weave four rows of alternating square knots as shown in the diagram. In the first row, weave one square knot below the vertex of the diamond pattern. In the second row, weave two square knots aligned with the end of the spiral knot. In the third row, weave four square knots spaced 4 to 5 cm apart from the second row, leaving two strands of cotton cord unknotted on each side. For the fourth row, spaced 7 to 8 cm apart from the third row, create alternating square knots (as shown in the diagram: three columns in each group, each column with two square knots), which will be used for the square knots at the bottom of the bottle in step 8. Leave four strands of cotton cord unknotted on each side.

Step 8 Place the small flower vase in the center of each group of woven patterns. Use the two strands of cotton cord from each side of the third row of square knots from step 7 to create a square knot around the middle of the vase. Then, use the remaining cords from the fourth row to create two columns of knots on each side, with each column consisting of two square knots. Finally, use a wrapping knot to gather the cords of each group, completing the bottom of the hanging planter.

Envelope Clutch

This clutch bag features a one piece design. The long woven piece is folded twice to create the finished product. Even with just simple square knots, the bag stands out beautifully due to the use of different colors. The carp embroidery patch adds a lively touch to the design.

Materials

Embroidered patch
Cord material: blue gray fabric strips (2 balls), bright orange fabric strips (1 ball), deep blue floral fabric strips (1 ball)

Tools

Large-eye needle, fabric glue

Cord Cutting Guide

Blue gray fabric strips: 70 cm × 1 piece (starting holding cord), 3.5 m × 16 pieces (32 strands)
Bright orange fabric strips: 3.2 m × 4 pieces (8 strands)
Deep blue floral fabric strips: 3.2 m × 4 pieces (8 strands), 1.2 m × 4 pieces (two sides)

Basic Knots

Reverse lark's head knot, square knot, diagonal double half hitch knot

Patterns

Alternating square knots pattern (No. 1), upside down triangle pattern with square knots (No. 32), V-shaped pattern with diagonal double half hitch knots (No. 66)

Starting Technique

Reverse lark's head knot starting method

Product Dimensions

Length 25 cm, width 22 cm

Steps

Step 5 Adhere the embroidery patch to the triangular flap area.

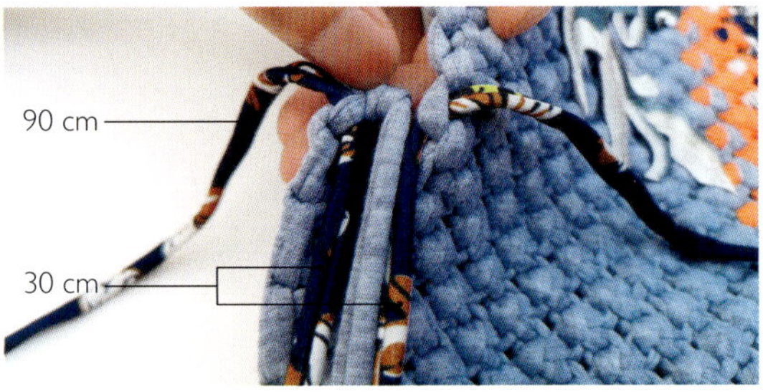

Step 6 Thread a 1.2 m long deep blue floral fabric strip through point C and another through point D. After folding the bag inward (i.e., C and D align, and C′ and D′ align), leave 30 cm of the deep blue fabric strip adjacent to the blue-gray fabric strip at point D. This will be used as the shared holding cord along with the blue-gray fabric strip, while the remaining 90 cm of deep blue fabric strips will be used as the working cords.

Step 7 Weave a square knot, then thread the deep blue working cords from both sides through the next set of reserved holes and continue weaving square knots. Each time you weave two square knots, thread the braiding strands through a row of reserved holes until you reach the bottom at points A and B. Repeat the same process on the other side to connect both sides of the envelope clutch together.

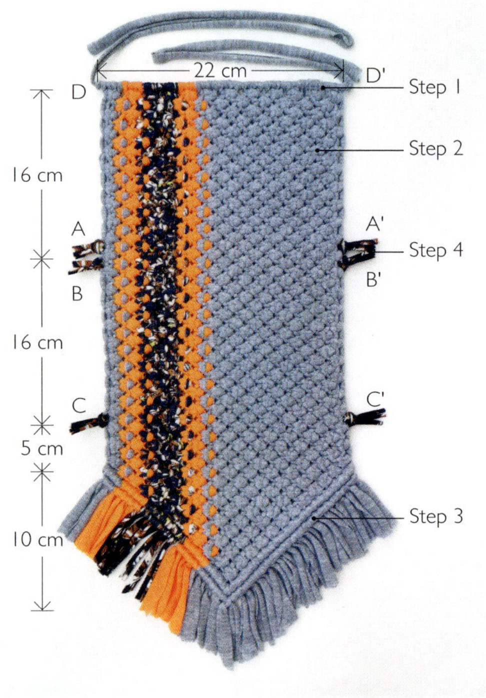

Step 1 Attach all fabric strips to the 70 cm long blue gray fabric strip using reverse lark's head knots, following this sequence: two blue gray strips, two bright orange strips, four dark blue floral strips, two bright orange strips, and 14 blue gray strips.

Step 2 Use all the fabric strips to weave approximately 37 cm of alternating square knots, then weave an upside down triangle pattern with square knots.

Step 3 Close to the upside down triangle, weave double-layer V-shaped pattern with diagonal double half hitch knot, then trim the cord ends evenly.

Step 4 On the flat woven surface, mark every 16 cm, such as points A, B, C, and A′, B′, C′. Fold along the lines connecting AA′. When folding, make sure to align the marked points on both sides. After folding, points A and B should overlap, and points A′ and B′ should overlap. The line connecting AA′ and BB′ will be the bottom edge of the clutch. Points C and D should overlap, and the line CC′ will be the top of the clutch.

Step 8 Turn the envelope bag inside out and hide five thread ends on each side inside the knot with a large-eye needle and reinforce with glue.

Single-Shoulder Cutout Bag

The single-shoulder cutout bag is a common bag style, suitable for matching with casual wear, vacation clothing, and cottagecore style outfits. The main body of this shoulder bag can be completed by only using square knot pattern by exchanging working cords and holding cords, and the shoulder strap is connected with metal clasps, so you can make up long or short straps to suit your needs as alternatives.

Materials

Drawstring pocket: length 40 cm, width 40 cm
Metal D-clasp: 4
Metal hanging clasp: 2
Cord material: 3 mm flesh pink core-spun cotton cord

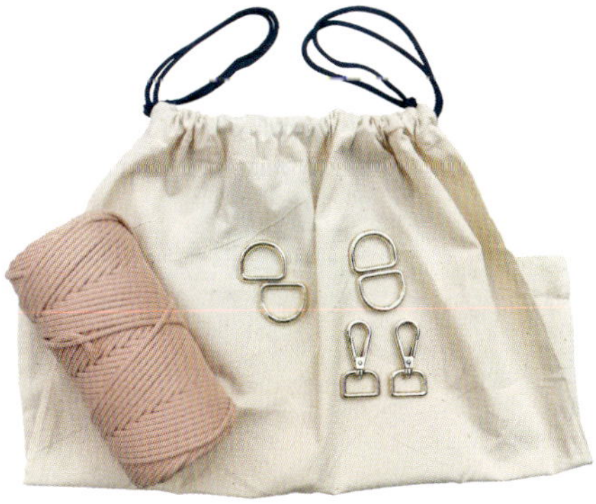

Tools

Large-eye needle, glue

Cord Cutting Guide

Bag body: 80 cm × 16 pieces (32 strands), 1.2 m × 20 pieces (40 strands), 50 cm × 5 pieces
Strap: 1 m × 4 pieces, 4.5 m × 2 pieces

Basic Knots

Reverse lark's head knot, alternating half hitch knot, square knot, lark's head knot, wrapping knot, overhand knot

Pattern

Square knot with exchanging working cords and holding cords (No. 9)

Starting Technique

Reverse lark's head knot starting method

Product Dimensions

Bag body: length 57 cm, width 32 cm, strap length around 34 cm

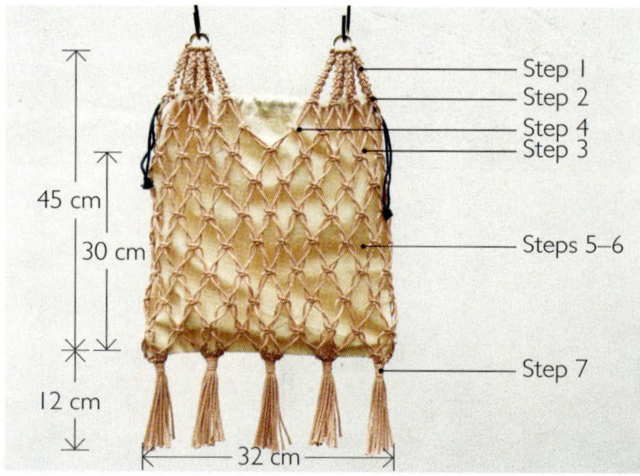

Steps

Step 1 Make the body of the bag first. Attach four pieces of 80 cm long cord to the D-clasp with a reverse lark's head knot. Weave 12 alternating half hitch knots for each two strands of cord and repeat the above operation on the other D-clasp.

Step 2 Use four pieces of 1.2 m long cord to add cord and weave a square knot each behind four sets of alternating half hitch knots. Increase to four strands of cord under each set of alternating half hitch knots.

Step 3 Weave three rows of square knot with exchanging working cords and holding cords in staggered rows of three, two and one respectively.

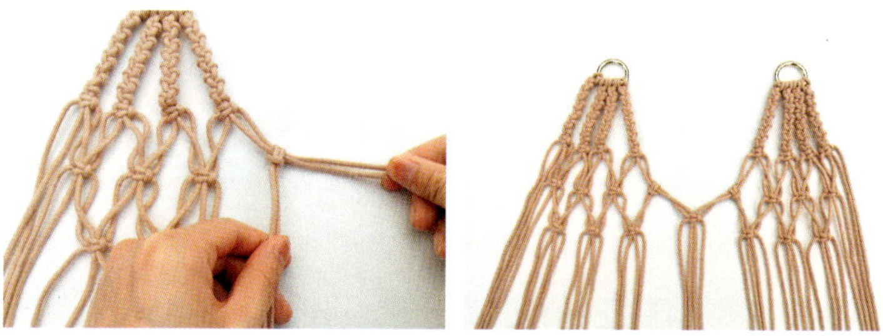

Step 4 Add a 1.2 m long cord with a lark's head knot on the two strands of cord on one side of the D-clasp weaving pattern, add cord on the symmetrical position of the other group of D-clasps, and weave a square knot with exchanging working cords and holding cords with four strands of cord on both sides to connect the two groups of D-clasps together. Repeat for the other two sets of D-clasps.

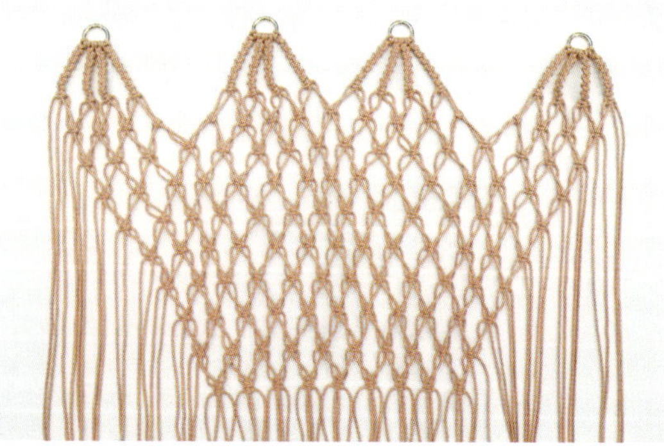

Step 5 Combine the two sets of D-clasps from step 4 using square knot with exchanging working cords and holding cords to connect them together. Weave ten rows of square knot with exchanging working cords and holding cords, decreasing by two strands of cord per row to form an inverted trapezoid. In the last row, use double square knots to increase the contact area of the base.

Step 6 Fold the expanded flat piece in half and connect the two sides using square knot with exchanging working cords and holding cords to form a cylindrical bag shape.

Step 7 Group the three square knots on each side and the four square knots in the middle together. Use a 50 cm long piece of cord to make five to seven wrapping knots to finish. If the wrapping knot is too short, it won't provide enough strength and if it's too long, the tassels will lose their fluidity.

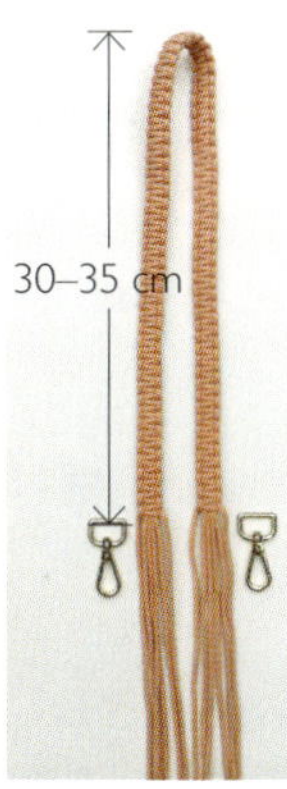

Step 8 Make the shoulder strap. Take four 1 m cords as the holding cords and two 4.5 m cords as the working cords. Align the midpoints of all the cords and temporarily secure them with an overhand knot. Then, weave square knots on both sides, weaving 33 to 35 cm on each side, for a total length of 66 to 70 cm.

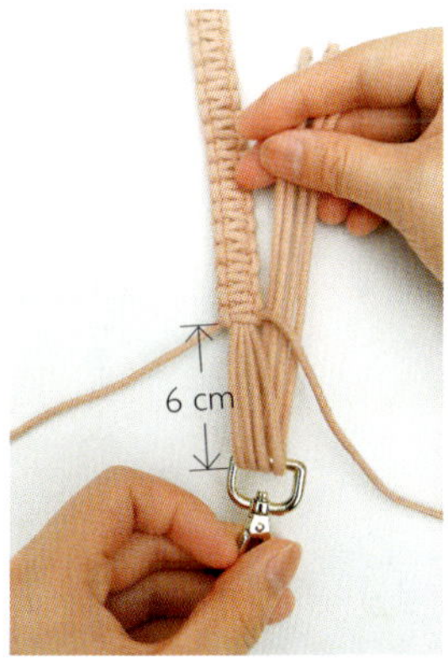

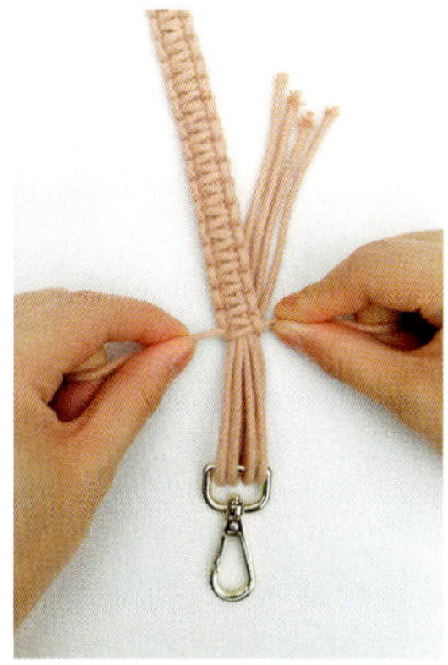

Step 9 Pass the holding cords on both sides through the hanging clasp, leaving about 6 cm of length. Fold the ends of the cords, overlapping them with the reserved cords. Using all the overlapped cords as the holding cords, continue weaving square knots until you approach the hanging clasp.

Step 10 There are six cord ends on each side. Use a large-eye needle to tuck the ends into the knots, apply a small amount of glue to secure them, and trim off the cord ends.

Composite Large Tapestry

The flexibility in making tapestries is very high. You can select various patterns or shapes and combine them to enhance the diversity of the tapestry design. You can increase or decrease the number of repeated patterns to create tapestries of different sizes, whether large or small. The tapestry in this project is 1 meter wide, making it ideal for decorating larger wall spaces, such as in a living room or bedroom.

Materials

Wooden rod: length 1.1 m, diameter 2.5 cm
Cord material: 3.5 mm white cotton cord, 3 mm beige cotton cord

Cord Cutting Guide

White cotton cord: 3.5 m × 90 pieces (180 strands), 40 cm × 25 pieces (adding cord tassel)
Beige cotton cord: 30 cm × 5 pieces

Basic Knots

Reverse lark's head knot, spiral knot, square knot, diagonal double half hitch knot, three-strand simple braid, alternating half hitch knot, wrapping knot

Patterns

Inverted V-shaped pattern with diagonal double half hitch knots (No. 65), V-shaped pattern with diagonal double half hitch knots (No. 66), V combination pattern with diagonal double half hitch knot, style D (No. 75), butterfly pattern with diagonal double half hitch knots, style A (No. 116), tassel, style B (No. 133)

Starting Technique

Reverse lark's head knot starting method

Product Dimensions

Length 60 cm, width 1 m

Steps

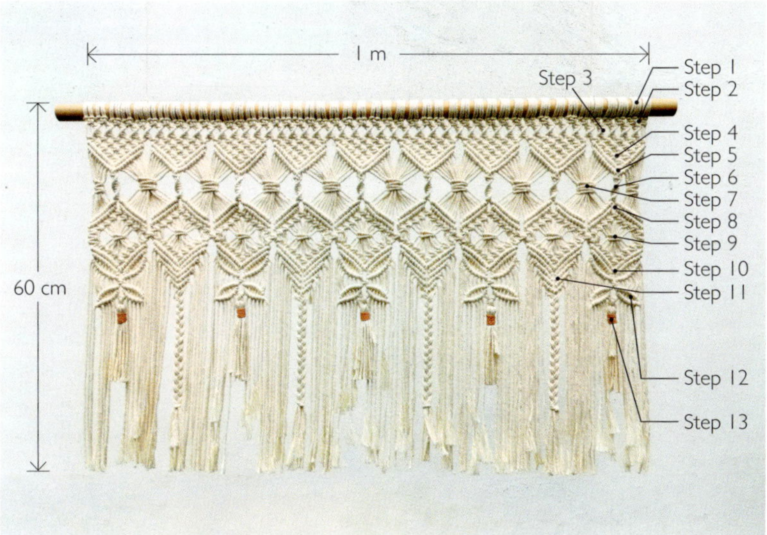

Step 1 Fold 90 pieces of 3.5 m cotton cord in half and secure them to the wooden rod using reverse lark's head knots.

Step 2 Use every four strands as a group to weave a row of 45 square knots.

Step 3 Weave five alternating rows of spiral knots, with a total of 44 groups of spiral knots in this row.

Step 4 Group every 20 strands together and weave a row of upside down triangle patterns with square knots.

Step 5 Directly beneath the upside down triangle, weave two rows of V-shaped patterns with diagonal double half hitch knots.

Step 6 Take the four cords at the top of the V-shaped patterns and weave 10 to 12 spiral knots.

Step 7 Use the 16 cords between each set of V-shaped patterns to weave two consecutive square knots. The outer two cords are the working cords, while the remaining cords serve as the holding cords.

Step 8 From the spiral knots, weave two rows of inverted V-shaped patterns with diagonal double half hitch knots towards both sides.

Step 9 Group every 20 strands together and weave diamond patterns with square knots, with a large square knot centered within each diamond. Note that adjacent diamonds need to be connected with square knots.

Step 10 Directly beneath the diamond patterns with square knots, weave a row of V-shaped patterns with diagonal double half hitch knots.

Step 11 In the 2nd, 4th, 6th and 8th groups, weave a V combination pattern with diagonal double half hitch knots. At the top of these V shapes, braid the six cords into a three-strand simple braid.

Step 12 In the 1st, 3rd, 5th, 7th and 9th groups, weave butterfly patterns with diagonal double half hitch knots. Note that the lower wings of the butterflies should use two strands fewer than the upper wings.

Step 13 Use the four cords below each butterfly to weave two alternating half hitch knots. Take five pieces of 40 cm long beige cotton cords and create tassels by weaving wrapping knots below the alternating half hitch knots.

Composite Small Tapestry

The design concept and overall framework are similar to the large tapestry in the previous project, but with changes in the details, resulting in a completely different design. Similarly, you can adjust the number of repeated patterns to create tapestries of different sizes.

Materials

Wooden rod: length 50 cm, diameter 1.5 cm
Cord material: 3.5 mm weave patterned cotton cord

Cord Cutting Guide

3.5 m × 32 pieces (64 strands)

Basic Knots

Lark's head knot, square knot, diagonal double half hitch knot, four-strand simple braid, three-strand simple braid, spiral knot, hitch knot, barrel knot

Patterns

Upside down triangle pattern with square knots (No. 32), inverted V-shaped pattern with diagonal double half hitch knots (No. 65), V-shaped pattern with diagonal double half hitch knots (No. 66), wave pattern with diagonal double half hitch knots, style A (No. 85)

Starting Technique

Lark's head knot horizontal starting method

Product Dimensions

Length 70 cm, width 40 cm

Steps

Step 1 Fold all the cotton cords in half and secure them to the wooden rod using lark's head knots. Weave a double square knot every four strands.

Step 2 Group every 16 strands together and weave upside down triangle patterns with square knots. Directly beneath the upside down triangles, weave two rows of V-shaped patterns with diagonal double half hitch knots.

Step 3 Take the four cords below the V shapes and weave four square knots.

Step 4 Use the 12 cords between each set of V shapes to braid a small section of a four-strand simple braid.

Step 5 From the square knots, weave two rows of inverted V-shaped patterns with diagonal double half hitch knots towards both sides.

Step 6 Braid the six cords below the top of the inverted V shapes into a section of a three-strand simple braid.

Step 7 Use the ten cords between adjacent V shapes to weave three diamond patterns with diagonal double half hitch knots with embedded square knots. Decrease by two cords for each subsequent diamond downwards. After the three diamonds, add a section of spiral knots and finish with a hitch knot.

Step 8 Weave diagonal double half hitch knot waves with the five cords on each side and finish with a hitch knot.

Step 9 Use the leftover cotton cords to randomly weave barrel knots as decoration.

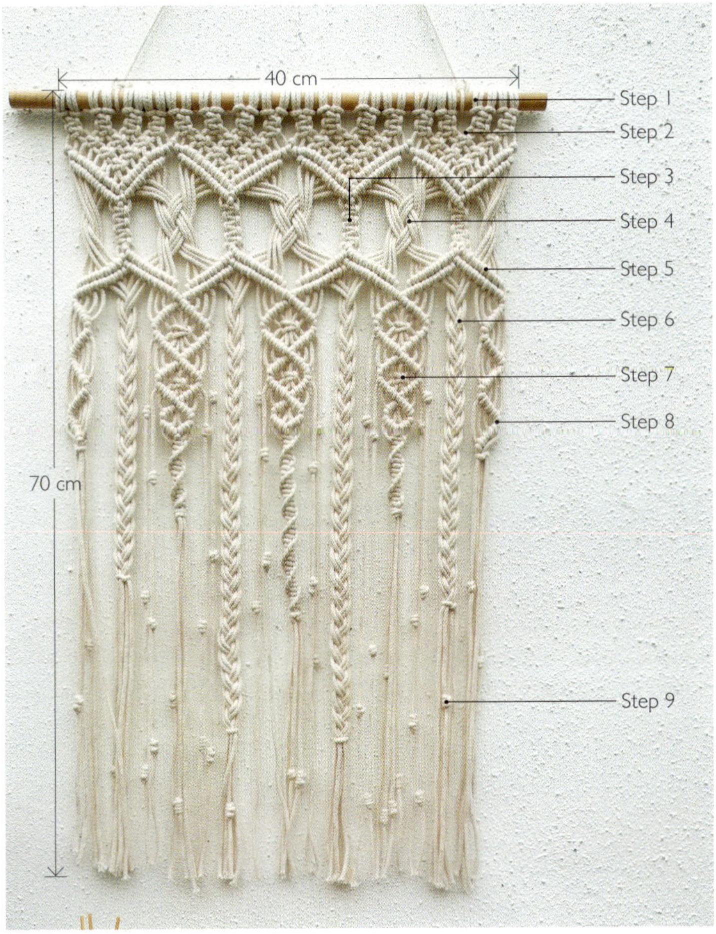

Curtain

Windows are a very important element in home decor. Curtains not only serve the purpose of providing shield, but also add aesthetic value to the space. Woven curtains in this project are truly unique, combining solid and hollow diamonds as design elements to create two layers of tassels—one long and one short. The versatility in adjusting the tassels for full or partial coverage adds both beauty and practicality to the design.

Materials

Wooden ring: 20, curtains need to be matched to the size of the curtain rod for proper fit
Wooden beads with large holes: 20
Cord material: 2.5 mm cotton cord

Cord Cutting Guide

Curtain body: 6 m × 242 pieces (484 strands)
Tassel: 40 cm × 80 pieces

Basic Knots

Lark's head knot, square knot, diagonal double half hitch knot, spiral knot, wrapping knot, barrel knot

Patterns

Single-layer V-shaped pattern with square knots (No. 28), solid diamond shape with square knots (No. 35), embedded diamond pattern with square knots, style B (No. 47), embedded diamond pattern with diagonal double half hitch knots, style A (No. 96)

Starting Technique

Lark's head knot starting method

Adding Cord Technique

Diagonal cord adding on both sides

Product Dimensions

Length 2 m, width 2 m

Steps

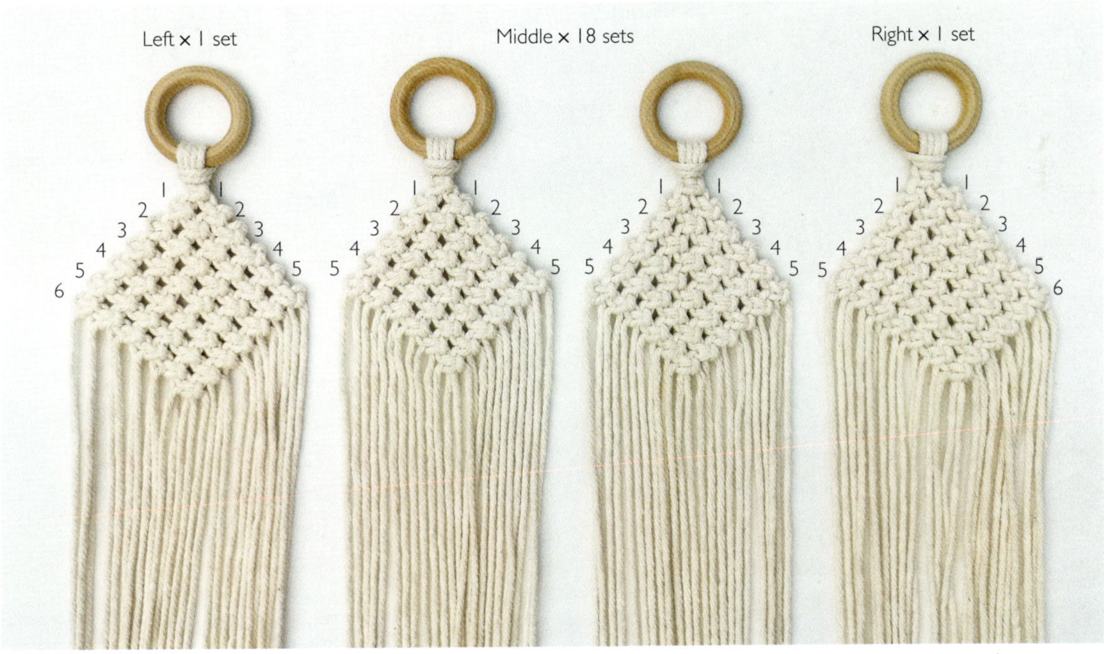

Step 1 Take two 6 m cords, secure them to a wooden ring using lark's head knots, and weave one square knot. Using the method of adding cords diagonally on both sides of the square knot, gradually add ten cords and weave them into a solid 24-strand diamond shape. Weave a total of 18 sets of solid diamonds, which serve as the middle section of the curtain.

Step 2 Based on step 1, add one extra cord on the left side to form the left part of the curtain, and add one extra cord on the right side to form the right part of the curtain. Make two sets in total. Arrange all the solid diamonds as shown in the diagram, positioning them in the left, middle, and right sections of the curtain.

Step 3 Following the arrangement from the previous step, connect the two adjacent solid diamonds with square knots. Then, weave an additional row of square knots along the lower edge of the diamonds.

Step 4 Between adjacent solid diamonds, weave square knots using 16 cords. Use two cords on each side as the working cords, with the remaining cords as the holding cords. Then, weave V-shaped pattern with square knots below the large square knots to create hollow diamonds.

Step 5 Weave solid diamonds in a 6 × 6 pattern as in step 2 between adjacent groups of hollow diamonds from step 4.

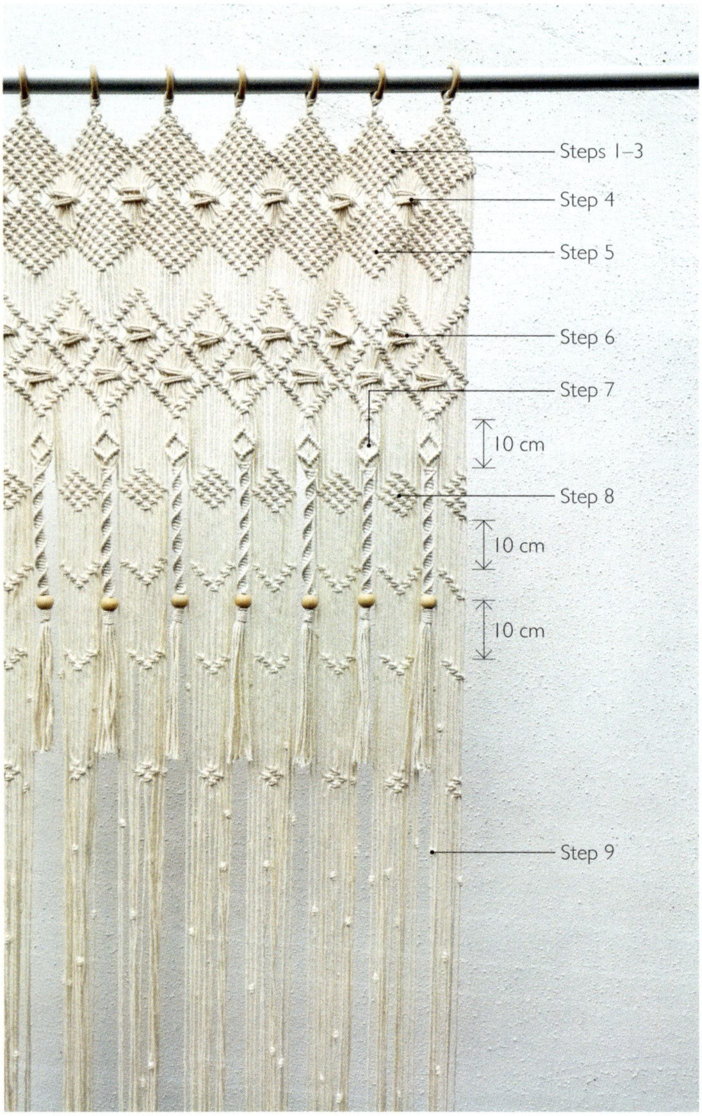

Step 6 At approximately 10 cm intervals, weave two rows of diamond pattern with square knots, with a large 16-strand square knot in the center of each diamond. Use two cords on each side as the working cords and the remaining cords as the holding cords.

Step 7 Use the eight cotton cords below each diamond to weave diamond patterns with diagonal double half hitch knots. Next, weave a section of spiral knots with a length of your choice (20 cm in this project). Thread the eight cords through a wooden bead. Take a 40 cm long cotton cord and use it to make wrapping knots, creating a tassel. If you find that eight cords for the tassel are too thin, you can add more cords. In this project, three additional 40 cm cotton cords were added.

Step 8 After completing step 7, the cotton cords naturally separate into groups of 16 strands each. As shown in the diagram, about 10 cm below step 6, weave a solid 16-strand diamond shape with square knots. At a distance of 10 cm apart, weave 16-strand V-shaped patterns with square knots. Another 10 cm down, weave 12-strand V-shaped patterns with square knots. Another 10 cm or more down, weave 12-strand diamond patterns with square knots.

Step 9 In the blank areas, randomly weave barrel knots as decoration. If the length is insufficient, you can also add more cord by using barrel knots.

Five-Layer Cloud Shoulder Tapestry

Among the various weaving patterns, select a few strip patterns and layer them in an overlapping manner. Hang tassels along the sides of some of the strip patterns. This design resembles the cloud shoulder decorations found in ancient Chinese clothing, so it is evocatively called a cloud shoulder tapestry.

Materials

Wooden rod: length 60 cm, diameter 2 cm

Cord material: 3 mm white cotton cord, 3 mm yellow cotton cord

Cord Cutting Guide	Main body	Tassels on the sides
First layer of white cord	2.5 m × 8 pieces	50 cm × 22 pieces
Second layer of yellow cord	80 cm × 4 pieces	
Third layer of white cord	3.5 m × 8 pieces	50 cm × 38 pieces
Fourth layer of yellow cord	1.2 m × 4 pieces	
Fifth layer of white cord	4.5 m × 8 pieces	50cm × 56 pieces

Basic Knots

Reverse lark's head knot, lark's head knot, diagonal double half hitch knot, square knot

Patterns

Square knot with exchanging working cords and holding cords (No. 6), embedded diamond pattern with diagonal double half hitch knots (No. 96)

Starting Technique

Reverse lark's head knot horizontal starting method

Product Dimensions

Length 70 cm, width 50 cm

Steps

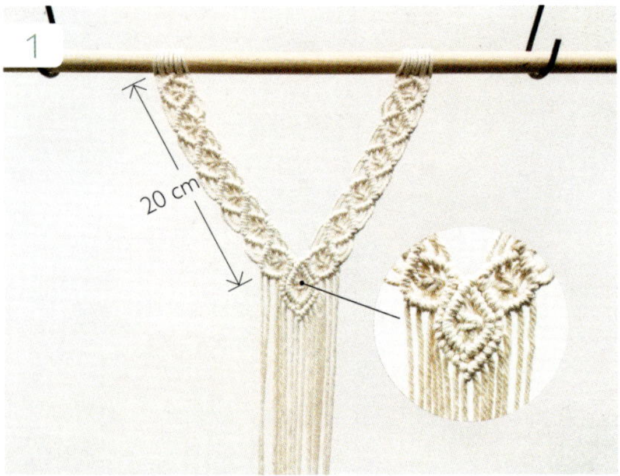

Weave the innermost first layer of the tapestry. Secure eight cords to a wooden rod using reverse lark's head knots, with eight strands on each side. Weave six embedded diamond patterns with diagonal double half hitch knots with embedded square knots. Next, gather the cords from both sides toward the center. Take ten strands and weave a double-layer embedded diamond pattern with diagonal double half hitch knots with an embedded square knot. Finally, attach 22 pieces of 50 cm long cotton cord using lark's head knots in the blank spaces between the diamonds, with 11 cords on each side.

Weave the second layer. On each side, use four strands to weave seven square knots with exchanging working cords and holding cords. Then, gather the cords from both sides toward the center and weave a embedded diamond pattern with diagonal double half hitch knots with an embedded square knot.

Weave the third layer. Repeat step 1, weaving ten embedded diamond patterns with diagonal double half hitch knots with embedded square knots on each side. Then, attach 38 pieces of 50 cm long cotton cord using lark's head knots in the blank spaces between the diamonds, with 19 cords on each side.

Weave the fourth layer. Repeat step 2, weaving 11 square knots with exchanging working cords and holding cords on each side.

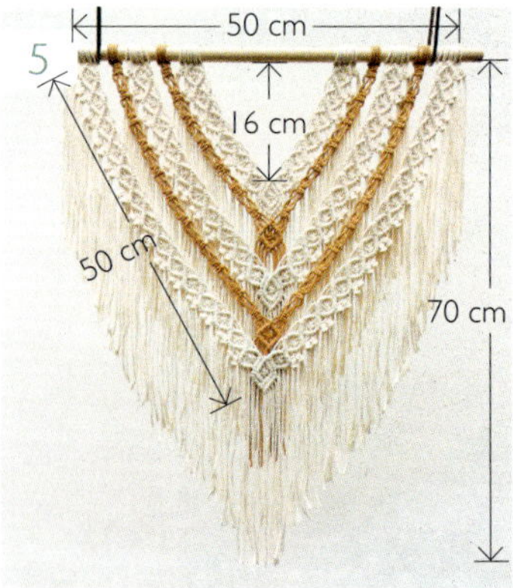

Weave the outermost fifth layer. Repeat step 1, weaving 14 embedded diamond patterns with diagonal double half hitch knots with embedded square knots on each side. Then, attach 56 pieces of 50 cm long cotton cord using lark's head knots in the blank spaces between the diamonds, with 28 cords on each side.

Composite Cloud Shoulder Tapestry

By combining more patterns and colors, you can expand the cloud shoulder design to create even richer variations. This project features a leaf-based design with three cloud shoulder combinations, a large main section, with smaller sections on both sides. The tassel sections are gradually trimmed from the inside out, making the design ideal for larger indoor walls or as a main installation in outdoor spaces.

Materials

Natural branch: length 1.1 m
Cord material: 3 mm white cotton cord, 3 mm mint green cotton cord

Cord Cutting Guide

	Main Body	Two Sides
First layer	2.5 m × 30 pieces (60 strands, white cotton cord)	2 m × 8 pieces × 2 groups (32 strands, white cotton cord), 80 cm × 16 pieces × 2 groups (white cotton cord)
Second layer	2 m × 6 pieces (12 strands, mint green cotton cord)	2 m × 6 pieces × 2 groups (24 strands, mint green cotton cord)
Third layer	3.3 m × 8 pieces (16 strands, white cotton cord), 60 cm × 46 pieces (white cotton cord)	2.5 m × 10 pieces × 2 groups (40 strands, white cotton cord), 20 cm × 24 pieces × 2 groups (white cotton cord)
Fourth layer	3.8 m × 10 pieces (20 strands, white cotton cord), 20 cm × 60 pieces (mint green cotton cord)	

Basic Knots

Reverse lark's head knot, lark's head knot, diagonal double half hitch knot, alternating half hitch knot, three-strand simple braid, square knot

Patterns

Alternating square knots pattern (No. 1), solid diamond shape with square knots (No. 35), diamond pattern with diagonal double half hitch knots (No. 96), leaf patterns with diagonal double half hitch knots (No. 115, No. 124)

Starting Technique

Reverse lark's head knot horizontal starting method

Product Dimensions

Length 85 cm, width 109 cm

Steps

Create the main body section. Secure the 30 cords of the first layer to a branch using reverse lark's head knots. Group every 20 strands together and weave leaf patterns with diagonal double half hitch knots. Connect each row of leaves with two alternating half hitch knots. After weaving the corresponding number of leaves as shown in the diagram, add two to six alternating half hitch knots at the tips and center of the leaves.

Weave the second layer. On both sides of step 1, weave a 30 cm three-strand simple braid using six mint green cotton cords and merge them. Then, continue braiding with 12 cords to create a three-strand simple braid of your desired length.

Weave the third layer. On both sides of step 2, weave 40 cm of alternating square knots using eight cords of 3.3 m each, and merge them. Then, use 16 cords to weave diamond patterns with diagonal double half hitch knots with embedded large square knots. Connect 60 cm long cords between adjacent square knots on the sides using lark's head knots, with 23 cords on each side.

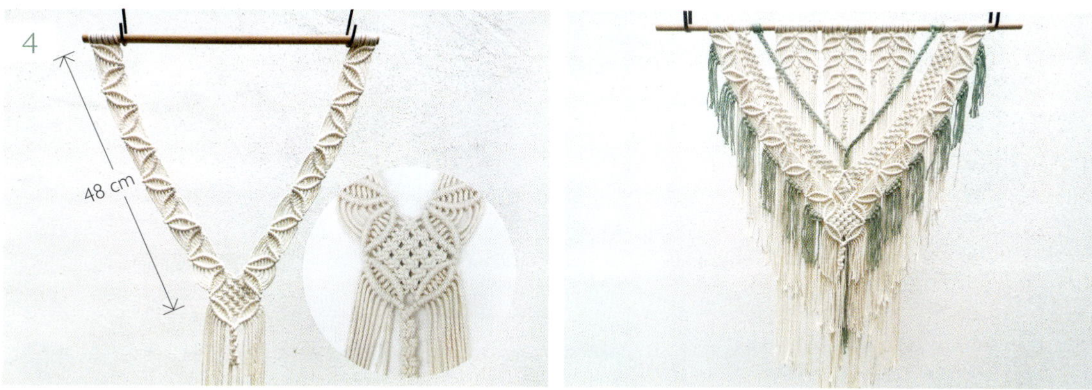

Weave the fourth layer. On both sides of step 3, weave a 48 cm long leaf pattern with diagonal double half hitch knots using ten cords, connecting the ends of the leaves together. In the center of the convergence area, weave a solid diamond shape with 16 cords using square knots. Gather the leaves around the diamond, and then weave alternating half hitch knots of your desired length. Connect 20 cm long mint green cotton cords between adjacent leaves on the sides using lark's head knots, with five cords between each leaf, totaling 60 cords.

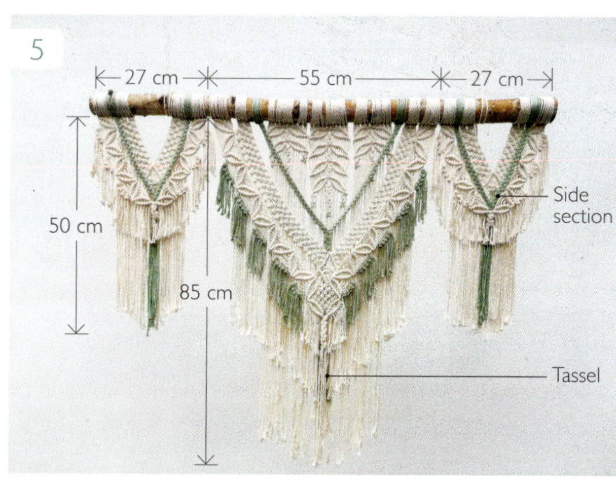

Weave the side sections by following the same method used for the main body section.

For the first layer, weave 15 cm of alternating square knots using eight cords. At the convergence points, use 16 cords to weave diamond patterns with diagonal double half hitch knots with embedded large square knots. Fold 80 cm long cotton cords in half and use lark's head knots to connect them between adjacent square knots on the sides.

For the second layer, weave a 2 cm long three-strand simple braid patterns using six mint green cotton cords. After merging, continue weaving three-strand simple braid patterns.

For the third layer, weave a 25 cm long diagonal double half hitch knot leaves using ten cords. At the convergence points, weave alternating half hitch knots of your desired length. Fold 20 cm long cotton cords in half and use lark's head knots to connect them between adjacent leaves on the sides.

Trim the tassels into the desired shape, typically a pointed or rounded tip.

Foliage Tapestry

Foliage tapestry is designed to mimic the shape of tree branches. It has no fixed style or direction, allowing for flexible design of the length and angle of the branches and leaves according to your preferences. In this project, the branch and leaf design is arranged in a downward-draping shape, with the overall flow directed downward. It also features a few leaves gently falling to create a dynamic effect.

Materials

Natural branch: length 40 cm
Cord material: blue flat cotton cord

Cord Cutting Guide

4 m × 30 pieces (60 strands)

Basic Knots

Lark's head knot, diagonal double half hitch knot, overhand knot

Pattern

Leaf pattern with diagonal double half hitch knots (No. 126)

Starting Technique

Lark's head knot horizontal starting method

Product Dimensions

Length about 90 cm, width 32 cm

Steps

Step 1 Attach all the cotton cords to a branch using lark's head knots.

Step 2 Refer to the weaving method from No. 126, weave from top to bottom in the sequence of green, white, yellow, orange, purple, blue, red. The branch and leaf design emphasizes the direction of the branches, giving you the freedom to weave the length and angle of the branches according to your preferences. If it is difficult to visualize the concept in your mind, you can start by sketching the general shape of the branches and leaves on paper.

Step 3 Once the branch and leaf section is complete, trim the cords to your preferred lengths, adjusting for both long and short strands according to your taste. In this case, after weaving an overhand knot at 90 cm, trim the cords to be even.

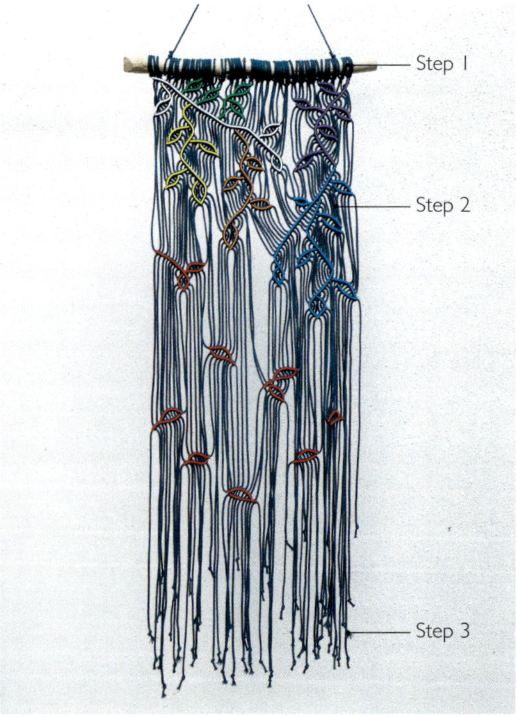

Tassel Tapestry

When weaving, it is common to end up with a lot of excess cord ends, which can lead to waste. To minimize this, you can use the leftover cords to create tassel designs, effectively using up the extra material. In this project, several striped weaving patterns were designed to complement the tassels. The color scheme primarily features off white and earth tones, with deep blue fabric strips added for highlights to make the tapestry more vibrant. The inclusion of lace yarn adds a touch of lightness to the piece.

Materials

Wooden rod: length 35 cm, diameter 1.5 cm
Cord material: 3 mm white cotton cord, 3 mm earth tone cotton cord, dark blue fabric strip, lace

Cord Cutting Guide

White cotton cord: 3.2 m × 3 pieces (6 strands), 3 m × 10 pieces (20 strands), 2.5 m × 4 pieces (8 strands), 1.8 m × 2 pieces (4 strands)
Earth-yellow cotton cord: 80 cm × 6 pieces
Dark blue fabric strips: 1.8 m × 2 pieces (4 strands)
Lace: 70 cm × 8 pieces
Gather 54 white cotton cord ends longer than 40 cm

Basic Knots

Lark's head knot, square knot, spiral knot, diagonal double half hitch knot, barrel knot, wrapping knot

Patterns

Square knot pattern with exchanging working cords and holding cords (No. 6), diamond pattern with diagonal double half hitch knots (No, 96), tassel, style B (No. 133)

Product Dimensions

Length 50 cm, width 30 cm

Steps

Step 1 Begin weaving from the center. Secure three strands of 3.2 m long white cotton cord to a wooden rod using lark's head knots. Weave a 35 cm length of diamond pattern with diagonal double half hitch knots.

Step 2 Hang four strands of 3 m long white cotton cord on each side of step 1 and weave a 32 cm length of spiral knots. In the spiral knot, the central holding cord is not involved in the weaving and uses very little cord length. Therefore, when securing the cord to the wooden rod, fold it at the 50 cm mark, placing the shorter two strands in the middle to serve as the holding cords.

Step 3 Attach 1.8 m of dark blue fabric strips and white cotton cord to each side of step 2. Weave a 30 cm length of square knot patterns with exchanging working cords and holding cords.

Step 4 Hang six strands of 3 m long white cotton cord on each side of step 3 and weave a 28 cm length of diamond patterns with diagonal double half hitch knots.

Step 5 Hang four strands of 2.5 m long white cotton cord on each side of step 4 and weave a 26 cm length of spiral knots. When securing the cords, fold them at the 40 cm mark and place the shorter two strands in the middle to serve as the holding cords.

Step 6 Interweave the earthy yellow cotton cord among the white cotton cords, randomly weaving barrel knots.

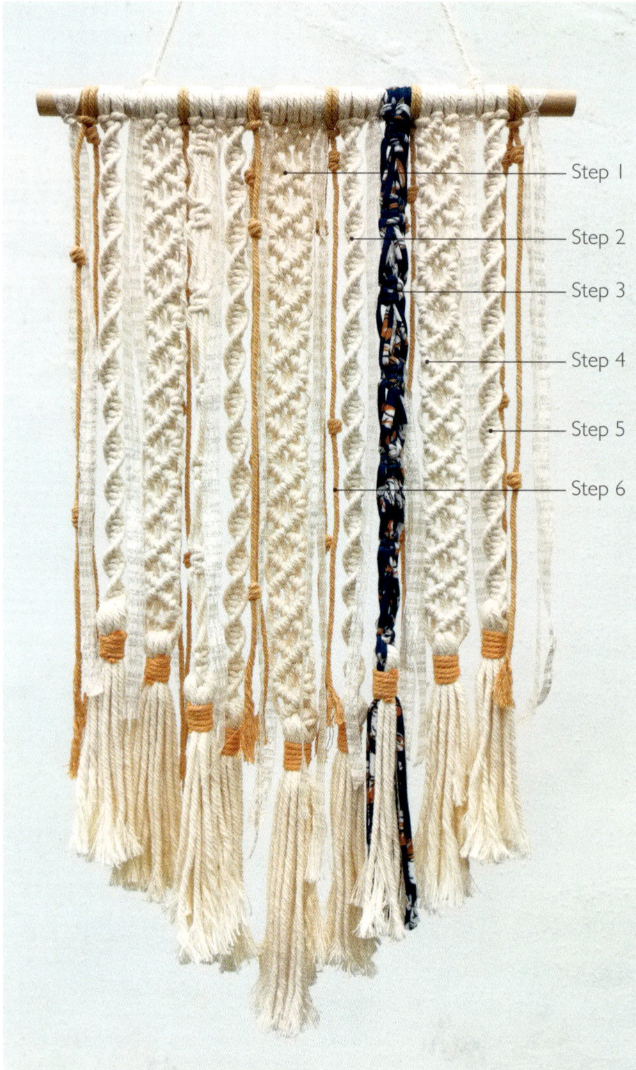

Step 7 Weave tassels using six white cord ends below each woven pattern.

Step 8 Weave lace yarn into the tapestry, gradually shortening from the center to the edges. Finally, trim the tapestry into a pointed shape.